THE ENCYCLOPEDIA OF
TRUE
CRIME

The paperback edition printed in 2006

ISBN 10: 1-86147-156-4
ISBN 13: 978-1-86147-156-7

3 5 7 9 10 8 6 4 2

Published by Abbeydale Press
An imprint of Bookmart Ltd
Blaby Road, Wigston
Leicestershire LE18 4SE
England

First published in hardback
by Bookmart Limited in 1993

Revised and updated in 2005

Every effort has been made to contact the copyright holders for the pictures.
In some cases they have been untraceable, for which we offer our apologies.
Special thanks to the Hulton-Deutsch Collection, who supplied the majority of pictures,
and thanks also to the following picture libraries and agencies:
Cassidy and Leigh, Mary Evans Photo Library, Express Newspapers, Robert Hunt, Imperial War Museum,
Marshall Cavendish, Midsummer Books, Peter Newark/Western Americana,
Popperfotos, Press Association, Rex Features, Frank Spooner Pictures,
Syndication International, Topham Picture Source.

The Author
Allan Hall is the American correspondent for for a major U.K. newspaper.
He has written several books on crime, the paranormal and the unexplained.

Printed in Thailand

THE ENCYCLOPEDIA OF
TRUE
CRIME

Abbeydale Press

TRUE CRIMES

Every society has its misfits; those who cannot, or will not, comply with the social consensus of behaviour. Most of these restless souls are harmless, petty villains, but every now and again there emerges a truly criminal type. And there are other – more horrifying – periods when a group, or even a nation, loses its head to commit hideous acts within and against itself.

True Crimes catalogues the full range of human frailty and weakness – and evil. Some misfits unconsciously seek each other out to form a strange partnership, a secret union of perversity and, as a couple, commit unthinkable acts. Others remain solitary: strange women who loosen the constraints of their sex to turn to murder, or the lonely men whose fantasies are dark dreams of power and strength. But these isolated cases of horror are but reflections of the madness that can overtake society itself – rounding up thousands of victims, imprisoning them, torturing and slaughtering in a mass blood lust. We need to understand what causes these outbursts of deviant behaviour, whether it is found in individuals or groups.

We need to absorb the facts, the dreadful details, because perhaps through knowledge we can stop the carnage, the exploitation of misery that criminals inflict on our societies. This volume chronicles the couples who join in crime, those whose mutual perversities unite in a life of evil. There are the stories of women who, to compensate for their inadequacies, will exploit and even kill to achieve money, power or love. And the men, who alone or in political and military groups, become bloodthirsty killers.

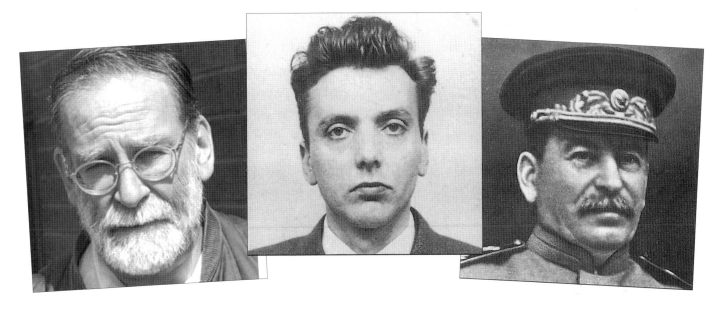

Contents

PARTNERS
IN CRIME

BONNIE & CLYDE
A Killing Love

The true story of Bonnie and Clyde is far more sinister than the movie. He was a homosexual and she a nymphomaniac, both were obsessed with guns and violent death and thrived on the publicity that surrounded them, even sending pictures of themselves to newspapers. Their small-time hold-ups were only an excuse for an orgy of killing.

Few villains achieve, in their own lifetime the status of folk hero. Robin Hood of Sherwood Forest was one who did, and in our own times, so has Ronnie Biggs, the Great Train Robber whose bravado and contempt for the law has earned him a certain popular respect. However, time adds lustre to even the most vicious criminals, and their evil is forgotten as myth gives them the glamour of brave individuals, outsiders who defy the constraints imposed by those in power.

Two such misplaced criminals are the professional thieves and murderers Bonnie Parker and Clyde Barrow, who went on the rampage during the Great Depression in America. Although they were ruthless killers, they have been immortalised in film, song and popular legend. They weren't very good robbers – most of their thefts were from gas stations, grocery stores and small-town diners. But they displayed a brutality and worked with a wild audacity that has earned them a place ias heroes in the myth of folk-lore.

Semi-literate and wholly without compassion, they roamed the Great Plains states of Missouri, Kansas and Oklahoma in their quest for easy cash. They loved their guns and their violent acts, cloaking themselves in the mystique of their 'mission' and recorded themselves for posterity in photographs.

With Buck Barrow, Clyde's brother, and other bandits, they formed the Barrow Gang, a nomadic outlaw tribe that criss-crossed state-lines, terrorising the small businessmen and farmers who were every bit as much victims of the Great Depression as themselves.

Their relationship was an odd one, for Barrow was a homosexual, Parker virtually a nymphomaniac. Together they found a kind of love, a bond between misfits, focussed on firearms and violent death.

Clyde was born on 24 March, 1909 into extreme poverty in Teleco, Texas. One of eight children, his older brother Buck – who would later take orders from him – taught Clyde how to steal and hot-wire cars. After petty crime as a juvenile, and time spent in a boys' reform school, Clyde graduated to robbing roadside restaurants and small, country filling stations.

Often there was no more than a handful of dollars and some loose change to steal from these places but Clyde reasoned they were safer to rob than banks. His brother was sent to prison in 1928 after he was caught on a raid on a diner. With the heat

Above: *The shattered Ford V8 in which the gangster pair met their death.*

Opposite: *Bonnie Parker and Clyde Barrow have passed into folklore as glamorous outlaws but they were really vicious killers.*

on him Clyde drifted to Texas. In January 1930, feeling peckish while wandering around Dallas, he dropped into a cafe called Marco's and was served a hamburger by a vivacious and pretty waitress. Her name was Bonnie Parker.

Parker, born on 1 October, 1910, was the daughter of a bricklayer, a petite blonde package of boredom – 'bored crapless' as she confided to her diary at the time. She listened to the tall tales that the customer spun her about life on the road. Later that night she met him for a date, but there was no sexual interest on his part. Rather, they fuelled their friendship with each other through tales of robbery and mayhem. Parker, married to a convict serving ninety-nine years for murder, moved into a small furnished apartment in Dallas with Barrow.

Guns became the consuming passion of this strange pair. Parker was thrilled by the pistols that her beau wore holstered beneath his coat, and they took regular trips to the farmland outside Dallas for target practice with revolvers, rifles and sub-machine guns. Soon Parker was every bit as good a shot as he was. Parker undoubtedly saw in her trigger-happy new friend the means of escape from the life of menial work that bored her so much.

They soon took to robbery, she driving the getaway car – despite the fact that

Clyde was a much better driver – while Clyde ran into the stores and cleaned them out at gunpoint. He would then run back to the car, jump on the running board and cover them as the car raced away. The thrill of these escapades was almost sexual for Parker, who could never find satisfaction with Barrow. He had confessed that he became homosexual in the reform school and she satisfied her considerable sexual needs with a series of one-night stands and with the men who would later drift in and out of the Barrow Gang.

Three months after they teamed up Clyde was behind bars, having left his fingerprints all over the scene of a burglary in Waco, Texas. He was arrested at the Dallas apartment and sentenced to two years, but he didn't stay to complete his sentence. His brother Buck had broken out of jail and Clyde wrote a coded letter to Bonnie asking her to spring him. Together, she and Buck travelled to Waco, with

Parker wearing a .38 police issue revolver strapped to her thigh. She escaped the attentions of prison guards due to an incompetent search and contrived to slip the weapon to Clyde. He managed to break out that same night and rode freight trains across the plains states to Ohio.

Clyde Barrow stayed free for just a week before he was arrested again and this time sent to Eastham Jail, the tough Federal penitentiary from which his brother had

beaten with a whips and made to perform exercises until he dropped. He also killed a man, Ed Crowder, a cellblock informer, with a lead pipe, but authorities at the penitentiary did not credit him with the killing until after Clyde's death.

Parker was the next to go to prison after they stole a car and were pursued by police. Clyde escaped after crashing into a tree and running across fields, but Parker was caught and sentenced to two months. While she was inside, Clyde continued to rob the small-town stores and highway gas stations. In Hillsboro, Texas, he murdered sixty-five-year-old John Bucher in his jewellery store after taking just ten dollars from the till. It was when Bonnie was released that their wild and cold-blooded-killing spree began in earnest.

On 5 August, 1932, Clyde murdered two lawmen, Sherrif Charles Maxwell and his deputy Eugene Moore. He intended to rob the ticket seller at a barn dance in Atoka, Oklahoma, when the lawmen saw him loitering suspiciously. 'You better come out into the light boy, so I can see you better,' said Sherrif Maxwell, the last words he ever spoke. Clyde lifted up his overcoat and shot the two men at point-blank range with two automatic weapons.

A BUNCH OF NUTTY KILLERS

The bizarre couple then began their deadly odyssey across America. They robbed an armoury in Texas of an arsenal of sub-machine guns, ammunition, small arms and rifles. They fired indiscriminately into a dozen state troopers who had set up a road-block in Texas, wounding several. They held up liqour stores, gas stations and grocery outlets, all for a few dollars. They even kidnapped a sherrif, stripped him and dumped him on the roadside with the parting words: 'Tell your people that we ain't just a bunch of nutty killers. Just down home people trying to get through this damned Depression with a few bones.'

escaped. His mother Cummie Barrow deluged the state governor with pleas for leniency; pleas which were answered on 2 February, 1932, when he was released on parole. The prison was a crucial turning point in his life – after experiencing it he vowed to Parker, who waited to greet him at the gates, that he would rather die than ever go back inside. He had been tortured in the jail dubbed 'The Burning Hell',

Above: *Clyde cuddling his beloved firearms. The pair often sent photographs of themselves to the press for they delighted in their notorious fame.*

On the road they lived like old-fashioned outlaws, sleeping by camp fires, surviving on wild fowl they shot and peanut butter sandwiches. At night they would get drunk on bootlegged bourbon whiskey and Parker would write turgid romantic poetry that bemoaned their lot in life – that they were persecuted by the establishment and that in

HE REGULARLY SLEPT WITH BONNIE... AND WITH CLYDE. THIS BIZARRE TRIANGLE SEEMED TO SUIT THEM ALL.

reality they were a new breed of hero. A sense of foreboding hung over the two of them; both sensed that they were not long for the world and that they would die young and die violently.

In the autumn of 1932, Bonnie and Clyde headed for New Mexico with gunslinger Roy Hamilton who joined them

house in Dallas for another robber, were gunned down when Clyde turned up instead. And together they kidnapped gas station attendant turned apprentice-robber William Jones, who was to travel with them for the next eighteen months. This fellow traveller would later give lawmen many details of the criminals' life.

Above: *Those in authority were appalled by the public's interest in Bonnie and Clyde. The pair were written about in popular magazines, their images were in all the papers. Here, 'souvenirs' of their vagabond life are assembled – stolen car plates, clothing and baggage.*

but they decided that pickings were not as rich there as Texas, so headed back. Hamilton, an accomplished robber, was also as perverted as the duo he now allied himself with. He regularly slept with Bonnie... and with Clyde. This bizarre triangle seemed to suit them all.

They killed indiscriminately and often. Clyde murdered a butcher with eight bullets when the man lunged at him with a cleaver after Clyde had stolen $50 from his store. He murdered Doyle Johnson in Temple, Texas, when he tried to stop them stealing his car. Two lawmen, staking out a

Like gypsies, they criss-crossed the southwest, continuing to hold up shops and garages. They picked up brother Buck again, together with his wife Blanche, and the robberies increased. In Kansas they robbed a loan company office where Bonnie saw her wanted poster for the first time. She was so excited that she and Clyde were 'celebrities', she fired off a dozen letters to prominent newspaper editors complete with snapshots of her and Clyde they had taken on the road. She perpetuated the myth that they were fighters against authority – authorities like the banks that were foreclosing on poor farmers and businessmen. She made no mention, of course, of the pathological delight they both took in killing.

At this time she was working on a turgid, autobiographical poem, 'The Story of Suicidal Sal' that would later reach the newspapers.

We, each of us, have a good alibi,
For being down here in the joint.
But few of them are really justified,
If you get right down to the point.
You have heard of a woman's glory,
Being spent on a downright cur,
Still you can't always judge the story,
As true being told by her.

As long as I stayed on the island,
And heard confidence tales from the gals,
There was only one interesting and truthful,
It was the story of Suicide Sal.

Now Sal was a girl of rare beauty,
Though her features were somewhat tough,
She never once faltered from duty,
To play on the up and up.

She told me this tale on the evening,
Before she was turned out free,
And I'll do my best to relate it,
Just as she told it to me.

I was born on a ranch in Wyoming,
Not treated like Helen of Troy,
Was taught that rods were rulers,
And ranked with greasy cowboys...

The poem was interrupted at this point due to a police raid on a hideout they used in Joplin, Missouri. Bonnie and Clyde, Buck and Blanche, fired more than one thousand machine gun bullets at the cops coming to get them, killing two of them. Later she finished the poem and mailed it.

Then I left my home for the city,
To play in its mad dizzy whirl,
Not knowing how little of pity,
It holds for a country girl.
You have heard the story of Jesse James,
Of how he lived and died,
If you are still in need of something to read,
Here's the story of Bonnie and Clyde.
Now Bonnie and Clyde are the

Barrow gang,
I'm sure you have all read
How they rob and steal
And how those who squeal
Are usually found dying or dead.

There are lots of untruths to
  their write-ups.
They are not so merciless as that;
They hate all the laws,
The stool pigeons, spotters and rats.
If a policeman is killed in Dallas,
And they have no clues to guide,
If they can't find a fiend,
They just wipe the slate clean,
And hang it on Bonnie and Clyde.

If they try to act like citizens,
And rent them a nice little flat,
About the third night they are invited
  to fight
By a sub-machine gun rat-tat-tat.

A newsboy once said to his buddy:
'I wish old Clyde would get jumped,
In these awful hard times,
We'd make a few dimes,
If five or six cops would get bumped.'

They class them as cold-blooded killers,
They say they are heartless and mean,
But I say this with pride,
That once I knew Clyde,
When he was honest and upright and clean.
But the law fooled around,

Above, left: W.D Jones and Henry Methvin (above) were part of the Barrow Gang but both were to betray Bonnie and Clyde.

SHE WAS SO EXCITED THAT SHE AND CLYDE WERE 'CELEBRITIES', SHE FIRED OFF A DOZEN LETTERS TO NEWSPAPER EDITORS.

Kept tracking them down,
And locking them up in a cell.
Till he said to me
'I will never be free
So I will meet a few of them in hell.'

The road was so dimly lighted,
There were no highway signs to guide,
But they made up their minds,
If the roads were all blind,
They wouldn't give up till they died.
The road gets dimmer and dimmer,
Sometimes you can hardly see,
Still it's fight man to man,
And do all you can,
For they know they can never be free.

They don't think they are too tough or
desperate,
They know the law always wins,
They have been shot at before
But they do not ignore
That death is the wages of sin.

From heartbreaks some people have
suffered,
From weariness some people have died,
But take it all and all,
Our troubles are small,
Til we get like Bonnie and Clyde.

Some day they will go down together,
And they will bury them side by side,
To a few it means grief,
To the law it's relief,
But it's death to Bonnie and Clyde.

Below: *Relatives of the Barrow Gang on trial for harbouring the criminals. Bonnie's mother is third from left, Clyde's mother third from right. The rest are sisters or sisters-in-law.*

Below: *Her family gave Bonnie a fine funeral ill-suited to a killer.*

The robbing went on. They switched mostly to small banks, in the rural towns of Indiana, Minnesota and Texas. A marshall was killed in cold blood outside the town of Alma and a two-hundred-strong possee set off after the gang. They were holed up in a rented log cabins at a country park near Platte City in Missouri but the manager became suspicious when they paid the rental in small change – the loot from several of their nickel-and-dime gas station hold-ups. The manager of the Red Crown Cabin Camp alerted police who, upon hearing the description of the guests, assembled a small army to lay siege to the rented cabin. It was 24 July, 1933.

In the ensuing confusion they escaped, leaving three officers dead. But Blanche had taken a slug in her leg, Clyde was grazed on the head, Bonnie was grazed with a bullet on her ribs and Buck... Buck was dying from a rifle bullet in his head.

NO PLACE TO GO

They escaped to a woodland area between Dexter and Refield in the rural state of Iowa where they did their best for Buck. But because they were always on the road, and without a network of contacts like those used by contemporary gangsters such as **Ma Barker** and **John Dillinger**, there was no place to hole up and get the medical attention Buck badly needed.

They were debating how to leave the wounded Buck when Clyde intuitively sensed a movement in the trees. Suddenly bullets began to rain down on their campsite. They returned fire with rifles and machine guns, even the mortally wounded Buck fired more than one thousand rounds at the lawmen. Bonnie and Clyde managed to bolt into thick undergrowth and escape but Buck was riddled with bullets. The posse found Blanche prostrate across his corpse, weeping inconsolably.

With the heat on, the duo headed back to the north and Minnesota, reasoning that

they do.' The following month Bonnie and Clyde drifted back to Texas for a meeting with his mother at a roadside picnic spot. But the pair barely escaped with their lives – his mother had been followed by a sherrif's posse who ringed the site. Once again alerted by some kind of sixth sense, Clyde drove straight past the rendezvous site. The back of the car was stuck by bullets and both he and Bonnie were wounded in the legs but not seriously.

After pulling off a few more small robberies, they teamed up again with Hamilton – after springing him from a jail

> 'IT'S THEM TWO,' HE SAID. 'I AIN'T NEVER SEEN ANYONE ENJOY KILLIN' AS MUCH AS THEY DO.'

there would be less trouble in a state where they had committed relatively few crimes. They were practically bums now, stealing washing from clothes-lines and foraging for scraps of food. Jones, the kidnapped garage attendant, was with them and he later told police: 'This was not the life I expected when I joined up with them. We was nothing better than hobos.'

In October, fed up with his diet of raw vegetables stolen from fields, Jones hopped a freight train back to Texas, was arrested, and told police about the antics of the gang making sure he disassociated himself from the killings. 'It's them two,' he said. 'I ain't never seen anyone enjoy killin' as much as

with minor thugs Joe Palmer and Henry Methvin – and the Barrow Gang was back to strength once more. The FBI, because of the murders and the transportation of weapons and stolen cars across state lines, was now in on the hunt and the officers were instructed to shoot-to-kill and ask questions afterwards. J. Edgar Hoover, celebrated head of the FBI warned his G-men that Clyde was a 'psychopath – he should be killed like a rattlesnake'. Even other gangsters, knowing about their bloodlust, decided that there should be no honour among thieves. Charles Arthur 'Pretty Boy' Floyd, the gangster, was furious when he learned that the psycho-

Above: *Police hold a distraught Blanche Barrow after they shot dead her husband, Buck Barrow.*

pathic pair had entered territory that he regarded as his own in the Cookson Hills, northern Minnesota. 'Don't feed them and don't give them shelter,' he ordered his cohorts and criminal associates. 'Stick the law on them if you can. They are vermin and have nothing to do with our people.'

Public opinion was rapidly turning against them. The banks they robbed were forced to close because they were suffering in the hard times, as were the businesses they raided. Soon the newspaper readers who had adored her romantic poem realised that there was nothing Robin-Hood-like about their exploits. They were simply greedy and ruthless killers.

KNOW THINE ENEMY

Soon only Methvin was left with the gang. Hamilton had argued with Clyde and gone his own way. Palmer dropped out with chronic stomach ulcers. The heat was on like never before, particularly in Texas, where a lawman called Frank Hamer, who had gunned down sixty-five notorious criminals during his career, was given the task of hunting down Bonnie and Clyde.

Hamer analysed every move they made, drew up maps and charts of all their movements over the previous years and discerned a pattern of sorts in the type of places they hit and the routes they took. 'I wanted to get into their evil minds,' he said. 'Know thine enemy was my maxim and I learned it well.' Several times during the early months of 1934 Hamer and his men came upon campsites that the duo had abandoned just hours before, but he was determined to stay on their trail.

In April that year, after hiding out on a farm in Louisiana, they returned to Texas to see Bonnie's relatives and hopefully lie low. But, as they neared the outskirts of the town of Grapevine, motorcycle police Ernest Wheeler and Harold Murphy rode past them. When they crested a rise in the road in front, Clyde pulled the car over and stopped. The motorcycle cops, their suspicions aroused, turned around and came back towards them. As they drew level with the car Clyde murdered them both with both barrels of a shotgun. Two weeks later in Oklahmoa, when their car got stuck in mud, they were approached by two police officers. One died with a

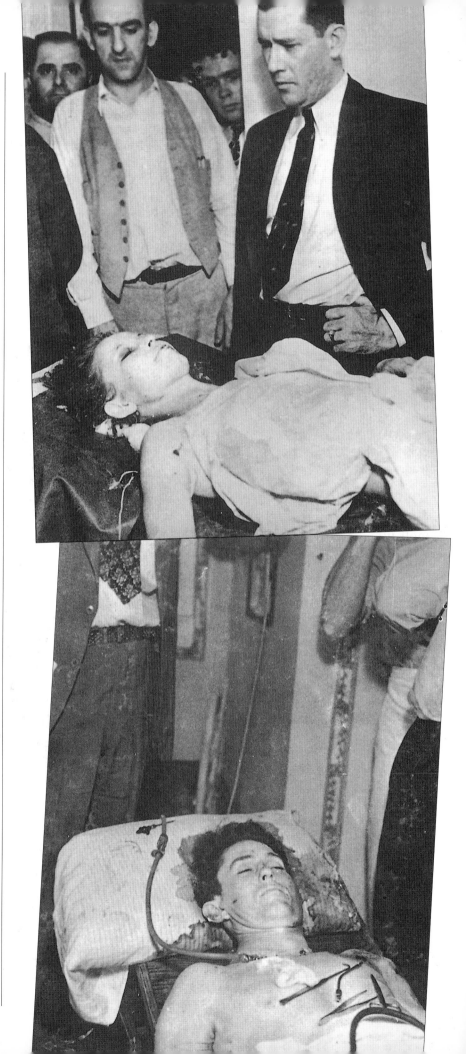

revolver bullet in the chest, the other was luckier - he was slightly wounded.

The key to capturing the outlaws lay with Methvin, who was still running with them. His father Ivan offered to help trap them if Hamer would agree to granting his son a pardon. Hamer, needing Bonnie and Clyde more than him, agreed to the deal. Henry Methvin, seeing a way out for himself, agreed to co-operate with his father when he next contacted him. Henry slipped away from a hideout shack in Shreveport, Louisiana, which was promptly surrounded by Hamer's armed Texas Rangers. Soon a posse had hidden themselves along the road leading to the shack; they were armed with Browning machine guns, high-powered rifles and numerous grenades and tear gas bombs.

At 9.15am on 23 May, 1934 the V8 Ford which the couple had been using for the past week – they changed licence plates every day – crested a rise in the road leading from the hideout. Clyde was at the wheel, his shoes off, driving with bare feet. He wore sunglasses against the strong spring sunshine. Next to him sat his deadly moll in a new red dress she had bought with stolen loot some weeks previously. Stashed in the car were two thousand bullets, three rifles, twelve pistols and two pump-action shotguns.

A FRIGHTENED DECOY

Methvin Snr has agreed to be a decoy. His truck was parked at the edge of the road and Clyde drew level with it. Clyde asked him if there had been any sight of his son. Methvin, almost quaking with fear, saw a truckful of black farm labourers coming down the road and he panicked, diving for cover beneath his own vehicle. A sherrif with the posse named Jordan suddenly yelled for the duo to surrender. But this was like a red rag to a bull for this homocidal pair. In one swift motion Clyde had his door open and a shotgun in his hand, Bonnie was equipped with a revolver.

This time there was no escape. A murderous rain of fire battered the car. More than five hundred bullets slammed into the bodies of the gangsters and they were literally ripped to pieces. Clyde was slumped backwards, his foot off the clutch pedal. The car was still in gear and it

Opposite: *Pictures of the dead desperadoes were circulated all over the United States. The public could not get enough to read about the gruesome lives and bloody deaths of Bonnie and Clyde.*

Below: *Bonnie Parker at peace at last after a wild and dangerous life.*

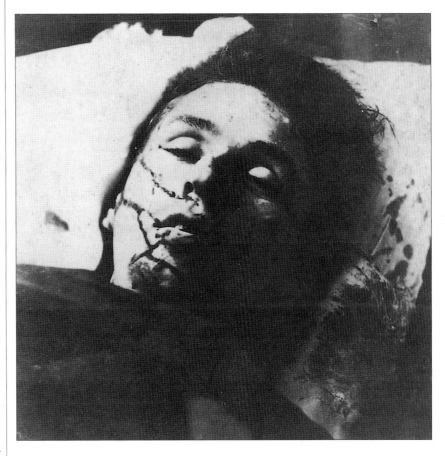

'THEY WERE DIRTY PEOPLE. HER BREATH SMELLED AWFUL AND HE NEVER TOOK A BATH. THEY SMELLED BAD ALL THE TIME. THEY WOULD STEAL THE PENNIES FROM A DEAD MAN'S EYES.'

inched ahead, coming to a halt in a ditch. The posse of lawmen continued to pour fire into the wreck for four whole minutes after it had come to a stop.

As newspaper headlines around the world shouted the news of their deaths, local residents were charged a dollar a head to view the mangled corpses on a morgue slab. Thousands paid to look.

Ray Hamilton, the robber who ran with them, was eventually executed less than ten years later for other murders. Just before his death, he accurately described Bonnie and Clyde.'They loved to kill people, see blood run. That's how they got their kicks.

There was many times when they didn't have to kill, but they did anyways. They were dirty people. Her breath smelled awful and he never took a bath. They smelled bad all the time. They would steal the pennies from a dead man's eyes.'

The Parker family tried its best to paint Bonnie in a different light. The horribly-inaccurate inscription on this murderer's tombstone reads thus: 'As the flowers are all made sweeter, by the sunshine and the dew, so this old world is made brighter, by the likes of folk like you.'

JUAN & EVITA
The Corruptible Perons

Proud dictator Juan Peron and his nightclub singer Evita presided over an evil and repressive regime. They brought their country to the verge of bankruptcy as they looted millions from charities and the state to fill their Swiss bank accounts. And they did it all in the name of the Argentinian people they claimed to love.

They were a most unlikely double act, this notorious nightclub singer and the ambitious army colonel but together they shaped the course of South American politics and still enjoy near-mythological status to this day.

Andrew Lloyd Weber's musical 'Evita' was not the only reason that Eva Duarte, mistress of Juan Peron, became a household name. In the southern hemipshere, in the land of the pampas, Peronism has become more than a political movement; it is almost a religious affirmation and to those who supported them; Juan and Evita were the demi-gods who put Argentina on the world stage.

However, it was, mostly, a clever show without real substance, for while the illusion created by this glittering twosome was lapped up by the masses, they used the peoples' ill-judged support to mask their own corruption – a corruption which channelled untold millions from the national coffers into Swiss bank accounts. They also supported the Fascist movements in Europe during wartime, clamped down on the press which opposed them, and even launched an anti-church campaign aimed at those ministers within the Catholic hierachy that they regarded as enemies.

While Peronism may still make the gauchos and the housewives of Buenos Aries misty-eyed for 'the good old days' it was in reality nothing more than a cover for a well-ordered fleecing of the state. It is an indisputable fact that before their rule Argentina was one of the wealthiest nations in the world; afterwards, the nation was ruined and bankrupt.

Before there was an Evita for the crowds in Argentina to cheer there was Colonel Juan Domingo Peron. Born in Lobos in 1895 to poor immigrant stock, he rose through the army ranks thanks to dilligence and ability. Equipped with charm, athleticism and that essential Argentinian characteristic, machismo, he was destined to go far. But he was also a moral and physical coward, a man who shunned reality if he thought confronting it would be unpleasant. He could not endure being unpopular and many of his ludicrous economic policies were pursued so he could enjoy the applause of the mob while he followed them through.

In 1943 Argentina was under the rule of President Ramon Castillo – at least until June that year, when the military decided to stage a coup. It was led by colonels calling themselves the Young Turks, Peron among them. The colonels claimed that the Ramon government was supporting the Allies in the war. This was alien to the Fascist-temperament of the officer corps, many of whom were of Italian extraction and saw

WHILE THE ILLUSION CREATED BY THIS GLITTER-ING TWOSOME WAS LAPPED UP BY THE MASSES, THEY USED THE PEOPLES' ILL-JUDGED SUPPORT TO MASK THEIR OWN CORRUPTION.

Opposite: *The glittering Eva and her husband Juan Peron managed to keep the adoration of the masses even as they stole from the nation's coffers.*

Below: *The successful politicians who promisd to turn Argentina into a paradise for the workers. But Eva and Jaun fulfilled little of their socialist programme.*

Mussolini in Italy as their kind of leader. At the time of the coup Peron was one of the keenest pro-Fascist officers among the colonels and worked in the Ministry of War, but by the end of October he was promoted when he was granted the critical job of running the Labour Department in the new military junta.

The labour movement in Argentina was split between trades unions and those workers on the ranches and in the slaughterhouses who had no organisation. Peron set out to mould the workers into a single, military-like unit, with the discipline and style of the black shirts he admired at rallies in Nazi Germany and Fascist Italy. Many workers' leaders had suffered cruelly under previous regimes, while the men they represented were mercilessly gunned down in the streets if they dared to strike.

Peron used his considerable charm to become the friend of the unions, the affable big brother who would ease their economic and social woes. Months earlier these same men had been called Communist scum and filth by the military but Peron believed flattery was a better way of attaining what he wanted from them.

What he wanted from them was subservience to the government. He made it, for instance, mandatory for wage negotiations between workers and bosses to go through his office. Kickbacks from the unions and the bosses were discreetly channelled into the seven-figure bank account he held in Switzerland. The more astute union leaders realised what he was up to but he outflanked the old guard. He

ordered free paid holidays, a month's bonus at Christmas for the meat packers and other fringe benefits. While the workers cheered at this short-term philanthropy, the bosses bemoaned the loss of their managerial rights, and the unions felt emasculated. They were both victims of Juan Peron's attempt to create a permanent Argentinian military dictatorship based on the solid support of the masses.

As the dictatorships which the Argentinian military so admired crumbled in Europe, so the movement for freedom and openness in Argentina grew. In August 1945, the military lifted a state of emergency that had existed throughout the war years – causing a half-a-million strong demonstration the following month on the streets of the capital from a populace seeking greater freedom and human rights. It was a frightening display of people-

Below, left: A young admirer approaches a delighted Eva and Juan in their presidential box at a social event on the River Plate.

Below, right: The Perons, while promising a socialist regime, brought expensive glamour into their own lives.

mistress Eva Duarte. Fierce and brave, she yelled abuse at the soldiers, while reliable sources have it that her colonel fell to his knees and begged for mercy. Eva, the nightclub singer who literally slept her way to the top, rallied support for Peron among the unions that he had helped so much and rioting broke out in the streets. For forty-eight hours, Buenos Aries was paralysed until the military backed down and Peron was released, his stature greater than ever.

power and sparked a Draconian response from Peron who ordered waves of arrests. But when disputes arose within the ranks of the military themselves (the air force officers standing with the workers while the army were against them), Peron played a gambling rusethat he was doomed to lose. He went on radio urging workers to 'rise up' and follow his path of liberation. It was a valiant but vain plea which ended with his own arrest and imprisonment.

With him when he was arrested in his apartment in the Calle Posadas was his

Opposite, above: Eva uses the state radio to thank the nation for electing her husband as president. He stands on the left, while the Interior Minister, Angel Borlenghi sits to the right.

Opposite, below: Eva loved the glamour of state occasions. The Perons step out at an Independence Ball.

With the adulation of the workers ringing in his ears, Juan Peron realised that his dreams of a neo-Fascist worker's militia had evaporated; instead he saw in the cheering *descamisados* – the shirtless ones – the roots of a new worker's revolution. So, believing this to be his chance, he resigned from the army and offered himself up as the leader of a new labour party.

His first step towaards domination of the workers was to ruin the unions of the shoemakers and the textile workers, two proud and disciplined welfare groups who

Above: *Eva Peron could rally the crowds, while winning over the army and the church.*

were not convinced by his scheme to bond workers to his state. Within six months they were finished, their leaders driven into poverty and exile. To gain credence for the free elections which were to be held in 1946, Peron also had to win over the Catholic church hierachy, especially because of his relationship with Eva Duarte – 'This woman Duarte' – as the newspaper *La Prensa* called her. Eva, born in 1919 into great poverty, was his real love and several years earlier he had divorced his wife, hoping to marry his 'Evita'. He peruaded the church to recognize his marriage to her in 1945, to view it as reparation for his sin of keeping her as a mistress. The church gave its blessings to the man who would soon be ruler.

> 'THE PURPOSE WAS NOT TO GIVE POWER TO THE WORKING CLASS, BUT TO ENCOURAGE THE WORKING CLASS TO GIVE POWER TO JUAN PERON.'

Below: *The Perons in Brazil (left) and in London the Worshipful Company of Butchers, pleased with the Argentinian beef trade, welcomed them (right).*

establishing the priorities which are necessary for the operation of any economic system. He taught the community to believe in the instantaneous and total pay-off, so that no one had any order of expectation.' Another study of Argentina, 'The Mothers of the Plaza', by John Simpson and Jana Bennett, says: 'It was all, essentially, a form of charity with Peron. Peron made working-class people feel they had dignity and an importance in the national life of Argentina. The purpose was not to give power to the working class, but to encourage the working class to give power to Juan Peron.'

His brand of socialism bound the workers and the bosses to the state as never before, while he wasted vast quantities of the nation's money by nationalising the run-down railways at super-inflated prices. He became a master of the pay-off, offering kickbacks to critics and bosses, while he remained the darling of workers who had never had it so good. But they never had it so good at the expense of a government that was rapidly paying out more than it was taking in. Peron's largesse in handing out holidays, pensions and bonuses was laying the foundations for Argentina's eight hundred per cent inflation rates of the 1970s and 1980s.

By 1949 his plans were badly adrift; inflation and unrest followed as a government of bribes and torture was exposed. Peron reacted harshly, arresting dissidents, purging churchmen and formulating a law which made it a serious offence to insult

In 1946 he attained his dream in one of the few fair elections ever held in Argentina. He gained the backing of the workers to take over the Casa Rosada, the pink palace of the national leaders, with Eva at his side; the country was his for the taking. Peron came to power with great expectations placed in him. The country was rich, it had been spared the war which had torn apart the Old World, business was booming and there was plenty of money in the bank. What went wrong?

'Indisputably, Peron operated his system extremely badly,' said historian H.S.Ferns in his authoritatve study 'Argentina'. 'Like a spoiled child he wanted everything and he wanted it at once. He revealed himself totally incapable of making choices and

the president or any of his public servants. He milked the agricultural aid programme for his own benefit and left the grain farmers and the beef herders increasingly impoverished. Newspapers that criticised him and Evita were closed down – like the honourable and influential *La Prensa*, which was seized and turned into a pro-government trade union sheet.

Evita, during these years, manipulated businessmen and landowners to contribute tinto what has been called the biggest political slush fund in history. The Eva Peron Foundation did indeed build schools, educate children, feed the hungry and shelter the homeless. However, the enormous amount of money that rolled in was administered by people who had to answer to no one but her. Her emissaries travelled to every factory, every workshop, every building site to take the tribute demanded by their new Cleopatra. Those who didn't 'contribute' voluntarily soon found their premises judged unfit by factory inspectors and were closed down.

Experts estimate that Evita stashed away as much as $100 million in hard cash into secret Swiss bank accounts from this fund, flown out twice a month to Geneva in suitcases. Gwyneth Dunwoody, the British MP said: 'With the euphemistically- titled Foundation behind her, Eva Peron handed out Christmas gifts for needy children to

Above: *Eva and Juan pose before their sumptuous country estate, paid for by funds siphoned from Eva's charity organization.*

Right: *Rapt attention on the faces of the leaders as they watch a boxing match.*

hospitals and schools, while ceaselessly driving home the message that it was because of the Peronistas that these remarkable benefits were available.

'What she omitted to say was that the Foundation, which had initially been billed as a society to be be supported by voluntary contributions, was rapidly taking on the air of a Godfather organisation. She did not hesitate to demand payment from every worker that obtained a rise and from every business that claimed that it needed the government's assistance.

'Every possible source of finance was milked so that this myth of Eva caring for the workers could be promoted. She was not a gentle and gracious woman – she relied on her own regime and army and police power to keep her where she wanted to be. In an organisation with astonishingly few accounts, the amounts of money that were spent were directly connected with what was useful for the Peronista regime. She was no Joan of Arc.'

MORE MONEY LESS LOVE

John Barnes, author of the book 'Eva Peron', says that after her death, investigators of defunct bank accounts traced to her found an estimated $14 million worth of money and jewels that she had literally forgotten she had. No doubt, much of this was stolen from the contributions to the Eva Peron Foundation.

'The love of the people feeds me,' Evita gushed, as large amounts of this unchecked and uncounted money were creamed off into her secret bank accounts. Whole government departments were taken over by her, many of them running twenty-four hours a day, to keep the Foundation supplied with untraceable money. On the government front, Colonel Peron bought off politicians to vote through legislation diverting $5 million worth of public funds into her Foundation. To this day, no one knows exactly how much was stolen from Argentina by the Perons, but it ran into the hundreds of millions of dollars.

She was as vain as she was greedy. Newspapers that did not print mentions of her glittering balls and glittering guests suddenly found that their supplies of newsprint had dried up. Although the workers cheered her and were solidly behind her, as they were behind her husband, she never gained the acceptance she craved from the upper classes. She knew the whispers surrounding her rise from the streets, the 'favours' she paid to men who helped her singing career.

Her revenge against the snobbish elite knew no bounds – once she paid a fish monger and gave him the necessary permits

Below: *General Peron, Eva and General Dutra of Brazil meet at the opening of a new bridge connecting the two vast countries.*

to sell fish outside the snooty Jockey Club in Buenos Aries for a whole long, hot summer. She saw conspirators everywhere and, when a union boss had the temerity to tell her that she would be better off at home in the kitchen than meddling in politics, she had him arrested and tortured with electric cattle prods. Another man, Victor Belardo, was arrested because he answered correctly the jackpot question on a radio quiz show – and then announced that he would give his money, a large amount, to a charity that

'THE LOVE OF THE PEOPLE FEEDS ME,' EVITA GUSHED, AS LARGE AMOUNTS OF THIS UNCHECKED AND UNCOUNTED MONEY WERE CREAMED OFF INTO HER SECRET BANK ACCOUNTS.

was not affiliated with or overseen by her omnipotent Foundation.

The Perons accumulated further millions from kickbacks they received for import-export permits. Traders literally had to grease their palms with millions of pesos – and do so willingly – in order to trade with the outside world.

Evita became a master of stage-managed rallies, copycat versions of those which the deposed dictators of Europe used to hold so regularly. Weeks before one particular event she invited Argentinian women from

Below: *Eva Peron died a young woman. This photograph was taken shortly after she had undergone surgery.*

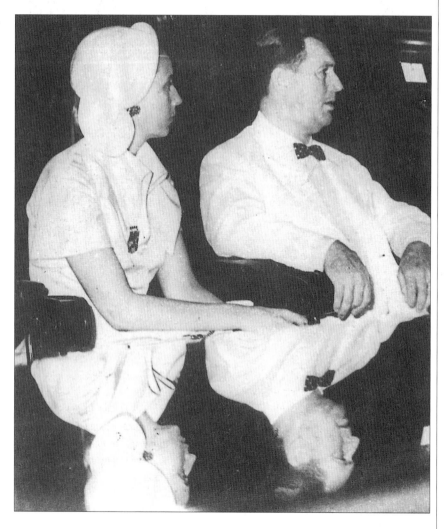

all over the country to bring their children to her to receive bicycles and dolls, a symbolic gesture to show that she cared for them, and that as the 'mother of the country' so all the children were her's to love and treat. It was a scene of chaos when they arrived outside the palace, so much so that police had to break up the crowds and at least two mothers went home without their offpsring – the children had been trampled to death by the mob.

In 1951 Peron's grip on polical power was faltering but his live-now-pay-later generosity with the workers still earned them both enormous support. He nearly lost this, however, in the 1951 elections by offering up his wife as the vice-president on his ticket. Much as the people adored Evita, this was still the land of machismo. The thought of Vice President Evita sent a shiver through the ranks of the military, upon whom Peron relied so much, and also troubled the workers deeply. A new slogan appeared on city walls – 'Long Live Peron – As A Widower!' Other graffiti depicted Evita naked, walking like a giant over masses of Lilliputian men. Juan Peron bowed to the pressure of the church and the military and his beloved Evita did not appear on his election ticket.

Shortly before the elections, which Peron was in danger of losing, there was another attempt at a military coup, this time put down by Peron and by the workers who idolised him. It ensured his victory in the October polling, giving him sixty-two per cent of the vote, ten per cent more than he had gained in 1946. And this, despite the faltering economy, the looted millions and the alienation of the ruling class.

But the following year one half of the double act was gone – Evita died from cancer. Juan Peron used her demise to canonise her in the eyes of an adoring people. She was only thirty-three and had recently toured the world, capturing hearts and minds for her country. Nevertheless, her death averted the fall from grace and power that would ultimately have been her lot. By dying, she became to her impoverished admirers a memory of diamonds and furs, not a woman who left her nation stripped of its wealth and teetering on the brink of bankruptcy while her detractors screamed under torture in filthy jails.

Economic conditions deteriorated after the death of Evita. The emperor was beginning to be seen without his clothes by the adoring masses burdened under hyper-inflation and suffering increasing harassment from his secret police and torturers. Moreover, the Catholic church, long the traditional dispenser of charity in the country, was beginning to feel aggrieved at having lost its place in society to the Foundation. The universities had been wrecked by semi-literate oafs who were given their posts by corrupt officials in return for kickbacks. Peron's goon-squads burned down the Jockey Club, which had spurned his late wife in the past, and he robbed the magnificent library and art gallery for his own pleasure.

In 1955 it all literally came crashing down when the air force bombed the Casa Rosada – missing him, but killing hundreds of civilians in the process – and armed gangs took to the streets, ransacking shops, businesses and even churches. The army garrison at Cordoba rose against him and there were no workers who believed in his Utopia anymore to save him. He went into exile aboard a Paraguayan gunboat.

A DAZZLING ALADDIN'S CAVE

In much the same way as the mob was allowed to look over the spoils of office of dictator Ferdinand Marcos in the Philippines years later, the poor of Argentina were given a glimpse of how their Evita had really lived when the portals of her stupendous palace were opened to the public after Peron's flight.

'It was a show which would outdazzle Aladdin's cave,' wrote Daily Express correspondent Jack Comben when he gazed at her riches. 'Glass shelves laid tier upon tier in the chandelliered brilliance of Peron's palace displayed gems which are estimated to be worth two million pounds. Diamonds almost as big as pigeons' eggs glittered and flashed. There was a two-inch thick collar encrusted with diamonds.

'I saw at least four hundred dresses – all perfect of their type and all expensive. And experts calculated that Evita owned enough shoes to last her for four hundred years. But all the treasures, the clothes, the pictures, are supposed to be only a fraction of what Peron and his wife acquired during nine years of power. The government believes he sent most of his fortune out of the country to Switzerland. And Peron was once quouted as saying: "The only jewellery I ever gave to my wife was a wedding ring".'

These event, had they occured in any other part of the world other than South America, would have been ended then. In 1973, however, after almost twenty years exile in Spain, Peron returned to power in Argentina with his third wife. Nostalgic,

perhaps, for the good old days that never really existed, the people embraced the man who threw his lot in with the workers,. They forgot all his sins, the massive amounts of money and assets that he looted from them in the past.

He died in 1974, the reins of power passing to Isabelita Peron, whom he had married in 1961. She excelled both her husband and his previous wife in the corruption stakes. Arrested in 1976, after she was deposed as president, she was charged with stealing $1 million intended for charity, convicted of embezzelling cash from a charity and for using government buildings for her own ends and was jailed. She was released in 1981 after serving two-thirds of her prison sentences.

Despite all this, the name Peron can still elicit nostalgia in Argentina – a land where 'strong' evokes a response than 'just'.

Above: *An Italian admirer sent this stone statue of Eva to the people of Argentina. It arouses mixed feeling among the citizens: some adore her memory, others despise her greed.*

EXPERTS CALCULATED THAT EVITA OWNED ENOUGH SHOES TO LAST HER FOR FOUR HUNDRED YEARS.

PARKER & HULME
Their Secret World

Pauline Parker and Juliet Hulme were anything but normal schoolgirls. These teenage lesbian lovers bashed in the head of Pauline's mother who had tried to separate them. Were they criminally insane or just murderous little minxes?

There is much in 'Partners in Crime' that dwells on the madness generated by two people that would not have have occured had the partnership never been formed. Normal lives and patterns of behaviour vanish as two personalities, each bland and safe on its own, ignite into intrigue and danger when combined.

Such was the madness that descended on two adolescent girls in New Zealand in the 1950s – girls who retreated into their own special world of aloofness, superiority and forbidden sex, a world that held murder.

When Juliet Marion Hulme and Pauline Yvonne Parker were brought before the Crown in Christchurch, New Zealand, in 1954 the case received worldwide attention because of its morbid themes. Like the case of Loeb and Leopold (Chapter xxx), psychologists were at pains to try to explain the fusion of two normal minds into a single entity bent on misery and death. For that is what happened to Juliet Hulme and Pauline Parker when their perfect world was threatened.

In order to prevent separation from one another, they plotted and carried out, the murder of Mrs Honora Mary Parker. Mrs Parker, forty-five, Pauline's mother, was bludgeoned to death by the two, who tried to cover their tracks by claiming she had fallen. But in the end their own inflated ideas of their intelligence and skill failed them badly and the most basic police methods proved that they were the killers.

The full extent of their wickedness and depravity revealed at the trial shocked this colonial outpost as nothing before or since.

It was on 22 June, 1954 that the two hysterical girls, covered in blood, shattered the tranquility of afternoon tea at a sedate Christchurch restaurant when they burst through the doors. 'Mummy's been hurt,' blurted out Pauline. 'She's hurt, covered with blood.' Tearfully they begged the manageress of the restaurant to phone for police while they gulped down sugared tea in an apparent attempt to ease their shock. Some of the customers went with police

and the girls to a beauty spot in a nearby park close to a small bridge over a stream. Lying in a pool of blood, her face unrecognisable, was Mrs Parker. Her head was brutally battered. It was a bad fall.

Initially the girls told police that Mrs Parker had fallen and slipped on a board. 'Her head just kept banging and banging,' blurted out Pauline to police, in a none-too-convincing explanation of why her mother came to have some forty-nine serious head wounds, any one of which would have been enough to render her unconscious. The

*Opposite: **Juliet Hulme**, on the left, and **Pauline Parker** were so in love that they were prepared to murder anybody who threatened their relationship.*

*Below: **The childish face of Juliet Hulme** hid a passionate nature and a wilful nature.*

> 'HER HEAD JUST KEPT BANGING AND BANGING,' BLURTED OUT PAULINE TO POLICE.

officers knew that they were dealing with something far more sinister than an accident and both young girls – Pauline was sixteen and Juliet fifteen years and ten months – were taken into custody for further questioning.

As they were led away a sharp-eyed policeman found near the pathway, a few feet away from the body of Mrs Parker, a

> 'AFTER THE FIRST BLOW WAS STRUCK I KNEW IT WOULD BE NECESSARY FOR US TO KILL HER.'

Above: *The distinguished father of Pauline, Dr H.R.Hulme, Rector of Canterbury University College, Christchurch. He intended to take his daughter away from her friend.*

brick wrapped in an old stocking. It was found to be covered in blood and great clumps of her hair were stuck to it. Clearly, this and not a board or a plank of wood had been the instrument which despatched the unfortunate woman. Later, a pathologist examined the corpse and said there was bruising around the throat consistent with her having been held down as blow after blow rained down on her head.

Once in custody Pauline confessed almost immediately to the murder. She said she had 'made up my mind' a few days before the event to kill her mother during an outing in the park and that Juliet, who was walking with them, was not implicated in the crime. She told detectives: 'She knew nothing about it. As far as I know, she believed what I had told her, although she may have guessed what had happened but I doubt it as we were both so shaken that it probably did not occur to her.'

But while she was being questioned, one of the officers guarding her turned his back to her, and she tried to burn a piece of paper on which she had written: 'I am taking the blame for everything.' This was seen as a message that she intended to smuggle to Juliet – Juliet, who, on learning of the abortive bid to contact her, changed her story immediately and confessed to being a willing accomplice.

IT WAS TERRIBLE BUT INSANE?

'I took the stocking,' said Juliet, 'and hit her too. I was terrified. I wanted to help Pauline. It was terrible – she moved convulsively. We both held her. She was still when we left her. After the first blow was struck I knew it would be necessary for us to kill her.'

There would have been no need for a protracted criminal trial, along with all its publicity, had the pair pleaded Guilty to murder. Instead, they chose to plead Guilty of murder by insanity – something the Crown was not prepared to accept. While in custody they had both seemed perfectly aware of what they had done, had both shown little remorse and had both only wanted to return to their 'perfect world'. Their insistence on a plea of insanity meant that the spotlight would now be directed at their dark world.

In his opening speech the prosecutor Mr Anthony Brown ominously told the jury: 'I feel bound to tell you that the evidence will make it terribly clear that the two young accused conspired together to kill the mother of one of them and horribly carried their plan into effect. It was a plan designed solely so they could carry on being together in the most unwholesome manner.'

Brown went on to explain how something 'unhealthy' had developed

between the two girls; how they had met at school as friends but then their relationship had deepened and broadened into something much more than girlish camaraderie. He remarked that it was a relationship 'more commonly seen between members of the opposite sex, and of a more advanced age', than that seen between two schoolgirls. Unhappy when apart, disturbingly attached to each other when together, Mr Brown painted a portrait of two girls sharing an unnatural love.

Above: *Juliet Hulme photographed at the time she was involved with Pauline but before they turned into killers.*

'WHY, OH WHY, COULD MOTHER NOT DIE? DOZENS OF PEOPLE, THOUSANDS OF PEOPLE, ARE DYING EVERY DAY.'

Mrs Parker, not surprisingly, was most unhappy about the relationship and was doing her best to break it up when she met her end. She had been in touch with Juliet's father, Dr Hulme, a Rector of Canterbury University College, New Zealand. Earlier that year he had resigned his post with the intention of taking a new position in Cape Town, South Africa. He agreed to take Juliet with him, to get her away from Pauline. The date agreed for his departure was 3 July – and the two girls vowed to kill Mrs Parker before then, her punishment for engineering their separation.

All this was corroborated in a sensational diary kept by Pauline Parker and in notes passed between the two – correspondence which the Crown said was definitely the work of people who were quite aware of what they were doing.

'In it,' said Brown, waving Pauline's leather-bound diary before the jury, 'she reveals that she and Juliet Hulme have engaged in shoplifting, have toyed with blackmail and talked about and played around in matters of sex. There is clear evidence that as long ago as February she was anxious that her mother should die,

Above: *The girls ran to the Victoria Tearooms, crying that Mrs Parker had fallen and was badly hurt.*

'Their first idea was to carry out this crime in such a way so that it appeared that it was an accident which befell Mrs Parker,' said Brown. They persuaded Mrs Parker, having pretended for a couple of weeks prior to her death that they no longer cared about being separated, to take them on a picnic to the country. Juliet Hulme brought along the brick from the garden of her home and the deed was accomplished.

and during the few weeks before 22 June she was planning to kill her mother in the way in which she was eventually to be killed.' It was damning evidence.

On 14 February, he read: 'Why, oh why, could mother not die? Dozens of people, thousands of people, are dying every day. So why not mother and father too?' Later, in April, she wrote: 'Anger against mother boiled up inside me. It is she who is one of the main obstacles in my path. Suddenly a means of ridding myself of the obstacle occurred to me. I am trying to think of some way. I want it to appear either a natural or an accidental death.'

In June it continued: 'We discussed our plans for moidering [sic] mother and made them a little clearer. Peculiarly enought I have no qualms of conscience (or is it just peculiar we are so mad!)' On 22 June, the actual day of the crime, Pauline penned this entry: 'I am writing a little bit of this up in the morning before the death. I felt very excited like the night before Chrismassy last night. I did not have pleasant dreams, though.' She did not elaborate on these.

The reading of the diary caused a stunned shock to the court. The two looked for all the world like normal schoolgirls and yet they had plotted and committed murder. There was even more damning testimony about them which showed that they were sneering, arrogant vixens who enjoyed illicit adult pleasures wrapped up in a fantasy world of their own making. And much of this damaging testimony was delivered by Juliet's mother.

THE STRANGE
DEBORAH AND LANCELOT

Mrs Hulme told the court how the girls were planning to publish a novel (although they hadn't yet written one) and practised writing in strange letters to each other using romantic pseudonyms. Juliet was often called Charles II, Emperor of Borovnia, then she changed to Deborah and then Bialbo. Pauline Parker, at the start of this bizarre correspondence, had called herself Lancelot Trelawney, a Cornish mercenary. Names of medieval drama.

The letters were initially full of romance as they created a fantasy world into which they escaped, but soon the tone changed to something far more sinister. They became violent, sadistic, with maidens raped and knights tortured as the girls' own lust for each other became ever more urgent. Soon they were sleeping together and even indulged in bondage. One said: 'I loved how we enacted how each saint might make love in bed. We have never felt so exhausted... but so satisfied!' It is no suprise that their parents wished to see the girls parted permanently.

Further details emerged of how they spent their days when they were supposed to be in school. They often slipped away to a country barn where they frolicked in the hayloft as lovers, finishing their day by washing each other in a country stream. They talked of going to America, of becoming rich and famous and buying a house together where they would have eunuchs as servants.

Juliet said she wanted to be 'safe' with Pauline – as a child she was brought up in the East End of London at the time of the London Blitz, something which traumatised her deeply. One of their 'games' involved Pauline cradling her as she made noises like bombs exploding around her. And all the while they played out this weird relationship, all schoolfriends and other playmates were excluded; it was, as described in one of Juliet's missives to Pauline, 'their perfect world', one to which no other was admitted.

Initially, Mrs Hulme, who had emigrated with her husband and Juliet when the child

Above: *Mrs Hulme broke down frequently during the trial of her daughter for murder. She refused to speak about the case for many years after the event.*

'I LOVED HOW WE ENACTED HOW EACH SAINT MIGHT MAKE LOVE IN BED. WE HAVE NEVER FELT SO EXHAUSTED... BUT SO SATISFIED!'

was five years old, welcomed her friend-ship with Pauline because it seemed to bring her out of her shell. 'Had I known where this would lead, I would have killed it stone dead there and then,' she sobbed.

Another entry in Pauline's diary, and one which was instrumental in proving their sanity, was the one which read: 'Prostitution sounds a good idea to make money and what fun we would have in doing it! We are so brilliantly clever, there probably isn't anything we couldn't do.' Was this, said the prosecution, the words of a pair who claimed they did not know what they were doing? Further, when Pauline was called to testify, her own arrogance virtually broke their defence. When asked if she knew that it was wrong to murder she sneered: 'I knew it was wrong to murder and I knew at the time that I was murdering somebody that it was wrong. You would have to be an absolute moron not to know that something was wrong.'

Lawyers for the two girls said there was no question that they were the killers but

'I KNEW AT THE TIME THAT I WAS MURDERING SOMEBODY THAT IT WAS WRONG. YOU WOULD HAVE TO BE AN ABSOLUTE MORON NOT TO KNOW THAT SOMETHING WAS WRONG.'

Below: *It was on this pathway, near the planking, that the two girls blud-geoned the mother to death.*

that they should not hang – a possibility, despite their age because they were being judged as adults – because of the abnormal-ity of their minds. One medical expert, a Dr Medlicott, pointed out that each of the girls had suffered bad physical health as toddlers and that their siblings were also prone to illnesses, suggesting somehow that this contributed to the unbalanced state of their young murderers' minds.

Discussing the bizarre relationship between them the doctor told the court : 'Juliet told me: "I do believe that we are indeed geniuses. I don't wish to place myself above the law – I am apart from it." And when I performed a medical examina-tion upon Miss Parker she turned to me and said: "I hope you break your flaming neck." In my opinion they are aggressive, dangerous, but most certifiably insane.'

It was not an opinion shared by expert Dr Charles Bennett who told the court: 'I find that they probably, very probably, knew what they were doing and knew it was wrong in the eyes of society at large.

But I doubt very much if they gave any consideration whatsoever to what society thought of them at all.'

In the end, after a careful summing up by the judge, it was left to the jury to decide whether the girls were mad or not. Mr Justice Adams said: 'The important word is the word "knowing". It has to be considered at the very moment of the commission of the crime. Were their minds so confused that they did not know this act was wrong? This is what you, ladies and gentlemen of the jury, have to consider.'

Consider it they did and in just two and a quarter hours returned a verdict of Guilty. There was a fleeting smile flashed between the two girls, these supreme egoists, when they were spared the rope by a merciful judge and ordered to be detained at Her Majesty's Pleasure – which meant indefinitely. But in a move which, to many, seemed to mock justice, they were freed just four years later after intense psychiatric counselling. They remained friends but the spark from that earlier relationship had been extinguished by the separation.

Herbert Rieper – he was with Pauline's mother for twenty-five years although he never married her – never recovered from her death. He never forgave the girl.and when his daughter was freed he said: 'It still doesn't make up for robbing a person of their life. It was evil between them that did it. Pure evil.'

Above: *The trial aroused tremendous interest. Crowds clamoured outside the court for a glimpse of the young lesbian killers.*

'PROSTITUTION SOUNDS A GOOD IDEA TO MAKE MONEY AND WHAT FUN WE WOULD HAVE IN DOING IT!'

BRADY & HINDLEY
The Moors Murders

Ian Brady and Myra Hindley arouse revulsion and hatred like no other murderers in British history. Together in an evil pact, they systematically tortured and killed more than six children. The real death toll is still unknown, forever locked up in the killers' deranged minds.

He was a twenty-seven-year-old stock clerk who idolised Hitler and sunk into horrible fantasies after drinking bottles of cheap German wine which transported him back in his imagination to the rallies and the marches of the Third Reich. Although the expression had not yet been coined in the Swinging Sixties, she would no doubt have been called a bimbo: a twenty-two-year-old peroxide-blonde typist who nurtured fantasies of eternal love. And, indeed, she did find immortality of a kind with the man with mesmeric eyes and a quick temper. Together they have gone down in British criminal history as the most wicked of the wicked, for they are the child-killers, Ian Brady and Myra Hindley.

Even today, in a world hardened by violent crime, their vile acts set them apart as monsters of a very special breed. At 16 Wardle Brook Avenue, on the sprawling Hattersley council estate and on the wild Pennine Moors, children abducted by these two died a gruesome death before being buried in unmarked graves. But death was not all these perverts visited upon their innocent victims who should never have accepted the lifts home they offered.

They were sexually assaulted, they were photographed and, in the case of one victim, her screams were even tape-recorded... screams that would later be heard in a criminal court, a shocking testament to evil.

Ian Brady and Myra Hindley are a classic case of partners in crime. Separate and alone, they were ordinary, if stunted, characters who might have lived their lives without ever plunging into the abyss of madness and depravity. Together, they fell prey to what the French call a *folie a deux* - the madness generated between two people. She was the girl he could impress; he was the errant knight for whom she would have sold her soul. In reality, they were bound by perversion and a taste for cruelty. Together they have left an imprint on Britain's national conscience that has not been faded or eroded by the passage of the years.

Brady and Hindley forged their relationship after meeting at work. He was a winkle-pickered youth with a fondness for crime B-movies and Nazi philosophy. An illegitimate child who had never known his father (widely believed to have been a reporter on a Glasgow evening newspaper),

Opposite: *Ian Brady and Myra Hindley frolic for the camera during the thrilling days of their perverse passion.*

he was brought up in the Gorbals slums of the city. His mother, coping with both the stigma of being unmarried and the burden of being poor, put him in the care of a family called Sloan when he was small, during the formative years of his life.

The kindness they lavished on him was misplaced; he became a cold, sneering, surly youth who shunned kindness as weakness, compassion as foolishness. Brick by brick, he built a wall around himself and

Above: *Police search for clues in the garden of the Hindley-Brady residence.*

convinced himself that he was better than everybody else and that society was against him.

After serving terms in Borstals as a teenager for housebreaking, he was finally given a chance to escape going to the 'big house' - adult prison - by a Glasgow judge who insisted that he live with his real mother. She, by the time he was a teenager, had moved back to Manchester with her new husband, an Irish labourer, but was willing to take a chance, putting her unhappy young son back on the straight and narrow. Here Brady's teenage rebelliousness metamorphosed into something altogether more sinister.

He began buying Nazi books like 'The Kiss of the Whip', which glorified the persecution of the Jews, and to drink heavily. Alternately in and out of work, in trouble with the law for drunkenness, he managed to land a job as a stock clerk at

Millwards Ltd, a chemical and soap company in Manchester. Here the partnership in evil would be irrevocably forged when Myra Hindley was introduced to him on 16 January, 1961.

Within weeks they had become lovers. Her diaries at the time show the student of crime as a pathetically ordinary, normal, unsophisticated suburban girl who confided to paper her childish hopes and fears: 'Not sure if he likes me. They say he gambles on horses. I love Ian all over and over again!'

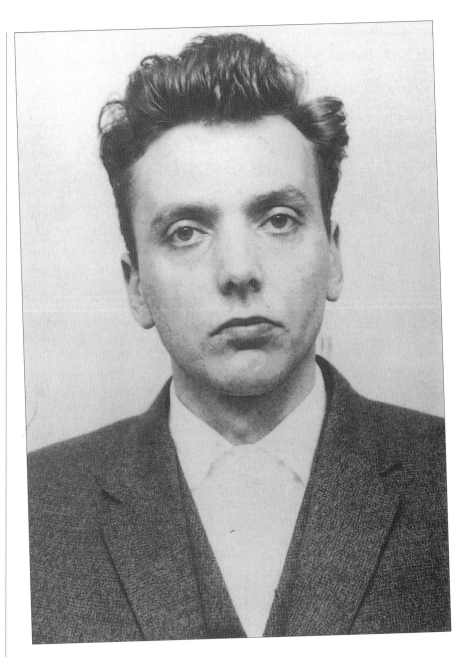

Above: *Ian Brady's image reveals an ill-tempered and defiant personality.*

Left: *The entrance to 18, Westmoreland Street, Manchester where Ian Brady used to live.*

Then: 'He has a cold and I would love to mother him.' Other times she is frustrated or cross with him, and determined to end their fledgling love affair.

Yet in the end he became her first lover, on a sofa-bed in the front room of the house she shared with her grandmother. It happened after they had seen one of his favourite films - 'Judgement at Nuremberg', a story of Nazi atrocities.

From these beginnings grew the seed of perversion and corruption. Brady's book collection of pornographic and sado-masochistic material had swelled now and his needs were more than conventional love-making. Soon he was taking lurid pictures of his girlfriend, complete with whips, a hood and even her pet dog. She

*Above: **Myra Hindley shows a hard, grim vanity in this photograph taken while she was on trial for killing small children.***

HE WAS TAKING LURID PICTURES OF HIS GIRL-FRIEND, COMPLETE WITH WHIPS, A HOOD AND EVEN HER PET DOG.

took pictures of him, too, surrounded by mirrors as he admired his body. But the thrill of this soon wore thin. Fuelled by the German wine he habitually drank, he drew her into his evil web of fantasy, when he talked of becoming a gangster and of her becoming his moll while they robbed and pillaged like a latter-day Bonnie and Clyde.

They did not have the courage for this, however; it was only Dutch courage inspired by the wine. But they did find the courage to satisfy their expanding sexual perversions, if courage is what is needed for two adult people to lure, humiliate, abuse and then murder little children.

No one knows at what precise moment they slipped over the edge and fantasy became action. Did they decide about it over tea, as the buses taking their neighbours to work roared along outside? Or perhaps it happened on one of their weekend excursions to the wild and lonely moors that ring Manchester. But Ian and Myra, the loving couple did cross the line between perversion and murder on Friday, 12 July, when Pauline Reade, aged sixteen, accepted a lift from them on her way to a social-club dance in Gorton.

Then on 23 November, 1963, they crossed it again when little John Kilbride, aged twelve-and-a-half, accepted a lift from them at the marketplace in Ashton-under-Lyne. On Tuesday, 15 June, 1964 Keith Bennett, aged twelve, became their third victim when he took a ride on a busy Manchester road after setting out to buy some sweets. On 26 December, 1964, Leslie Ann Downey, born on 21 August, 1954, died at the age of ten years and four months after she climbed into their car parked at a fairground near Ancoats.

THE HOME OF MURDER

After the disappearances of these children, there were the usual appeals of help, the usual sad pictures of the missing kids were plastered all over their neighbour-hoods and beyond. No clues linked their disappearances to each other, there was no reason to believe an evil pied piper was claiming them one by one. It took the brutal murder of an innocent teenager in the front room of the home Brady shared with his accomplice, to lead the police to uncover the horrific crimes of this couple.

On the morning of 7 October, 1965, David Smith, married to Hindley's sister Maureen, made a frantic 999 telephone call at 6.07am from a coin box on the edge of the housing estate where Hindley and Brady lived. He was a young man with a stammer, who was already known to the police for a string of petty offences, and he blurted out a tale of murder perpetrated, he said, the previous evening in the living room of Brady's house.

Smith said the victim, later identified as seventeen-year-old Edward Evans, had been axed to death by Ian Brady to 'impress' Smith. Brady had often talked of robbery and murders with Smith but Smith had put it down to an overworked imagination fuelled by the wine. This time the fantasy became reality before his very eyes. Brady had murdered a boy and Smith was asked to help clean up the blood after witnessing the ghastly scene.

In a calm monotone, he described how the young man had been lured to the house by Hindley, was set upon by the axewielding Brady and was finally 'finished off' by a length of electrical flex with which

Below, left: *Ian Brady is driven in a police car to the court to answer murder charges.*

Below, right: *Hindley was hysterical at leaving her dog when police bundled her off in their barred van.*

Millwards. The letter was an excuse to explain why he wouldn't be at work that day - he claimed he had hurt his ankle. In reality, he was planning an excursion to his private cemetery on the moors to make room for one more corpse.

Talbot, upon being greeted by Myra Hindley at the doorway, pushed past her into the house announcing that he was a police officer. Hindley tried to block his entrance to the bedroom but Brady, nonchalantly still lying on the divan, told her: 'Ye'd best give him the key.' Once inside the bedroom Superintendent Talbot discovered the corpse of the young man who died for their thrills.

With Brady in custody, charged with murder, the police re-interviewed Smith who told them that Brady had boasted of killing 'three or four others'. These others were allegedly buried on the bleak, beautiful Saddleworth Moor outside of Manchester. Talbot logged the numbers carefully in his orderly policeman's brain, for he believed he had seen in Brady's arrogant eyes and surly manner the mark of a very dangerous predator indeed.

Brady told police a bland story. He said

Brady throttled him. Brady asked Smith to help him in his macabre clean-up afterwards, saying: 'This one's taking a time to go. Feel, Dave, feel the weight of that. That was the messiest yet.' Afterwards, with the glow of a sexual, murderous frenzy bathing them, Ian Brady and Myra Hindley made love as Edward Evans's mutilated body lay upstairs.

A FATAL DELIVERY OF BREAD

Police decided that there was more to Smith's tale than hysteria or mischief. The house in Wardle Brook Avenue was approached and police superintendent Bob Talbot put on the white coat of a local breadman, borrowed his loaves and knocked on the door of number sixteen. Hindley answered it; Brady was inside on a divan writing a letter to his bosses at

he had met Edward Evans, the victim, in a Manchester pub. The youngster had come to his house afterwards, they had rowed and, unfortunately, he had killed Evans with a hatchet. Talbot's superior officer, Arthur Benfield, Detective Chief Superintendent for the whole of Cheshire, was down at the police station by noon to investigate the drunken death but he was worried by the boast of 'three or four others'.

A search of the house revealed notebooks with ruled columns in which Brady had written down a series of what appeared to be coded instructions. There was 'meth' for method, 'stn' for station, 'bulls' for bullets, 'gn' for gun. After staring at it long and hard, Benfield realised he was looking at a shopping list for murder weapons. But whose murder?

Days later, as he sifted through the paraphernalia of Brady's bedroom, he came upon a tattered school exercise book filled with scribblings and graffiti. There was a list of names that apparently meant nothing, jotted down by the day-dreaming clerk during moments of boredom. But Benfield read through all the names nonetheless - Christine Foster, Jean Simpson, Robert Uquart, James Richardson, Joan Crawford, Gilbert John, Ian Brady, John Sloan, Jim Idiot, John Birch, Frank Wilson, John Kilbride, Alec Guineas, Jack Polish, J. Thompson. John Kilbride... the name hit Talbot like a hammer blow and suddenly the feeling washed over him that he was on to a monstrous crime, something bigger than he had ever imagined.

The search of the house brought to light the pornographic photographs Brady and Hindley had taken of each other and the sado-masochistic and Nazi book collection. And there were other pictures too of Hindley and Brady taken on the moors. One in particular caught his eye, that of Myra sitting on the ground, looking wistfully at the gorse and peat beneath her, staring at

Above: *Myra Hindley's peroxide has faded, but her sneering defiance remains and can be discerned even in this partial view of her.*

'THIS ONE'S TAKING A TIME TO GO. FEEL, DAVE, FEEL THE WEIGHT OF THAT. THAT WAS THE MESSIEST YET.'

Above: Mr David Lloyd Jones, in front, and Mr Philip Curtis counsel for Brady and Hindley respectively. The defence had an unenviable task.

Right: Scenes outside the courtroom as Lesley Anne Downey's uncle lunged at the man who murderd the child. Police restrained him but the public did not.

The police had two lucky breaks. Everyone was eager to help catch the murderers, and the police received vital information from a neighbour's twelve-year-old daughter who accompanied Auntie Myra and Uncle Ian on excursions to the moors to 'help them dig for peat'. Then, a car hire company confirmed that they had rented a car to a Myra Hindley on 23 November, 1963, John Kilbride's last day alive. The police used photos removed from the couple's bedroom to locate the burial places of the murdered children. They were helped by the girl who, though she had been taken to the moors by the pair, had survived the trip.

A CASE OF LEFT-LUGGAGE

The body of Lesley Ann Downey was found by the police searchers on 16 October, ten days after the death of Edward Evans. Police thought that they would find the body of John Kilbride but they only found the little tartan skirt belonging to the trusting little girl. Two days later another

nothing in particular except the ground as if ... as if she were staring at a grave.

Brady played mind games with the police, claiming the stories he told to Smith were lies to build up an 'image'. He said there were no more bodies and that the name Kilbride in the exercise book was an old chum from Borstal days. Police made door-to-door inquiries in their neighbourhood.

policeman on the team made an even more startling discovery. Hidden in the spine of Myra Hindley's communion prayer book was a left-luggage ticket for two suitcases at Manchester Central Station. Once retrieved, they yielded up more porno-graphic books, small-arm ammunition, blackjacks, wigs, tapes and photos of moorland views.

And other pictures. Pictures of a little girl with her eyes bulging in terror, naked save for her socks and shoes, bound and gagged. Talbot felt the tears well up in his eyes as he looked into the helpless face of Lesley Ann Downey.

Later, the tapes were played. The first one was a hotch-potch of Hitler marches and the BBC *Goons* show, interspersed with a documentary on Hitler's life. Then the second one was played - the tape that numbed the policemen present, would later make hardened journalists weep and would finally nail Brady and Hindley for the cruel and evil monsters they were. 'Don't... please God help me. Don't undress me will you... I want me mam...'. Interspersed with screams, pleas and futile whimpers, against the barking commands of Hindley and Brady, these were the final words of Lesley Ann as she met her unspeakable end at the hands of the sinister people who gave her a lift at the fair.

Below, left: *Ian Brady takes a last look at the world where he behaved with such depravity.*

Below, right: *Patricia Cairns, second on the right, the lesbian warder who plotted to free her lover, Hindley.*

On 21 October the body of John Kilbride was found in the spot where Myra had been photographed with her beloved dog Puppet. John's underpants had been pulled down to below his thighs, knotted hard in the back to prevent him from moving his legs. He had been sexually assaulted and buried face down. Britain and the world were inflamed with anger at the killers now branded the Moors Murderers. Myra Hindley was now

under arrest to face charges of murder along with her lover, Ian Brady.

The trial gripped the public attention as no other had done when the pair came before Chester Assizes on 19 April, 1966. Both pleaded Not Guilty to murder and maintained an arrogance and swagger throughout that earned them the hatred of prosecutors, police, journalists, the judge and the parents of the dead.

In the Evans case, Brady maintained that it was Smith's idea to 'roll a queer' for money and that he had participated in the killing. In Lesley Ann's case, Brady gave the court a totally implausible story that he had taken photos of her after she had been driven to their home by men he didn't know and that he turned her over to them afterwards. In the case of John Kilbride, he denied murder and sexual assault.

It was the tape, however, which dominated the proceedings and for which they will always be damned. Emlyn Williams, in his authoritative chronicle of the crimes and aftermath 'Beyond Belief'

Opposite: *The pair had many snapshots of their excursions with dogs on the moors. Myra, particularly, was fond of animals. However, the police were able, with the help of these 'family' snaps, to locate the burial grounds of murder victims. The photos were grotesque 'souvenirs' of grotesque crimes.*

Right: *Hindley's sister, Maureen with her husband, David Smith. He was seduced by Brady's ideas on dangerous sexual thrills, but the reality disgusted him. Smith reported Brady and Hindley to the police after he witnessed them killing a young man.*

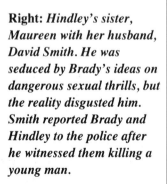

BRADY, WHEN ASKED WHY HE KEPT THE TAPE RECORDING, SAID IT WAS BECAUSE IT WAS 'UNUSUAL'.

wrote: 'This tape was to become the most scaring object ever to lie on the exhibits table below a judge at a murder trial... the tape began. And played for seventeen intolerable minutes. To listen to it was made doubly dreadful by the very nature of the invention which made the experience possible. In the course of murder trials, for centuries dreadful things have had to come to light, not only visually but mumbled by unwilling witnesses. Never before, however, has the modern phenomenon of preserved sound been put to such a grisly use as was "the Moors tape".' The courtroom listened in shocked horror and disbelief to the pleading of the little girl as she begged for life and her mam, to the backdrop of Christmas carols and the barking commands of Brady for the child to pose in immodest positions.

Brady, when asked why he kept the tape recording, said it was because it was 'unusual'. It was a gross answer.

Hindley, in particular, became the focus of public curiosity. Men like Brady - well, there are many perverts and murderers down the ages, men who have killed to sate their demonic urges. But women were supposed to be the gentler sex, the givers of life, the nurturers of children. How could she have slipped into such an abyss? She gave little indication that she had a 'feminine' heart at her trial. Scrutiny of testimony during examination by the Attorney General Sir Elwyn Jones shows that she had little remorse for what had taken place, even though she pleaded Not Guilty to all charges. The following is an extract from the trial.

Attorney General: Time and again you were driving into this child's ears your orders, 'put it in'.

Hindley: I just wanted her to not make a noise.

Attorney General: Then you say, 'Will you stop it. Stop it'. Did you think there was the most terrible threatening note in the second order to stop it, Miss Hindley?

Hindley: No, it was a desperate tone.

Attorney General: Then one hears the poor little child making a retching noise. This thing was being pushed down her throat, was it not?

Hindley: No,

Attorney General: Who do you say undressed this child?

Hindley: Herself

Attorney General: Can you therefore explain the child's saying: 'Don't undress me will you? That was precisely what you were trying to do with the child?

Hindley: No, I was not.

Attorney General: A little further on Brady is saying: 'If you don't keep that hand down I'll slit your neck.' That is why you do not want to be landed with hearing that, is it not?

Hindley: No.

Attorney General: Then when the child was whining you say, 'Sh. Hush. Put that in your mouth again and...'. Then there follow the words 'packed more solid'. Why did you want the mouth to be packed more solid?

Hindley: Why more solid? I don't know.

Attorney General: That was preparatory to suffocating her in due course, was it not?

Hindley: No.

Above: Police with long poles search near the site where they unearthed the body of Lesley Anne Downey. They were looking for other victims.

THEY KILLED FOR SICK AND TWISTED KICKS. THEY ARE NOT FIT TO MIX WITH HUMANS.

But no one in the court believed they were innocent. On 6 May, 1966, both were found Guilty of murdering Edward Evans and Lesley Ann Downey, Brady further found Guilty of the murder of John Kilbride with Hindley being an accessory after the fact. Brady was jailed for life on each of the three murder charges, Hindley for life on the Downey and Evans murders with a further seven years for her part as an accessory to the Kilbride slaying.

They were driven off to separate prisons with the screams of the mob outside ringing in their ears, and the lovers were never to see each other again. Hindley appealed her conviction but three appeal judges ruled against her.

The grisly saga of the Moors Murders might have ended then but the disappearances of Pauline Reade and Keith Bennett remained unsolved. Police officers who had worked on the case felt in their bones that these two monsters had something to do with the disappearances of these two but there were no photographs or tape recordings to link them with the youngsters.

These suspicions continued down the years as Myra Hindley became a model

prisoner, then was involved in a lesbian love-affair that sparked a failed escape plot. She became an Open University graduate, converted to Christianity and established communication with Lord Longford, the prison reformer who is one of very few people who believed that Myra Hindley had been rehabilitated and deserved to be released.

The correspondence between her and Brady was furious and passionate in the first months of separation, but time cooled the love while Brady slipped deeper into madness before he was finally moved, in November 1985, to a maximum-security hospital. But he was not so mad as to be incapable of thwarting the long-cherished dream that his former lover clung to throughout her long years of captivity.

A LOVER'S FURY

When Brady heard of Myra's attempts to be released, he broke his silence regarding the deaths of Reade and Bennett, prompting police to visit Myra Hindley in her jail cell. On 15 December, 1986, Myra Hindley returned to Saddleworth Moor, her first breath of the moors since the terrible events of more than two decades previously. Her memory, perhaps faded with time, perhaps by the enormity of what she had done, failed to pinpoint any graves, although she was sure she had the right area. But police searched diligently and in June the following year the body of Pauline Reade was discovered. Pathologists analysed that she had been sexually assaulted and her throat slashed from behind.

Her confession to the Reade and Bennett murders effectively stifled any hope that Myra Hindley would ever be freed and she was said to have resigned herself to death in jail. After unconfirmed media reports that Hindley was suffering with advanced lung cancer, she did eventually die in prison at the age of 60.

Brady's mental degeneration continued. Declared clinically insane, in the winter of 1987 he mailed a letter to the BBC containing sketchy information about five further murders, including unsuspected Moors victims, a man murdered in Manchester, a woman dumped in a canal and two victims gunned down in Scotland. He remains alive in the high security Ashworth hospital on Merseyside. After failing several attempts to starve himself to death, he remains on continual hunger strike being force-fed through a plastic tube.

Other victims of the killings are the families of the murdered children. Mrs Ann West, mother of Lesley Ann, was a vociferous campaigner for Hindley to stay behind bars. On the twenty-fifth anniversary of her child's death she wrote to Home Secretary Kenneth Baker, saying: 'Though a generation has passed since those evil monsters were put behind bars the horror of their crimes remains as fresh as ever. I beg you to turn a deaf ear to those well-meaning but tragically misguided do-gooders who would now set them free on compassionate grounds. Ignore, at all costs, those who would forgive and forget. For just as there is no parole for we who still grieve, so must there be no parole for them.

'Every night I am haunted anew by the memory of that courtroom. I can still hear the taped screams of Lesley Ann begging for mercy...

'The enormity of those murders has not diminished. They killed for sick and twisted kicks, and showed no compassion. They are not fit to mix with humans. I implore you to make sure they do not.'

Below, left: *The bleak burial grounds of two murdered children.*

Below: *Ian Brady after years in prison. He has grown madder and madder and is in a psychiatric unit.*

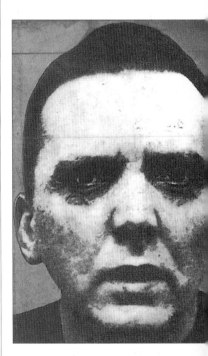

DOWNEY'S BODY FOUND OVER RIDGE

KILBRIDE'S BODY FOUND HERE

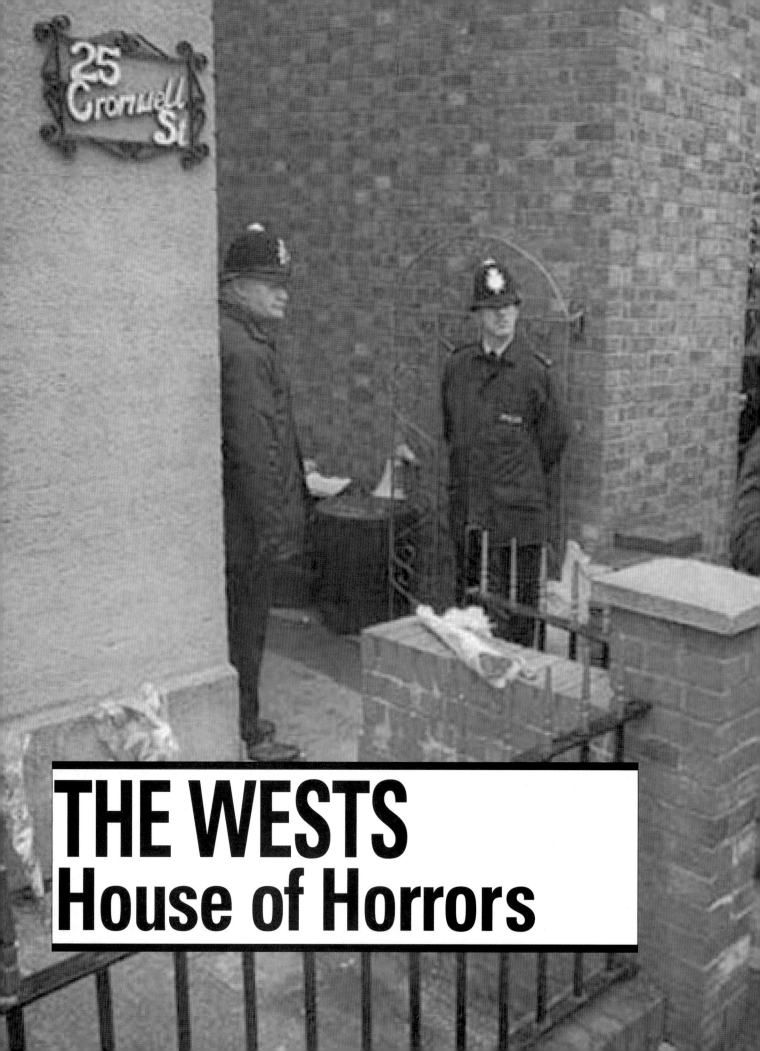

25 Cromwell St

THE WESTS
House of Horrors

On 24 February 1994, police began to dig up the garden at 25 Cromwell Street to look for Heather West, daughter of Rosemary and Frederick West. On 13 December 1994, Frederick West was charged with twelve murders. Rose also received life imprisonment on each of the ten counts of murder.

Young women would go and stay at 25 Cromwell Street, either as nannies, lodgers or friends, but very few of them made it out of the West house alive. It was slowly becoming a House of Horrors.

FRED'S CHILDHOOD

Frederick West was born in 1941 to Walter and Daisy West, who lived in Much Marcle, a village about 120 miles west of London. After Fred, Daisy had another six children during the following ten years.

As Fred grew older, he developed a close relationship with his mother, doing everything she asked. Fred also had a good relationship with his father whom he admired as a role model.

While being a scruffy looking boy, Fred inherited some of his mother's features, a rather large mouth with a gap between his big teeth, resembling the looks of a gypsy.

At school, Fred was always in trouble for which he was frequently caned. His mother, Daisy, would then go to the school and yell at the teacher, which made Fred the victim of many jokes.

Opposite: *Police guarding 25 Cromwell Street as evidence is being removed.*

Right: *Fred and Rosemary West, the happy couple.*

At the age of fifteen and virtually illiterate, Fred left school and went to work as a farm hand. By the time he was sixteen, he had become very aggressive to the opposite sex and persued any girl that took his fancy.

Fred, recognised as a notorious liar, claimed that his father had sex with his daughters using the excuse 'I made you so I'm entitled to have you'. Then at seventeen, he was seriously injured in a motorcycle accident. After a week in a coma, a broken leg and having a metal plate inserted into his head, Fred was left with one leg shorter than the other. This head injury may have resulted in

Fred being prone to sudden fits of rage and the loss of control over his emotions.

After this accident Fred met a pretty 16-year-old called Catherine Berna-dette Costello. Nicknamed Rena, she had always been in trouble with the police since early childhood and was an accomplished and experienced thief. They quickly became lovers. The affair ended months later as she returned to Scotland. Then, after plunging his hand up a young woman's skirt while on a fire escape at a local youth group, Fred

Left: *Rosemary as a child.*

fell, banged his head and lost consciousness. It may be that he suffered brain damage due to his two head injuries and this could have been the cause of a lasting impact on Fred's behaviour.

After being fined for theft in 1961, Fred was accused of getting a 13-year-old girl pregnant. He couldn't understand that he had done anything wrong, as this girl was a friend of the family, it caused a scandal and he was told to find somewhere else to live. Working on construction sites, it wasn't long before he was caught stealing and having sex with young girls.

At the age of 20, although he got off without a prison sentence, Fred had become a convicted child molester and petty thief; a complete disgrace to his family.

ROSE'S CHILDHOOD

Daisy Letts was hospitalized in 1953, due to her deepening depression, and trying to cope with a violent husband, three daughters and son, she had electroshock therapy. Shortly after this treatment she gave birth to Rosemary. Rosemary Letts was born in Devon in November 1953. Her mother suffered from severe depression and her father, Bill Letts, was a schizophrenic. Bill

'DOZY ROSIE' — AS SHE WAS CALLED, WAS NOT VERY INTELLIGENT ALTHOUGH SHE WAS SMART ENOUGH TO BECOME HER FATHER'S PET, ALWAYS DOING WHATEVER HE WISHED IMMEDIATELY.

was a violent and dominant man, demanding obedience from both his wife and children and enjoyed looking for reasons to beat them. The family was short of money because Bill was not an ideal employee and only maintained a series of unskilled and low paid jobs.

Rose had developed a habit of rocking herself in her cot and as she became older, she would swing her head for hours until she reached semiconciousness. Being quite pretty, if a little chubby, she was called 'Dozy Rosie', although she was smart enough to become her father's pet. But at school, due to cruel jokes and teasing, Rose was recognised as an ill-tempered, aggressive loner.

In her teens she walked around naked after baths, fondled her brother and became sexually precocious. As boys were not interested in her she focused her attentions on the older men of the village.

During 1968 Rose was raped by an older man who had taken advantage of her innocent ways. Then at the beginning of 1969 Daisy, her mother, took 15-year-old Rose and moved in temporarily with one of her other daughters to escape from Bill. At this time Rose began to spend a lot of time out with men. Later that year, Rose moved back home with her father.

As Rose Letts was not a very smart nor good tempered girl she became unfocused towards any productive goal except finding a lover older than herself.

THE FIRST VICTIM

In 1962 Fred was allowed to move back home in Much Marcle. Rena Costello returned from Scotland in the summer and they met up immediately, continuing their relationship. Although Rena was pregnant by an Asian bus driver, she and Fred secretly married and moved to Scotland. Charmaine was born March 1963. They both wrote to Fred's parents, stating that their baby had died at birth, therefore they had adopted a child of mixed race.

Fred's interest for normal sex was small, although he had a voracious appetite for oral sex, bondage and sodomy. As an icecream man, his apparent politeness and sincerity attracted teenagers around his van. This led to many sexual encounters. With his growing number of infidelities, Rena and Charmaine were pushed out of his mind.

FRED AND ROSE

Rena gave birth to Fred's child in 1964, and they named her Anne Marie. During their turbulent marriage, the West's embarked on a friendship with Anna McFall. Then Fred, Rena and their two children, as well as Anna, moved to Gloucester where Fred found work in a slaughterhouse. This is probably where Fred developed a morbid obsession with blood, corpses and dismemberment.

As the marriage fell apart, Rena returned to Scotland alone. When she returned to Gloucester in July 1966, she found Fred living in a trailer with Anna McFall. Due to pressure from Anna to marry her, Fred responded by killing her and her unborn child sometime in July 1967. He slowly and methodically dismembered her and the foetus, cutting off her fingers and toes, and buring her body somewhere near the trailer park.

Rena then moved back in with Fred, earning money as a prostitute, while he began, openly, to fondle Charmaine.

Then in February 1968, due to his mother dying, Fred started a series of petty thefts, which caused him to change his job frequently. In November 1968, while on one of these many jobs,

Left: *Anne Marie daughter of Fred and Rena Costello.*

Fred met Rose Letts, his future wife.

Although Rose's father did not approve of Fred, she carried on seeing him until she found herself pregnant with his baby. At the age of 16, Rose left home to take care of Charmaine, Anna Marie and Fred.

CHARMAINE

Rose gave birth in 1970 to Heather. While Fred was in jail, Rose was left at home with the all the children whom she treated quite badly. Then one day during the summer of 1971, Charmaine went missing. Although this happened while Fred was in prison, he probably helped to bury her body under the kitchen floor of their home in Midland Road, removing her fingers, toes and kneecaps, only to be discovered 20 years later. It was only a matter of time before Rena came looking for Charmaine. When she found Fred, he got her drunk, then strangled, dismembered her body and buried her as he had done with Anna, cutting off

HE WOULD DISMEMBER THE BODY, CUTTING OFF THE FINGERS, TOES AND KNEECAPS — THEN PUT THE REMAINS INTO BAGS READY FOR BURIAL.

Below: *Leading into the cellar at 25 Cromwell Street.*

her fingers and toes.

Fred and Rose married in Gloucester registry office in 1972, then Rose gave birth to a daughter, Mae West. As the family increased in size, they moved to 25 Cromwell Street, where Rose also had room for her prostitution business.

As the cellar was soundproof, they used it as a 'torture chamber'. Anne Marie, their 8-year-old daughter was the first victim, her mother held her down and her father raped her. The pain was so bad that she could not attend school.

CAROLINE OWENS

The couple hired a nanny, 17-year-old Caroline Owens. They abducted, raped and threatened her but she got away and reported this to the police. There was a hearing. At this time Fred was thirty-one and Rose only nineteen, and they were found not guilty.

LYNDA GOUGH

Lynda Gough, a friend who helped take care of the children, became the next victim. She was dismembered and buried in a pit in the garage, having had her fingers, toes and kneecaps removed.

A terrible pattern was beginning to develop.

CAROL ANN COOPER

In August 1973, Stephen, their first son was born. Fred and Rose abducted 15-year-old Carol in November, abusing her sexually until they strangulated or suffocated her. They dismembered and buried her body at the growing graveyard of 25 Cromwell street.

LUCY PARTINGTON AND THE REST

The cellar was enlarged and the garage was transformed into an extension of the main house, all done by Fred at strange hours of the day. On December 27, 1973, Lucy Partington went to visit her disabled friend but had the misfortune to bump into Rose and Fred. She was tortured for a week and then murdered, dismembered and buried under one of Fred's many construction projects at 25 Cromwell Street.

During the period from April 1974 to April 1975 another three women became victims like Carol and Lucy. They were Therese Siegenthaler 21, Shirley Hubbard, 15 and Juanita Mott, 18. The Wests buried these bodies under the cellar floor. Juanita had been gagged by a ligature made from a pair of white nylon socks, two pairs of tights and a bra, then tied up with plastic covered rope, the type used for a washing line. Tied up so tightly so that she could hardly move, she was probably suspended from the beams in the cellar. As for Shirley Hubbard, her body was wrapped entirely with tape, a plastic tube had been inserted up her nose, allowing her to breathe.

Fred continued to get into trouble with the police with thefts and stolen

> NOT ONLY DID HE KILL HIS MISTRESS AND THEIR UNBORN CHILD, HE SLOWLY AND METHODICALLY DISMEMBERED HER CORPSE AND BURIED HER ALONG WITH HER FOETUS.

Above: *Fred West – the last photograph before his death.*

> FRED'S INTEREST IN 'NORMAL SEX' WAS MINIMAL. HE WANTED ORAL SEX, BONDAGE AND SODOMY — AT ALL HOURS OF THE DAY AND NIGHT.

goods, which he needed to maintain his home improvement projects.

The Wests took in lodgers. One of these, Shirley Robinson, 18, a former prostitute, developed a relationship with them and later became pregnant with Fred's child. Rose had also became pregnant, but by one of her black clients. Rose became uncomfortable with this situation and wanted Shirley to leave. Seven months later, Tara was born to Rose in December 1977, Shirley and her unborn baby became the next victims and were buried in the garden of Cromwell Street. Yet another baby girl, Louise, was born to the Wests in November 1978, making a total of six. Fred's daughter, Anna Marie also became pregnant by Fred, although this was terminated.

After Rose's father died in May 1979, the Wests raped, tortured and murdered their next victim, Alison

Above: *The house in Northam, Devon where Rose West lived as a child.*

WHEN HE CUT OFF HER HEAD, IT MADE A SOUND, 'A HORRIBLE NOISE... LIKE SCRUNCHING — VERY UNPLEASANT.' BUT ONCE HER HEAD WAS OFF, HE STARTED ON HER LEGS, TWISTING HER FOOT UNTIL ONE ALMIGHTY CRACK.

Chambers who was only 17. She was also buried in the garden at Cromwell Street. The rest of the children in the West household were aware of strange happenings. They knew that their mother was a prostitute and that Anna Marie was continually raped by her father. Anna moved in with her boyfriend, so Fred made advances towards his other daughters, Heather and Mae. Heather was beaten for trying to resist her father's advances. Rose gave birth to Barry, Fred's second son in June 1980, followed by Rosemary junior, who was not Fred's, in April 1982. She also had Lucyanna in July 1983, who was half-black like Tara and Rose junior. With all these children to contend with, Rose became extremely bad tempered.

After Heather broke the silence and told her girlfriend of the abuse from her father, she too was murdered This happened after an argument with her father got out of control. Fred grabbed her round the neck, she went blue and stopped breathing. After trying to revive her, he dragged her to the bath and ran cold water over her. After taking all her clothes off and drying her, he tried to fit her in the rubbish bin. But as she did not fit, strangled her with tights just to make sure she was dead, and then cut her up into smaller pieces. Stephen, Fred's son, helped his father dig a hole in the back garden for Heather's dismembered body.

Katherine Halliday began to participate in the West's prostitution business, although this did not last long as she became very alarmed at their collection of suits, whips and chains and left abruptly.

Due to one of Fred's young rape victims talking, Detective Constable Savage, who had experience in dealing with Rena, was assigned to his case. On 6 August, 1992, Police arrived at Cromwell Street with a warrant to look for child abuse and pornography. Fred was arrested. While the Police had enough evidence to bring child abuse charges against Fred, Detective Constable Savage was curious as to the disappearance of Charmaine, Rena and Heather.

The West's children were put into care and with Fred in prison, Rose attempted suicide but failed. After rumours emerged that Heather was apparently buried under the patio, the house and garden were searched. Fred confessed to killing his daughter when human bones, other than Heather's, were found in the garden. The police began to dig the garden and it became only a matter of time before they found the first remains of a young woman, dismembered and decapitated.

Fred then told the police of the girls in the cellar, admitting to murder but not rape. In the cellar, nine sets of bones were discovered, although the police could not identify them and Fred was no help as he couldn't remember the victims.

Rena, Anna McFall and Charmaine's bodies were found, although Mary Bastholm was not.

At the joint hearing, Fred tried to console Rose, but she brushed him off, telling the police that he made her sick.

GUILTY

Fred was charged with twelve murders on December 13, 1994. After being devastated by Rose's rejection, Fred hung himself with his bedsheet on New Year's day at Winson Green Prison, Birmingham.

On October 3, 1995, Rose went to trial linking her to the murders and sadistic sexual assaults on young women. Among the witnesses were Caroline Owens, whom they had hired as a nannie in 1972, along with Anna Marie. The defence, led by Richard

AFTER BRUSHING OFF FRED, HE WROTE A LETTER SAYING THAT SHE WOULD ALWAYS BE HIS MRS WEST, THEY WOULD ALWAYS BE IN LOVE.

Below:
Rosemary West

Ferguson QC, tried to show that Rose was unaware of what Fred was up to, and that the evidence of sexual assault was not the same as evidence of murder. But after taking the stand, the jury were left believing that she ill-treated her children and was completely dishonest.

The most dramatic evidence was given by Janet Leach, who witnessed Fred's police interviews. During these interviews, Fred had said how he had involved Rose with the murders and that Rose had murdered Charmaine and Shirley Robinson on her own. After this testimony, Janet Leach collapsed and was admitted to hospital.

It did not take the jury long to find Rose guilty of murdering Charmaine, Heather, Shirley Robinson and the other bodies all buried at Cromwell Street. With ten counts of murder, the judge sentenced Rose to life imprisonment.

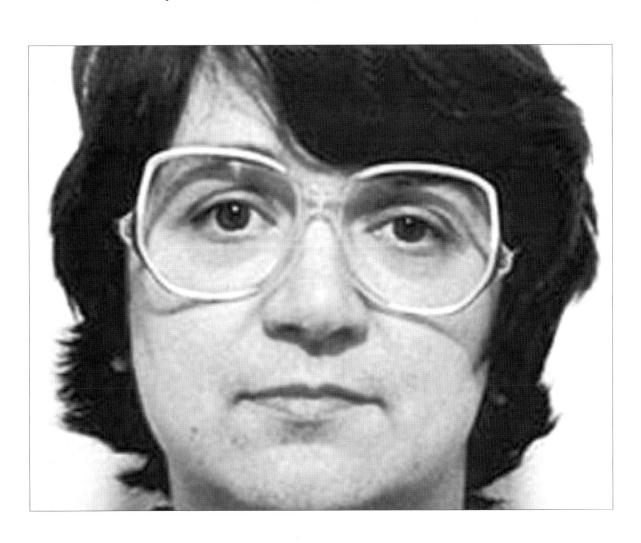

THE ROSENBERGS
The A-Bomb Spies

No-one ever thought there was anything special about Julius and Ethel Rosenberg, until they were tried and executed in the electric chair as spies. This ordinary couple were at the heart of a traitorous network which passed the secrets of America's first atomic bomb to the Soviet Union.

Julius and Ethel Rosenberg were the children of dispossessed Russian Jews who went to the New World determined to make a different and better life. Julius and Ethel were both born in the USA. Of course, as they matured they also nursed their hopes and their dreams. But their dream was not the same dream as that of their family and neighbours; it was one that could only be fulfilled by an alien creed hostile to their homeland, the government of the United States.

For Ethel and Julius Rosenberg were America's 'atomic spies', the suburban couple enmeshed in a plot to sell America's nuclear secrets to their Kremlin enemy. The Rosenbergs were the only Communist agents ever to be executed in peacetime and, while apologists and historical revisionists have argued down the years that the pair were the victims of a ghastly frame-up, experts conclude that the verdicts and sentences passed upon them have stood the test of time.

When the switch was thrown on them in the death chamber at Sing-Sing prison in New York on 19 June, 1953, it was the end of one of the grimmest chapters of international espionage. Many thronged the streets in the hours before they were executed, some protesting their innocence, others merely asking for clemency. The problem

with both Julius and Ethel Rosenberg, for those who believed them innocent, was that they looked so damned ordinary. But that, say the counter-intelligence chiefs who trapped them, was precisely what made them so damn good.

Outwardly, there was nothing to distinguish this married couple from their fellow citizens. Ethel, whose maiden name was Greenglass, had graduated from high school on the lower east side of Manhattan – a neigbourhood that embraced most of the races on earth. She left school at sixteen, was employed in various clerical jobs and secretarial posts before becoming an active trade unionist.

Opposite: *Ethel and Julius Rosenberg who played no small part in the Cold War when they sold A-bomb secrets to the USSR.*

Above: *The A-bomb explosion over Japan in 1945.*

Julius, the bespectacled electrical engineer who once underwent religious training in the hope of becoming a rabbi, sprang from similar roots. A graduate of the same high school as his future wife, he studied the Torah for a year before abandoning his religious leanings in favour of a degree in electrical engineering from the City College of New York. He knew Ethel at school as a friend, but when he met her later at a dance, their friendship blossomed into love. In 1939, while the storm clouds of war were gathering over Europe, he married her shortly after his twenty-first birthday.

Below, left: *Given the innocuous name of 'Little Boy' this is an A-bomb, capable of a dreadful, long-term destruction of mankind.*

Below, right: *Dr.Enrico Fermi, the Italian who escaped Fascism in his own country, and worked in the USA. He was the scientist who first produced the chain-reacting fission that led to the A-bomb.*

expelled from the Army when his covert membership of the organisation was discovered by the FBI. America was yet to reach her peak of anti-Communist hysteria under the McCarthy hearings, but to be 'red' was still an alien and utterly distasteful concept to the majority of her citizens. Unemployed and with a family to feed, Julius launched his own business with capital from Ethel's brothers, David and Bernard.

David Greenglass was an integral part of the conspiracy to sell USA secrets to the USSR that Julius and Ethel Rosenberg had willingly joined several years previously. For Greenglass worked during the war at the Los Alamos research centre, the top-secret New Mexico site where Robert Oppenheimer and his scientists worked in a desperate race to build the first atomic bomb before the Axis powers did. This remote site, formerly the home of a boys school, was the centre for the greatest and most destructive scientific achievement of this or any age... and David Greenglass systematically stole its secrets for traitorous sale to the Russians.

Just like the British-born Soviet spies Burgess, Philby and Maclean, who were recruited as agents while at British universities, so Greenglass saw the Soviet Union

A SOCIALIST FAMILY MAN

After a year of odd-jobs Julius became a junior engineer for the Army Signal Corps. In the spring of 1942 he and Ethel, who had been living in cramped conditions with his mother, rented a small apartment in a housing development on the east side of Manhattan. Life was sweet for the Rosenbergs during the war years; he had a desk job which didn't require him to serve abroad, and there were few of the economic privations in America which tested British familes during the War. They had two sons, Michael and Robert and the young Rosenbergs doted on them.

But Julius was already a keeper of secrets. Years earlier he had joined the Communist Party, impressed by what he saw as the 'new order' shaping world events from Moscow. In 1945 he was

*Above: **Julius Rosenberg is arrested by FBI agents on charges of espionage.***

as the way of the future. But the FBI later maintained that it was his sister and Julius who had recruited him to the cause. And the Rosenbergs kept him sweet on the idea of world socialism with liberal handouts of money. With the family as his puppet-masters, he agreed to use his work position to deliver the stolen blueprints for the bomb to their Kremlin bosses. When Greenglass eventually came to trial, he turned on his family to save his own neck. By pinning the blame exclusively on the Rosenbergs, claiming their own fanatical Communist leanings were used to intimidate him, he saved himself.

It was the Rosenbergs who were the lynch-pin for the entire spying operation which began to unravel in 1950 with the arrest of thirty-nine-year-old Harry Gold, a bachelor employed as a chemist at a Philadelphia hospital. He was named by the

HE HAD JOINED THE COMMUNIST PARTY, IMPRESSED BY WHAT HE SAW AS THE 'NEW ORDER' SHAPING WORLD EVENTS FROM MOSCOW.

FBI and the US Attorney General as being the accomplice of the disgraced nuclear boffin Klaus Fuchs, who was behind bars in England after pleading guilty to selling nuclear secrets to Moscow.

REVELATIONS OF A BRITISH SPY

Fuchs, a brilliant physicist who had fled his native Germany when Hitler came to power, was part of the British mission that was given access to the highest security levels surrounding the development of the bomb. He received a fourteen-year sentence for his treachery. He admitted that he used Gold as the courier, although it is still unclear to this day whether Fuchs had any contact with the Rosenbergs.

He was indicted on wartime espionage charges that carried the death penalty, even though the War was over. Gold, who had been the contact in America for Fuchs, was a wretched little man who sang like a canary once he was in custody. His confession that David Greenglass, the Los Alamos worker, had fed him atomic bomb secrets throughout the War years, exploded like the bomb itself across the front pages of the nation's newspapers.

The FBI built up a dossier detailing Grennglass' spying activities inside the Los Alamos complex. Greenglass had frequent access to top secret material on the 'lenses' for atomic bombs – the detonators that released the plutonium and uranium to create the single critical mass. On 17 July, under intense pressure from his captors, Greenglass sold out his brother-in-law. His sister's arrest was to follow shortly. Anti-Communist hysteria was rising in America now and Americans were fighting once again, this time against the menace of Communism in Korea.

The Department of Justice press release on the arrest of Rosenberg proclaimed: 'J. Edgar Hoover, the director of the FBI, said that Julius Rosenberg is a most important link in the Soviet espionage apparatus.

'Rosenberg, in early 1945, made available to Greenglass while he was on leave in New York City one-half of an

irregularly cut jelly-box top, the other half of which was given to Greenglass by Gold in Albuquerque, New Mexico, as a means of identifying Gold to Greenglass. Rosenberg aggressively sought ways and means to secretly conspire with the Soviet government to the detriment of his own country. Investigation to date also reveals that Rosenberg made himself available to Soviet espionage agents so he might "do something directly to help Russia".' This was all denied by the Rosenbergs who said they were trapped in a nightmare of which they had no part.

But the FBI had indeed assembled a massive body of evidence which they would later use against the couple at their trial. Another member of the spy ring to be arrested was Morton Sobell, a friend of the Rosenbergs who had studied electrical engineering with Julius. He was charged on a separate indictment of passing to them the details and plans of America's latest radar on its ships and submarines. This too would be used against them when they came to trial in March 1951.

A MISTAKEN IDEALISM

The full weight of the US government's case had shifted from Gold and the other arrested spies to the Rosenbergs. The FBI evidence depicted them as the architects of the spy ring who forged the contacts with the Soviet diplomats and agents. J. Edgar Hoover said that American intelligence predicted that Russia would not have the atomic bomb until the 1960s. But thanks to the secrets passed along by the Rosenbergs, they exploded their first device in 1949, rocketing them into the nuclear age and laying the foundations of the Cold War. This, he said, was the end result of the American spies' 'misty eyed idealism'.

Irving Saypol, the government prosecutor at the trial, left no one in any doubt, when he rose to open the case, that he intended to go for the death penalty. He said: 'We will prove that the Rosenbergs devised and put into operation, with the aid of Soviet agents in this country, an elaborate scheme which allowed them to steal, through David Greenglass, this one weapon which might well hold the key to the survival of this nation and means the peace of the world, the atomic bomb. This

Below: 'Old Sparky' the electric chair that despatched many felons in Sing-Sing, the prison in New York State.

Opposite, above: Enrico Fermi whose brilliant war effort was wasted by the treachery of the Rosenbergs.

Opposite, below: Sing-Sing prison where the traitors, Julius and Ethel Rosenberg, were executed.

love of Communism and the Soviet Union led them into a Soviet espionage ring.'

The fifteen-day trial was a sensation, the more so because of the spectacle of a brother betraying his own sister. But there was a parade of witnesses who testified that the Rosenbergs had sold their souls to the beliefs of the hammer and sickle, not the stars and stripes. Max Elitcher, the first witness, testified that Julius Rosenberg had badgered him, asking him if his job in the Navy Department in Washington gave him access to secrets that he could pass on to the Soviets. Elizabeth Bentley, a Columbia University graduate, told how she was lured into the espionage web through a series of disasterous love affairs with Soviet agents. She testified that the bond was between the Rosenbergs and Moscow was unusually strong.

Undoubtedly, it was the evidence of David Greenglass which sealed their fates. He testified that he worked in Los Alamos and had access to the greatest secrets which he passed to his sister and brother-in-law. 'They preferred Russian socialism to our system of government,' he said. Greenglass said that he began passing on information, initially about the personnel at the closely-guarded complex, later on about the explosives used to trigger the detonator and the detonator mechanisms themselves. He detailed the jelly-box story that had been revealed by the Department of Justice press release at the time of the traitors' arrest. The words 'I come from Julius' displayed on the top of the box flashed by Gold, meant that the coast was clear and that the Rosenbergs required more information for their Russian bosses.

Greenglass passed on data and sketches and in one despatch, for which he received $200, he typed up twelve pages of notes about the mechanism of the bomb. He went on: 'Working in the Rosenberg's living-room Ethel did the typing and Julius, Ethel and my wife Ruth corrected the grammar. Julius told me he communicated with his Russian contacts by leaving microfilm in an alcove at a cinema. He said he had received an alcove table from the Russians as a reward – I saw this table at his apartment. It was used for microfilming.'

A BROTHER'S BETRAYAL

Greenglass said the spying operation was finished with the arrest of Fuchs in 1950. He said that Julius visited him, Greenglass, and said: 'You remember the man who came to see you in Albuquerque? Well, Fuchs was one of his contacts. Doubtless this man will be arrested soon and this might lead to you.' He was referring to Gold and he was correct on both counts. Greenglass said he offered money for him to go away to Mexico and later came back with $4,000 for the purpose. But the plot was already unravelling because, by then, Greenglass was under surveillance .

Ruth Greenglass stepped into the witness box to corroborate everything her husband

'THEY PREFERRED RUSSIAN SOCIALISM TO OUR SYSTEM OF GOVERNMENT.'

Below: *Hiroshima, Japan after the A-Bomb was dropped.*

had said. She produced bank deposit receipts that showed large amounts of cash being placed in their account – sums far larger than her husband's salary at Los Alamos could have provided. She also recalled the last visit Julius made to their apartment, when he said they would have to flee before the arrests began. 'I was worried about my baby,' she said, 'and he at first said we should go to the Soviet Union. When I said that I could not travel with an infant he said: "My doctor says that if you take enough canned milk and boil the water, everything will be all right." He said that they were closing the net, that we could expect arrests soon. But we never intended to go.'

THE MEANING OF TREASON

Harry Gold, the US contact to the now-imprisoned Fuchs, also delivered damning testimony. He said that Anatoli Yakolev, the Soviet Union's vice-consul in New York City, was the paymaster with the money man who controlled him and Rosenberg. He said: 'Yakolev reported that the information I had given him had been sent immediately to the Soviet Union. He said that the information I had received from Greenglass was extremely excellent and very valuable.' Yakolev had left America rather rapidly on a ship bound for Europe in 1946 and was never quizzed on his role in the atom spy ring.

Julius Rosenberg took the stand and answered every specific allegation of treachery with the three words: 'I did not.' He denied giving the Greenglasses any money other than some cash he owed David from the business that he helped finance. But he refused to say whether or not he was a member of the Communist Party – he was – although he admitted that he did have sympathy for the Soviet political system 'as it has done much to improve the lot of the underdog.'

Ethel, too, denied all allegations of espionage. She said she loved the brother who had branded her and her husband as traitors, but could offer no explanation why he had implicated them other than as a ploy to save himself. Observers at the time thought that she didn't help herself by refusing to explain why so often she had pleaded the Fifth Amendment – the right to

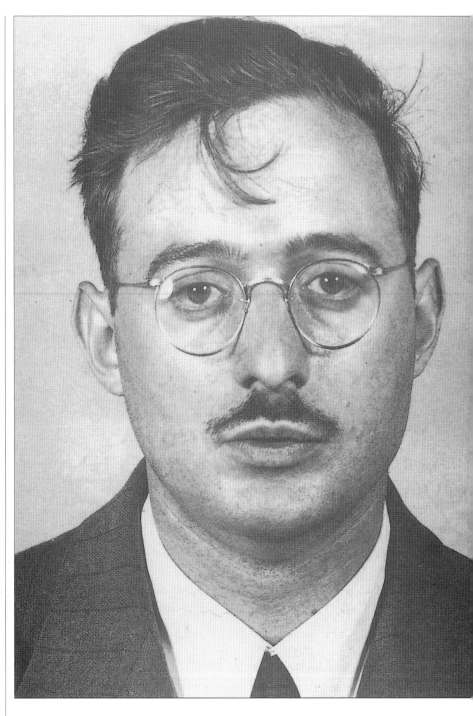

Above: *Julius Rosenberg.*

remain silent – during the grand jury hearings which led to her trial.

Morton Sobell refused to take the stand at the trial of the traitors.

In his summing up the prosecutor was emphatic that the accused were spies. Saypol said: 'This is one of most important cases ever submitted to a jury in this country. We know that these conspirators stole the most important scientific secrets ever known to mankind from this country and delivered them to the Soviet Union. David Greenglass' description of the atomic bomb was typed by Ethel

JULIUS TOLD ME HE COMMUNICATED WITH HIS RUSSIAN CONTACTS BY LEAVING MICROFILM IN AN ALCOVE AT A CINEMA.

Above: 'Save the Rosenbergs'. In Paris, certain groups decried the death sentence on the traitors.

'I BELIEVE YOUR CONDUCT IN PUTTING THE ATOM BOMB IN THE HANDS OF THE RUSSIANS... HAS CAUSED... CASUALTIES EXCEEDING FIFTY THOUSAND.'

Rosenberg, just so had she, on countless other occasions, sat at that typewriter and struck the keys, blow by blow, against her country in the interests of the Soviets.

'When Fuchs confessed, the Rosenbergs' position in the Soviet espionage hierachy in this country was jeaopardised. The evidence of the guilt of the Rosenbergs is incontrovertible. No defendants ever stood before the bar of American justice less deserving than them and Sobell.' Their defence lawyers tried to pin the guilt on Greenglass, but were unable to dismiss the fact that

Gold was involved with the Rosenbergs. They were all traitors.

On the morning of Tuesday, 29 March the jurors returned with Guilty verdicts on Julius, Ethel and Sobell. Judge Irving Kaufman told the Rosenbergs: 'The thought that citizens of our country would lend themselves to the destruction of our country by the most destructive weapons known to man is so shocking that I can't find words to describe this loathsome offence.' A week later, on 5 April, 1951, as they appeared for sentencing, he told them: 'I consider your crime worse than murder. Plain deliberate contemplated murder is dwarfed in magnitude by comparison with the crime you have committed. I believe your conduct in putting the atom bomb in the hands of the Russians has already caused the resultant aggression in Korea with casualties exceeding fifty thousand.

A CONTROVERSIAL VERDICT

'It is not in my power, Julius or Ethel Rosenberg, to forgive you. Only the Lord can find mercy for what you have done. You are hereby sentenced to the punishment of death, and it is ordered you shall be executed according to law.'

Morton Sobell got thirty years, of which he would serve sixteen. Later, Greenglass, who stole the secrets, got a remarkably light fifteen years, as did his wife Ruth Greenglass, who collapsed in the dock as the sentence was handed down.

There was to be no reprieve for the Rosenbergs, despite twenty-two appeals and numerous stays of execution. Julius, thirty-five, and Ethel, thirty-seven, died in the electric chair on the night of 19 June, 1953. Ever since then debate has raged about the possibility of their innocence, but top legal experts say their guilt is more than likely. Alexander Bickel, a Yale University law professor, said: 'It was a ghastly and shameful episode, but I believe they were guilty beyond a doubt.' And Roy Cohn, one of the prosecutors, added: 'I feel the guilt was overwhelming. Their apparent "ordinariness" made it possible for them to get away with it for so long.'

Only Cuba, satellite of the now-defunct Soviet Union for which they served, commemorated them as 'assassinated heroes' on a set of postage stamps.

EVIL WOMEN

PAMELA SMART
Mistress of murder

She was a teacher, a person of some standing and authority. She was a wife. But Pamela Smart was also crazy for sex with a teenage boy, so maddened by lust that she was driven to commit a gross and ugly murder.

Pamela Smart was young, she was beautiful and she was ambitious. She lived in the small town of Derry, New Hampshire on America's eastern seaboard, and she was restless. Bored with her life as a teacher, bored and unhappy as a wife, she sought excitement in a love affair with an adolescent boy. But this illicit passion was to lead her and her young lover to disaster and tragedy.

Shortly after 10pm on 1 May, 1990, police patrolman, Gerald Scaccia, received an urgent call to investigate a crime at number 4E in Misty Morning Drive, Derry. Scaccia had been cruising for the usual drunks and speeders when his despatcher announced an emergency call at the address – something about a body. He found a sobbing Pamela Smart sitting on the stoop of a neighbour's house. Hysterical with grief, she pointed into the open doorway of her own home, saying: 'He's in there – my husband's in there.' Scaccia entered with his flashlight, saw a man lying face down, his heels toward him in the hallway of the residence. He turned the body over and was about to begin mouth-to-mouth resuscitation when he spotted the small circle in the man's temple, a wound caused by a bullet, fired at point-blank range from a snub-nosed .38 revolver.

Neighbourhood sympathy for the young widow was widespread. Friends appeared to comfort the popular and personable high school teacher whose husband, Greg, had been so cruelly murdered just six days before their first wedding anniversary.

Pamela, who was a director at a media studies' centre that managed a number of projects in local schools, was interviewed by the police. She explained that she had been at a school meeting that night. She and Greg had moved to Derry a few months ago. He worked as an insurance salesman with the Metropolitan Life Company and, no, she did not know why anyone would want to kill him. But a detective at the interview said: 'There was something strange about her. Her world had fallen apart and, well, she seemed very, very calm about it all. I thought it was a bit weird. Call it a cop's intuition. There was nothing I could put my finger on at the time.'

Above: *The doomed husband, Greg Smart, on his wedding day in 1989.*

Opposite: *Pamela Smart proved to be an accomplished liar, a philandering wife and a conspirator to murder.*

Smart described to reporters the crime scene. She revealed details that the police would have preferred to remain confidential as they tried to track the killer.

PAMELA'S VERY YOUNG VISITORS

Four days after the murder, Dan Pelletier, a detective on the homicide squad, took an anonymous phone call from a woman who claimed that a minor, named Cecelia Pierce, was the person the police should interview in connection with the killing. The caller then claimed that Pamela had confided, to Cecelia, her plot to kill Greg.

Captain Loring Jackson was the officer put in charge of the investigation. He was to uncover a story of manipulation, obsession, greed, sex and lust. Just as his detective had felt, so Jackson, too, was puzzled by the widow's apparent calm, and there were aspects of her husband's murder that did not fit the story she was telling, and neither was there was any sign of a burglary. A diamond ring had been left on the murdered man's hand. There was no cash in his wallet, but all his credit cards were there.

In the days following the killing, numerous rumours began to circulate about Pamela and Greg Smart, that the couple dabbled in drugs and held wild parties at the house. Pamela telephoned a local television station so that she could make a public statement, denying the truth of these rumours. She seemed very composed for one so recently, and tragically bereaved, thought Jackson. And he was very annoyed when, just two days after the murder, Mrs

Above and right:
Erotic poses from the sexually-bored Pamela Smart. She gave similar photographs to her student and lover, Billy Flynn. He kept them in his wallet.

The detective remembered that Pamela had supplied a list of the people who had been in her home a month prior to the murder. Cecelia Pierce was on that list, and the police were now interested to note how many other very young people visited the school teacher in her home. Billy Flynn, for instance, was a visitor.

Billy Flynn was fifteen when he met Pam Smart in her role as teacher, when she came to Winnacunnet High School to organise a series of lectures on the dangers of drug and alcohol abuse. A female friend recalled that the first time Billy saw Pamela, he turned and said: 'I'm in love.'

People noticed that Pamela enjoyed flirting with her students; and the police were to hear that she seemed to favour Billy Flynn.

Cecelia Pierce was also close to Pamela, pleased because the twenty-two-year-old woman did not treat her as a big child, as her mother and other teachers did. Cecelia worked with Smart on the drugs and alcohol project, and was soon confiding her romantic problems to the older woman. It seemed Pamela knew how to empathise with the adolescents she taught.

Pamela Smart began a love affair with Billy Flynn. Her marriage to Greg, the man she met when she was a college student, was volatile, and they had violent rows. Billy Flynn would never forget his first sexual experience with Pamela. He visited the older woman at her home when her husband was away. She put the steamy Kim Basinger film '9¹/₂ Weeks' on to her video recorder. Then, leading Billy to the bedroom, she mimicked the striptease act performed by the actress in the film. To the music of Van Halen's 'Black and Blue', they had sex. Later, again copying a scene from the film, Billy rubbed Pam's body with ice cubes before they made love again.

Later he would say: 'I was kind of shocked. It's not every day that a teenage kid gets to do this with an older woman who says she likes him a lot. I was totally infatuated with her. I was in love with her.'

BILLY'S JEALOUS HATRED

They made love in her Honda car, at her office in school and at her home. She was compiling an anti-drugs film for a Florida orange juice company, and as Billy was her student on this project, he was able to skip school. They spent a lot of time together. She gave him sexy pictures of herself in a bikini, that he kept in his wallet, and the boy began to develop a jealous hatred of his lover's husband, Greg. Pamela portrayed Greg as evil, a man who cheated on her, abused her. She wanted to get rid of him… have him killed. Soon, the idea of murder took root in Billy Flynn's mind. Pamela told him that, if she were free of her husband, she could be with Billy for ever.

Pamela Smart was not only persuading Billy Flynn to kill her husband. She influenced Cecelia Pierce, manipulating the girl into feeling a strong dislike of Greg Smart.

Above: *Pamela Smart tried to convince the police that her husband had been killed by burglars, but they arrested her for conspiracy to murder.*

'IT'S NOT EVERY DAY THAT A TEENAGE KID GETS TO DO THIS WITH AN OLDER WOMAN WHO SAYS SHE LIKES HIM A LOT. I WAS IN LOVE WITH HER.'

Billy told the police that it was Pam's idea to make the murder look like the act of a violent burglar. He said that Pam even revealed details of the plan to Cecelia Pierce, who treated such conversations as part of some sort of macabre game of love enjoyed by Pam and Billy.

Stephen Sawicki, in his book 'Teach me to Kill', a study of Smart, analysed the motives: 'Perhaps it had become something of a perverse game that had nothing to do with reality for Billy and Cecelia. Maybe it was the thrill of flirting with danger, a dance along the edge of a precipice. Or maybe it was simply the lack of a sound-minded adult that the kids felt comfortable with, someone who could point out just how crazy it had all become. Whatever the

As Billy's infatuation for Pamela grew, so did his determination to kill her husband. He enlisted the aid of Patrick Randall, seventeen; Vance Lattime, eighteen, and Raymond Fowler, nineteen. All were promised a reward by Pam and Flynn, a little something for their trouble – a stereo, some cash or some other item of value from the house. Pam's only stipulation was that they hid her beloved Shih-tzu dog, Halen, away from the murder scene – she thought that witnessing the death of his master might disturb the animal.

A TOWEL WAS ALREADY SPREAD ON THE CARPET

The quartet's first attempt to kill Greg Smart failed when, travelling in Pam's Honda, they lost their way to the Smart's address. They planned to hide inside the house, waiting for Greg's return from work, killing him on arrival. However, when they finally arrived he was already at home.

On the second occasion there were to be no errors. This time, Flynn and Randall were dropped off near the house, and then changed into tracksuits they had bought for the occasion. As they started to move towards the home of Greg Smart, a couple appeared near the corner ahead of them. The two boys broke into a jog, pulling the tracksuit hoods over their faces. They broke into the house through the metal doors of the basement, and they began to vandalise the master bedroom, the bathroom and the lounge, hoping to create the scene of a frantic burglary. The other two accomplices, Lattime and Fowler, were waiting in a nearby plaza with a getaway car.

The killing took a few seconds. Greg was ambushed in the hallway of his own home. Grabbed violently by the hair and pummelled in the face by Randall, the man was brought to his knees. 'Don't hurt me dude,' pleaded Smart as Randall waved a long-bladed knife in front of his eyes. Randall told the police that he did not have the stomach to murder in cold blood. It was Flynn who pulled a gun out and shot Greg Smart, who dropped dead on to a towel that had been spread on the carpet. Pamela had made it quite clear she did not want blood on her precious hallway tiling and carpet.

The anonymous phone call that led the police to these confessions came from

case, being around Pam, even with all the strange talk of murdering her husband, offered a form of sustenance. Pam provided it in different ways for the boy and the girl, but when it came right down to it, their needs were the same. Both Cecelia and Billy deeply wanted to feel that they were good and loved and special. It was madness, but without abhorrence the kids continually accepted the small steps that in the end pointed to a death.'

Louise Coleman, a friend of Cecelia Pierce. Thirty-one and pregnant, Louise had been told by Cecelia that she knew of a woman planning to 'snuff' her husband for the insurance money. Louise thought at the time that Cecelia was acting out some kind of fantasy, or that her wires had become crossed. When Greg Smart was murdered, Louise felt it was her duty to tell the police about Cecelia's conversations.

A month after the murder, Captain Jackson was convinced that Pam was guilty. Her own behaviour combined with the gossip indicated that she was not innocent. She was, once again, hanging around with her adolescent friends – which, under the circumstances, smacked of impropriety. Captain Jackson decided to enlist the aid of Greg's father, Bill. Smart Snr was appalled by Pam's callous indifference to the murder of his son, her husband, and he realised that, probably, Pamela had killed his son. He would co-operate with the police in their investigations.

The police questioned Cecelia again and again. But the girl was loyal to Pamela Smart, and, although Cecelia had nothing to do with the murder, she refused to say anything against the woman whom she believed was her closest friend.

However, the young killers were unable to resist boasting of their exploit, and soon their school was abuzz with gossip. One of the students, Ralph Welch, did not view the adventure as part of a game, and after Randall and Fowler boasted to him of the murder, Welch told Vance Lattime's father that his gun had been used in a murder and that his son was invloved. Lattime checked his weapon and noticed it was dirty, although it was clean when he had put it away in his gun cabinet. He went straight to the police. Soon the four boys were rounded up for questioning.

CECELIA AGREES TO WEAR A 'WIRE'

Pam's wicked world was falling apart, but she was determined that she would not crumble. The boys gave their statements, in which Flynn admitted his role as killer, while the others claimed that they thought it was a game, that they had no idea they were part of a murder plan, but they all implicated Pam, insisting that she made Flynn kill her husband. But it was not enough to arrest Pamela Smart. The boys' claims needed to be supported by evidence of her part in the crime.

'We had to get some proof,' explained Captain Jackson after the investigation. 'We needed Pamela Smart to convict herself. Luckily, Cecelia Pierce came around for us after two more interviews. Like the rest she realised that what had happened was ugly and filthy and vile. She finally, finally helped us nail Pamela Smart.'

Cecelia agreed to wear a 'wire' to record her conversations with Pamela Smart in a bid to get her to implicate herself in the death of her husband. Cecelia was coached by lawmen to ask leading questions. Pamela Smart must have been very concerned that now her accomplices, the boys, were in custody, telling police her role in the drama, but she maintained a facade of calm composure. In the first few conversations with Cecelia she gave nothing away, and even denied that she was having an affair with Billy. But as the conversations proceeded, the police coached Cecelia and told her to mention to Pam that the district attorney wanted to interview her over a love note that she had written to Billy. This was the conversation between Pam and Cecelia:

Pam: All I can say is that no matter what they try and make you talk about, if I were you I didn't know a damn thing.

Cecelia: Well, all I know is that I had to come and talk to you because I... I mean I don't know what to do. I have to go talk to the district attorney. I'm just sick of lying, you know.

A MONTH AFTER THE MURDER, CAPTAIN JACKSON WAS CONVINCED THAT PAM WAS GUILTY.

PAM'S WICKED WORLD WAS FALLING APART, BUT SHE WAS DETERMINED THAT SHE WOULD NOT CRUMBLE.

slammer or you don't or if anybody sends me, it's gonna be you and that's the big thing, and that's what it comes down to. But what good is it gonna do you if you send me to the slammer? Because if you think that's gonna be the end of your problems... don't think it's the end of your problems. It's gonna be like your whole family going: "You knew about a murder, how could you have lived like that?" And the newspapers are gonna be all over you. And you're gonna be on the witness stand a million times, you know?'

THE GOOD NEWS –
AND THE BAD NEWS

Pamela Smart began to incriminate herself in these conversations with her good friend – someone whose destiny was closely tied up with her own. In one of the final wiretaps Pamela said: 'Bill coulda told them all I'd pay them. I don't know what Bill told them to get them to go, and then that was just a lie. You know. They're not going to have any proof. There's no money. So they can't convict me 'cause of a sixteen-year-old's word in the slammer, facing the rest of his life. And me, with a professional reputation and a course that I teach. You know, that's the thing. They're going to believe me.'

Pamela Smart was taken by surprise when Detective Dan Pelletier entered her school on 1 August and confronted her in her office with the words: 'I have some good news for you and I have some bad news for you. The good news is that we have solved the murder of your husband. The bad news is that you are under arrest for first degree murder.'

When she was arrested, the boys admitted they had been involved in the murder plan and told the police that they did it because of Billy's love affair with Pam. But Pamela maintained that she was innocent, the victim of a teenager's infatuation. She said she had never encouraged Billy Flynn, had never slept with him and had not solicited any of them to commit murder. But it was clear in the first days of her trial in March, 1991, that her story was difficult to believe; she may have been adept at manipulating impressionable youngsters, but she did not impress the prosecutors or jurors given the task of weighing up the facts.

Above and opposite: *These pictures reveal the cool detachment of the chief accused. Pamela Smart treated her court appearances as a fashion show and bemoaned the fact that there was so little time to fix her make-up. The court revelations of her sordid sex games with youngsters did not shake her demeanour and she maintained her plea of innocence to the end.*

Pam: Well, you know, I'm just telling you that if you tell the truth, you're gonna be an accessory to murder.

Cecelia: Right.

Pam: So that's your choice. And not only that, but what is your family going to think? I mean, they're like, 'Cecelia, you knew about this.' You know?

Cecelia: Yeah.

Pam: Nothing was going wrong until they told Ralph.

Cecelia: No.

Pam: It's their stupid-ass faults that they told Ralph.

Cecelia: I can't even believe they told him.

In another conversation she tried to keep Cecelia on her side: 'I think I've been a very good friend to you and that's the thing, even if you send me to the f***ing

Pamela Smart could not believe it when the verdicts were read out. She turned to her attorney and said: 'First Billy took Greg's life, and now he's taking mine.' But Captain Loring Jackson, who has met a fair cross section of criminals in his twenty-five years service with the police, was not impressed. He said: 'She not only took Greg's life but she also took away the lives of these bright, impressionable young men when she enlisted them in her scheme of murder. She is cold, calculating, manipulative, self-centred, totally unfeeling for anybody but herself. I have never met such a cold person as her. I think life in prison is, for this young lady, very, very fitting.'

Billy Flynn gave damning witness when he was under oath. He told how he had loaded the weapon with hollow-point ammunition, bullets designed to cause maximum destruction to a human target. He said he held back a moment after aiming the gun at Greg's head. 'A hundred years it seemed like,' he sobbed. 'And I said: "God forgive me".' He paused before admitting: 'I pulled the trigger.'

SHE TOOK MORE THAN GREG'S LIFE

The recordings, made by Cecelia, were played in court. Pamela Smart did not sound like a grieving young widow. The court heard her boast that her position in the community would give her an edge over her accusers. Smart's lawyers denounced the state case against their client as 'toxic soup', claiming Flynn and his cohorts were no more than deranged thrill-killers who had murdered Greg Smart because he was a romantic rival. The jury of seven women and five men took just thirteen hours of deliberation to decide that Pamela Smart had set out to teach the boys the business of murder and that she was Guilty as charged. Judge Douglas R. Gray imposed the mandatory sentence of life, without the possibility of parole, on Pamela Smart; Billy Flynn and Patrick Randall received sentences of not less than twenty-eight years each, while Vance Lattime was given eighteen years. Raymond Fowler's case has yet to be tried.

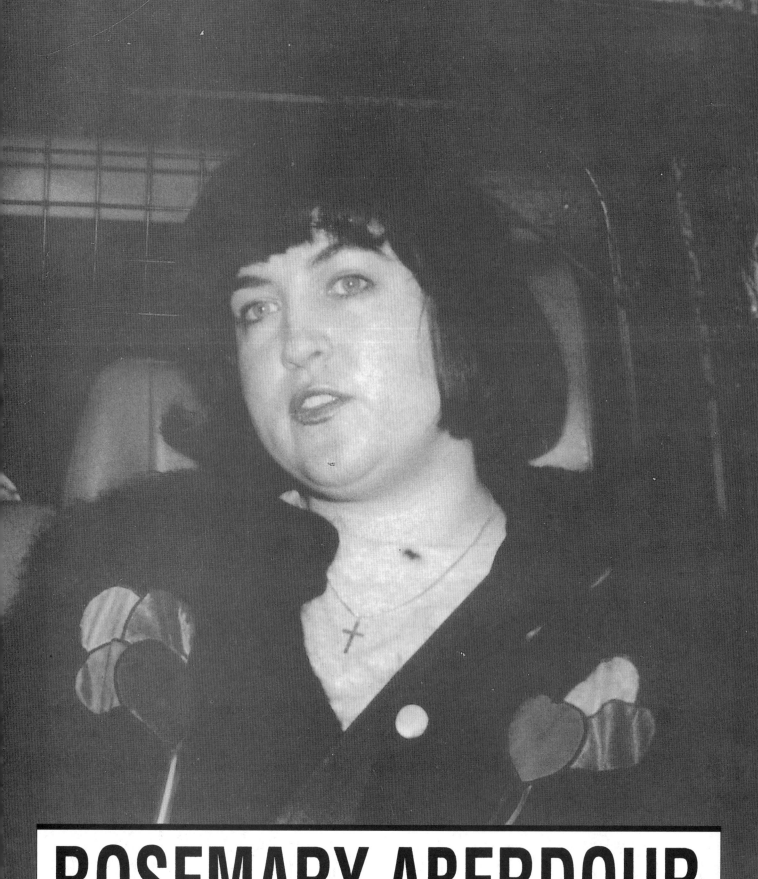

ROSEMARY ABERDOUR
The Lady is a Thief

She was plump, generous and fun-loving. She was also a lonely little fraud. Rosemary Aberdour gave herself a grand title and stole a vast sum from a charity. She spent it on parties, inviting all the friends that money could buy, but the only return on this investment was a prison sentence.

There is no denying it – when Rosemary Aberdour lived it up, she did it in style. She bought herself a Bentley turbo car worth £50,000 and promptly hired a chauffeur to go with it. In the course of a few years, she splashed out an amazing £780,000 on parties, once setting up an entire funfair in London's docklands. She bought a string of luxury cars, including a Mercedes and five other smaller models for her staff at a cost of over £200,000. In one lavish week Rosemary poured two hundred and forty bottles of Dom Perignon champagne into a bathtub for a friend to bathe in.

SWINDLING IN STYLE

There were Caribbean yachting holidays, buying trips to London jewellers and clothes purchased from the best couturiers in London and Paris. Once in London, when her black labrador dog Jeeves was looking a little ill, she decided to take it for a walk... in the Scottish hills. So she hired a chauffeur-driven car to take the dog for walkies in Scotland. Excess was the motto of her life. But so was cheating, for 'Lady' Aberdour was nothing more than a swindler, a fake aristocrat who decieved many good and trusting people, so that she could use their money to finance her lifestyle. She fiddled almost £3 million from a hospital charity before she was

EXCESS WAS THE MOTTO OF HER LIFE. BUT SO WAS CHEATING, FOR 'LADY' ABERDOUR WAS NOTHING MORE THAN A SWINDLER.

Opposite: *Rosemary Aberdour was trusted with large sums of money. She used the funds to transform her own dull life.*

Below: *Flanked by family and legal men, Aberdour makes her way into court as a common criminal.*

*Above: **Rosemary grew up in a semi-detached home in Worcester Park, Surrey (lower picture) but she wanted the secluded luxury of a house hidden in private gardens. She stole the money to pay for her dreams.***

detained as a guest of Her Majesty, in surroundings that bear little resemblance to those she left behind.

Her rise to riches was the result of a carefully orchestrated plot. Rosemary Aberdour was born in 1961, neither titled nor rich, but with lashings of that essential ingredient necessary for any good thief – greed. The daughter of Kenneth Aberdour, an Essex radiologist, and his wife Jean, once a secretary at the National Hospital, Rosemary was brought up at Witham, near Chelmsford, and had an ordinary education at a local school. She was a bright child who left school with several 'A' levels and then trained as an accountant with a city

firm. After working in various jobs, she landed the plum job of book keeper to the National Hospital Development Foundation in 1987. It was the beginning of her trek down the pathway of deceit.

During the first two years in this position, Rosemary worked exceedingly hard – and honestly – raising cash for a new wing and for medical equipment. The National Hospital, in London, is recognised internationally as centre for the treatment of multiple sclerosis, Parkinson's and Alzheimer's diseases, epilepsy and strokes. One of Rosemary's early successes came after she convinced the hospital trustees that the annual Queen's Square Ball, which got its name from the hospital's Bloomsbury address, could be promoted as a profitable fundraising event.

HAVING A BALL FOR CHARITY

The ball was little more than a staff party, but Rosemary knew that, if society folk and celebrities could be persuaded that this was a grand charity ball, worth the expense of the highly-priced tickets, the hospital would make a good deal of money. The Queen's Square Ball was so successful, that Rosemary organised three more similar occasions, as well as other fundraising events, some of which were attended by the Princess of Wales, the charity's patron.

Rosemary won the respect of the charity's bigwigs, who were impressed by her remarkable energy and genuine talent for persuading the rich and famous to donate large sums to the National Hospital Development Foundation. She was very persuasive, as her words in a society brochure reveal: 'I have gained great motivation from meeting patients who show immense courage in coping with their illnesses, often against incredible odds.' However, Rosemary was to lengthen those odds when she stole the money, that should have been used to treat these sickly patients, to top up her own income.

SHE BEGAN TO DOCTOR THE BOOKS

She crossed the line into criminality in 1988, when she began filching small amounts of the cash donated to the charity. Because she was held in such high esteem by the trustees of the charity, Aberdour had wide control of the charity's finances. There were several accounts in banks and building societies in which cheques, donated to the charity, were deposited. Aberdour became a signatory on these accounts when she organised the first re-vamped Queen's Square Ball. However, other signatures, like those of Richard Stevens, the charity director, were required on each cheque, and Rosemary began to forge these. Initially, she took enough money to pay for a car. She simply doctored the books so that the amounts she stole never appeared in the charity's legitimate accounts. She quickly realised that this was a very easy way to siphon off cash for her own purposes, and the horizons of her world were broadened considerably.

The bulk of the cash disappeared between April 1989 and 1991, when she was caught. And as the money flowed into special bank accounts she set up for herself, Rosemary Aberdour set about spinning a web of lies to give herself a completely new persona.

John Young, the chairman of the charity, recalls the day he became aware of her metamorphosis. He was used to seeing Rosemary arrive at work in her modest saloon, so he took a double-take when she

pulled up outside the offices in a gleaming Bentley, complete with chauffeur and bodyguard. 'We might have thought the queen was arriving,' he said to her jokingly at the time. Aberdour replied gravely: 'You must understand that I have inherited £20 million and I have to have a minder because I might be kidnapped.'

She informed anyone who cared to listen that her windfall also gave her the right to assume the title of 'Lady' Aberdour.

After her enormous inheritance, 'Lady' Aberdour began to collect the trimmings necessary for her new status in life. She moved to a Thameside penthouse, complete with indoor swimming pool that had an ivy-covered swing suspended from its atrium roof. There were maple wood doors,

Below: *At the Red October Ball in 1990, Rosemary, third from right, waits eagerly in a line-up to shake the hand of Princess Michael of Kent.*

pink marble bathrooms, outstanding views of the Thames and celebrity neighbours like the actress Brigitte Neilsen. Her lavish bedroom was swathed in blood-red and gold silks, while a cushion, placed on an antique chair, had been embroidered in her own hand. It read: 'I love old money, young men and me.' The chandelier in the living room – in the corner of which nestled a baby grand piano – was worth £10,000. In a valuable antique cabinet in her bedroom she kept her supply of bargain-basement Marks and Spencer knickers. Careful to avoid old friends and family, who might blow the whistle on her, Rosemary Aberdour began to cultivate the 'right' people who would appreciate the finer things in life that she now enjoyed.

WILD TWO-WEEK PARTY

Rosemary Aberdour was a brilliant party hostess. At one, held in the thirteenth-century Thornton Watlass Hall, in North Yorkshire, the revels continued for two weeks, with new guests coming and going every two to three days. A fleet of rented cars ferried the guests to and from airports and railway stations, and bottles of vintage champagne were cracked open for every arrival. It took weeks to fix the ancient mansion after the Bacchanalia had ended.

Tim Mudd, who ran the estate, said: 'They damaged silver and furnishings and left, owing a great deal of money to local tradespeople. The saddest thing was that

SHE HANDED OUT CARIBBEAN AND INDIAN OCEAN CRUISES, AND INVITATIONS TO THE BEST PARTIES IN LONDON.

SHE HAD AN INCREDIBLE BEACH PARTY AT HER FLAT WHERE THE WHOLE PLACE WAS EMPTIED OF FURNITURE AND THE FLOORS WERE COVERED WITH SAND.

Below: *This note to the media reveals the love and support the sad little fraud received from her family.*

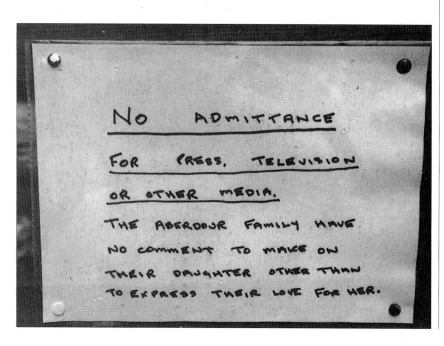

they put silver salvers worth thousands of pounds in the oven, melting the lead which secured the handles. Some became stained with carrot juice – so they cleaned the silver with scouring pads, totally ruining it. On Hallowe'en night she staged the biggest party of the lot and totally tore the place apart. One room was stripped of all its antique furniture and another was turned into a dance hall. There were imitation dead bodies everywhere and "live" bodies which jumped out of coffins. The bill for that one alone must have run to thousands a head.'

ROSEMARY AS QUEEN OF THE CASTLE

There were other memorable events. To mark the birthday of a girlfriend, Aberdour hired Conwy Castle in North Wales. To get there she rented a helicopter, and she planned an elaborate medieval-style pageant to greet it on arrival. The pampered labrador, Jeeves, was not allowed in the chopper but joined his mistress later... after a newly-hired flunkey drove him down the M4 in the Bentley. As the helicopter bearing Aberdour and her friend landed, minstrels, in elaborate costume, blew a triumphant fanfare on the battlements while a menacing black knight, replete with mock-armour, approached the giggling girls. They were saved by a dashing 'white' knight who fought his 'black' counterpart to a fake death. Rosemary was then playfully-crowned 'Queen of the Castle'.

Following this little display – estimated cost, £10,000 – she flew her friend on to another castle, where the reception committee consisted of a brass band and a full Welsh male voice choir. The whole day ended with bucketloads of champagne and elaborate food. The estimated cost of the fantasy jaunt was £40,000.

To her frequent hangers-on and staff, it soon became apparent that the plump charity queen was an unloved, lonely person who hoped to buy friendship with her lavish generosity. Rosemary handed out Caribbean and Indian Ocean cruises, and invitations to the best parties in London. She housed her London butler, Manuel Cabrera, a Filipino who worked for her for eighteen months, in a luxurious flat. He claimed, that although she had a fiancé, British Army Captain Michael Cubbins,

Rosemary also entertained a boyfriend. It was Cabrera's job to help her keep this secret, and to prevent the two men from bumping into each other.

A £60,000 VALENTINE'S PARTY

Cabrera described his employer: 'When Michael and Rosemary got engaged he gave her a fantastic diamond ring but she didn't like it, and bought herself another for over £8,000. She seemed to think money could always buy happiness. She meant to throw a hen party in the Grenadines but she didn't go because it would have meant leaving Michael – so she paid for all her girlfriends to go while she stayed home. Once she had an incredible beach party at her flat where the whole place was emptied of furniture and the floors were covered with sand. The bath was filled with bottles of Dom Perignon champagne that were just poured in one after the other. Another time she had a Valentine's party – and that was really one to remember.'

She called it the St Valentine's Day Massacre party and she spent £60,000 on it.

Top: *Mr and Mrs Aberdour outside the Old Bailey where their daughter stood trial.*

Above: *Her parents were driven away in shock after Rosemary was given a prison sentence.*

Guests were handed exotic cocktails as they entered her flat, then were led to tables groaning under the weight of fabulously cooked food. After the meal, guests went upstairs to her swimming pool where they were invited to change into costumes especially laid on for them. Pink heart-shaped balloons festooned the place and

Above: *Captain Michael Cubbins, Rosemary's fiance, who persuaded her to return to London for her trial.*

Below: *Her solicitor tried to justify Rosemary's crime when he claimed she lacked self-esteem and was immature.*

the fun began with a jolly water fight that ended in more champagne, more frolicking and more indulgence. It was a never-ending cycle of fun for 'Lady' Rosemary.

The National Hospital Development Foundation hoped to collect £10 million, intended to pay for a complete refurbishment of the hospital. So clever was Rosemary Aberdour at juggling figures in the foundation's accounts, that twice the accounts passed the scrutiny of top city

auditors and were declared to be perfectly in order. Nothing could have been farther from the truth. Aberdour used to give the auditors her accounts in sections, allowing herself time to move funds from one to the other, so that no discrepancies would show in the section she sent to the auditors. It seems foolish that the trustees of the charity allowed her this access to, and control over, their finances. But they trusted her and she abused their faith.

THE REAL LADY ABERDOUR

With such a successful system of fraud, greed grew fat and demanding. 'Lady A' became more and more extravagant, stealing £1 million in the first six months of 1991. In an ironic, some would say callous twist, she signed over a cheque for £100,000 from a personal account – money she had diddled from the charity – and 'donated' it to the hospital. It was an act of great magnanimity from the aristocrat who worked so hard for them and her generosity was not lost on the grateful trustees.

Such extensive embezzlement would not, of course, go unnoticed for ever. But long before the fraudster was rumbled by her bosses in London, there was, on a Scottish estate, a Lady Aberdour who was aware that something strange was afoot when her husband, Lord Stewart Aberdour, began receiving thank-you mail from guests who attended parties at strange venues, not in his home. Christmas cards, addressed to his wife, were signed by people neither the lord nor his wife had ever met.

'WHO WAS THIS WOMAN IMPERSONATING MY WIFE?'

'There was one incident,' said Lord Aberdour, 'when I was at a shooting weekend and this chap came up to me and said: "I met your wife recently – she's hosting the most amazing parties." He had never met my wife, Mady, so he just assumed she was this person. I was perplexed. I said: "My wife's up in Scotland having a baby so I don't see how you could have done." I told him he must have met someone who was pretending to be Lady Aberdour. I thought about turning up at one of her parties and exposing her as a fake. Another time I saw an article in a Sunday

newspaper describing this woman as my daughter. When letters started arriving I sent them back to the post office saying "person not known at this address". When you discover someone is an impostor there is not really very much that you can do.'

Two weeks before she was caught, Rosemary, a hopeless romantic, hired a grand hotel in Sussex, then rented the services of a professional video company. She dressed as Scarlett O'Hara, one of her favourite screen heroines, and kitted her friends out as other characters from 'Gone With The Wind' to create her own version of the screen classic. She spent £50,000 of charity funds on this little lark.

When her tissue of lies and deceit unravelled, it unravelled rapidly. One careless slip on her part caused her downfall – and saved the remaining cash in the bank accounts for the hospital. Rosemary Aberdour grew complacent, was less meticulous about covering her tracks. In June 1991, she left her office for a few days to take another of her fabulous holidays. But on her desk, she left, unhidden, a copy of a £120,000 cheque which had been drawn from one of the Foundation's building society accounts. With this copy, was a letter authorising the transfer of the cash to a Barclays Bank account which was one of five used by Aberdour to 'launder' the charity cash. Both the letter and the cheque copy were found by Richard Stevens, the charity director. He knew that the building society account did not allow Aberdour as a signatory to it and realised with horror that the signatures on the cheques were crude forgeries of the legitimate signatories' writing.

TREASURES AND RARE WINE

The following day, 14 June, fraud squad officers visited Aberdour's apartment to take stock of the Aladdin's Cave of furnishings and fittings that graced Aberdour's home. Box after box of papers, and other evidence relating to her mammoth swindle, were removed from the flat as neighbours of the fake aristocrat stared. The police inventory of luxury goods found in the Battersea apartment ran to thirty-seven pages and included over three hundred bottles of old and rare wine.

Above: Michael Cubbins and Rosemary's vicar leave the Old Bailey. They both attended Rosemary's trial to give her some comfort and support.

THE SIGNATURES ON THE CHEQUES WERE CRUDE FORGERIES OF THE LEGITIMATE SIGNATORIES' WRITING.

But there was no sign of the fraudster. She fled Britain after hearing that Fraud Squad officers had been to her apartment. In the footsteps of Great Train Robber Ronnie Biggs, she escaped to Rio de Janiero, as the horrified trustees of the charity began to realise the massive scale of her fiddling. From a rented flat near the Copacabana Beach, Aberdour contacted her parents and called her fiance Cubbins in Germany. There were numerous telephone conversations, over several days, during which they tried to persuade her to return to Britain. Finally the Ministry of Defence allowed Cubbins leave from his regiment to fly to Rio in a bid to bring her back to face the music. An old school-friend, called Sarah Boase, was also instrumental in trying to coax her back.

LAST FEAST BEFORE PRISON

Finally, Rosemary agreed but her journey back was in the high style that she had grown accustomed to. She forked out, presumably with charity money, for business-class seats for herself and her fiancé. On board she tucked into filets of beef and fine wine… the last meal before prison food faced this woman, ruined by her own greed. When the aircraft landed in Britain, detectives and security men escorted the ashen-faced Rosemary to an ante-room in the terminal building. She was cautioned by Fraud Squad officers. Then the woman who was used to being chauffeured in a green Bentley limousine, was sandwiched between two burly detectives in the back of a Montego police car. She was driven off to face questioning at the Fraud Squad headquarters which are in Holborn, Central London.

There followed a drastic change in lifestyle for the bogus aristocrat. Stripped of her Hérmes and Chanel creations, it was strictly prison flannel for Rosemary when she was remanded without bail although she was allowed to visit home for Christmas.

SHE LIVED IN A FANTASY WORLD

Rosemary Aberdour came to settle her account – not with the charity, but with justice – in March 1992, when she appeared at the Old Bailey. She pleaded guilty to seventeen charges of fraud and remained motionless as a litany of her crimes was read out in court by the prosecution; a £65,000 surpise party for a friend, £80,000 for the rental of a yacht in the Caribbean, £780,000 in all on parties, £134,000 on personal staff and £280,000 on cars.

In her defence, Graham Boal said: 'She is not an ordinary criminal or a sophisticated fraudster, stashing away funds. She had absolutely nothing to show for her crimes, nothing except shame, remorse, poverty and the courage to answer the indictment.' He said all the so-called friends who had wined and dined off her had evaporated like so many champagne bubbles. Aberdour had poured money down other people's throats. He said that she suffered from an impenetrable lack of self-esteem, insecurity and immaturity. He said she was a victim of the hard-bitten and glossy world of high-society fund raising. 'Eventually,' he said, 'the fantasy world became reality. Self-deception started to take over.' He added: 'This binge, this gorging, became a disease.'

The prosecution painted a rather different picture. Brendan Finucane said: 'It is clear many people were taken in by her, close friends and even her boyfriend. Thousands of pounds was given away to hangers-on and spongers. She had started

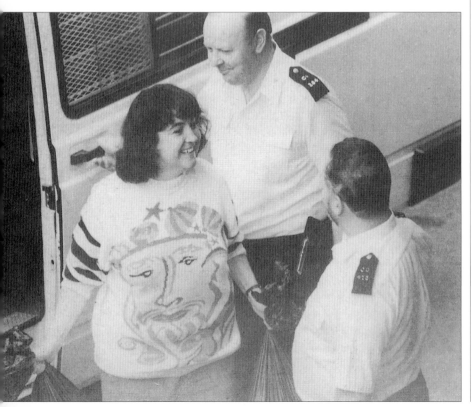

Below: Rosemary returned from her refuge in Brazil and was whisked off from the airport in a police car that took her to for questioning at the Fraud Squad headquarters.

humbly and then had grander designs. She was bound to be caught and fled to Brazil when the crime was discovered.'

Sentencing Aberdour to four years in jail, a sentence perceived as remarkably light by many at the charity, Mr Justice Leonard said: 'You spent the money on gross extravagance. It is said the motivation which brought you to these offences was complex or unusual. So it was, I am sure, but for two and-a-half years you went on milking this fund. You were trusted and you abused that trust.'

Rosemary Aberdour was certainly a rogue, and one of the greatest swindlers in British criminal history, but there is a certain sadness in her story, for the money she stole was used to buy friendship. Even as a schoolgirl, it is reported, she had used bribery to attract loyalty and company.

But there is one man who would like to befriend her. He has issued an invitation to 'show her the sights' of the Rio Janeiro she missed. Ronnie Biggs, who has holed up in the Brazilian sunspot for sixteen years ever since his jailbreak from a London prison, said: 'I could have given her so much pleasure around town before she went back. It's the perfect place for a girl who loves parties and she would never have had to flash that much cash.

Above: *As she was taken off to start her prison sentence, Rosemary Aberdour managed a smile for the press.*

Right: *The grand riverside block where Aberdour installed herself using money she swindled from charity funds.*

'I don't think she's mad to give herself up. In the circumstances I think she did the right thing. She is a young woman and has her whole life ahead of her. But you can be sure I will not be on the next plane. When she comes out I hope she comes to visit me – I'll show her what a true friend can be.'

IMELDA MARCOS
The Steel Butterfly

Imelda grew up in poverty, but her beauty lifted her out of the slums. A powerful politician wooed and married her. Imelda Marcos became a wildly greedy woman who robbed her own kind to pay for her extravagances.

The wife of the last of the great dictators walked free from court after a trial which ended in humiliating defeat for the American government. As Imelda Marcos emerged blinking into the Manhattan sunlight on 2 July, 1990, she carried in her heart a dark secret... the whereabouts of the missing millions she and her husband milked from his impoverished land. Ferdinand Marcos ruled the Philippines in the manner of a robber baron.

He used foreign aid and stole national treasures to finance a luxurious lifestyle. But he did not escape the consequences of his greed, for he died in exile and shame. His wife Imelda, dubbed the Steel Butterfly by peasants who gazed in awe at her extravagance and her ruthlessness, survived to face charges of fraud, grand larceny and racketeering. She had the dubious honour of being the first wife of a head of state to stand trial in the USA.

SHE HAD NO REGRETS

At her trial she gave no hint of the repentance that her accusers expected; rather they were subjected to Imelda's arrogant boasts about her lifestyle. From the first day she stepped into the dock in New York to face charges of racketeering, conspiracy and fraud and a possible sentence of fifty years in prison, she happily revealed the fabulous wealth she had enjoyed as wife of the president. Imelda and Ferdinand had viewed the Philippines as their personal fiefdom and appropriated, for their own use, bundles of aid-dollars donated by America. But their rule came to an end when Cory Aquino ousted the Marcos

Opposite: Imelda, former beauty queen, who became more famous for her greed than her looks.

Above: Grace and corruption marked the Steel Butterfly.

SHE HAD THE DUBIOUS HONOR OF BEING THE FIRST WIFE OF A HEAD OF STATE TO STAND TRIAL IN THE USA.

couple from power and then pressed the US to put the pair on trial. But Imelda Marcos was moved neither by the accusations nor the anger of her people. She did not regret her old life. Instead of feeling shame over her wealth, Imelda flaunted it. 'I get so

in jeopardy if Imelda Marcos was not prosecuted by the US government.

But the Justice Department was hindered in its investigations by the Swiss banking system that prides itself on its total secrecy regarding clients' finances, while allowing

tired of listening to "one million dollars here, one million dollars there,"' she yawned in court. 'It is so petty.'

When Imelda Marcos was found Not Guilty of the charges brought against her, observers thought that heads would roll in the US Justice Department because, it was felt, they had not properly prepared the case against Marcos. The Justice Department spent £20 million preparing this case and they had all the resources of the State Department, the FBI and the CIA behind them. But they lost their case.

SACKS OF MONEY WERE DELIVERED TO HER HOTEL ROOM

The American government was under pressure from Marcos' successor, Cory Aquino, who hinted that the important US military bases in the Philippines might be

the clients the same discretion – they do not have to reveal the source of their money. Vital documents relating to the Marcos' personal accounts were hidden in the vaults of banks in Geneva and Zurich and they were not released to the US prosecutors. Despite damning testimony from Phillipine National Bank officials who could show documents and who claimed that, although she had never earned a penny during her rule, Imelda had sacks of cash delivered to her hotel in New York every time she visited the city. But there was not enough evidence against the woman and she was found Not Guilty.

Despite her acquittal, the Phillipine government insists that Marcos and Imelda may have salted away as much as £7 billion worth of national treasures, hard currency and bullion in banks and investments around the world. The arrest of the

MARCOS AND IMELDA MAY HAVE SALTED AWAY AS MUCH AS £7 BILLION WORTH OF NATIONAL TREASURES, HARD CURRENCY AND BULLION.

billionaire arms dealer, Adnan Khashoggi, on charges that he 'laundered' the Marcos' fortune so that the US government would not be able to trace the money, were also dropped. His case only served to further the speculation that the Marcos couple were thieves on a fabulous scale.

In twenty years of power, initially as a democratically-elected politician but later as a despot who imposed martial law, Marcos and his Steel Butterfly drained the national economy. America supported his regime on the strategic Pacific islands because they saw the Philippines as a bulwark against Communism. They maintained important military bases in the country, and pumped in millions and millions of dollars intended to improve the economic growth of the sixty-two million inhabitants of the islands.

Instead, these funds fell into the personal piggy bank of the state leader and his wife.

Imelda, a former beauty queen, became a symbol of grotesque greed to her fellow Filipinos, most of whom lived in frugal poverty. At the height of her career as 'leader's wife', she was spending £300,000 a week on clothes. Designer gowns from

AT THE HEIGHT OF HER CAREER AS 'LEADER'S WIFE', SHE WAS SPENDING £300,000 A WEEK ON CLOTHES.

Below: *Imelda Marcos playing stateswoman at her desk in the Plaza Hotel in the Philippines.*

Paris and Rome were jetted over to her and she spent weeks touring Europe on shopping expeditions. After one shopping trip, she filled three sea containers with goods. Shoes were her quirky addiction. Three thousand pairs of Gucci, Christian Dior and Karl Lagerfeld designs were found in her wardrobes.

While she spent, her husband – a wily, shrewd politician – was gradually dismantling the democratic state which the world believed he was protecting.

A PRESIDENT WITH A PAST

Marcos was born on 11 September, 1917, the son of a lawyer and schoolteacher, in a small town two hundred and fifty miles from the capital of Manila. He trained as a lawyer and qualified for his bar exam with flying colours. In 1939, he was arrested on charges of murdering his father's political rival, and was sentenced to life imprisonment. But in a re-trial, when he cleverly conducted his own defence, the charges were dropped. During the Second World War, he claimed that he led guerilla fighters

Above: *The Marcoses entertained the great and the good. Here, Princess Margaret is led aboard their private yacht.*

Opposite: *The former First Lady suffered the indignity of police fingerprinting sessions when she returned to her homeland. She was charged with tax fiddling, and later for keeping unauthorised foreign bank accounts.*

against the Japanese conquerors, although this is disputed. Nevertheless, the story helped him become a representative in the Philippines Congress when he was only thirty-one years old, the youngest politician in the country. In 1954, after an eleven-day courtship, he married Imelda. Ferdinand marcos said that her love for him 'drove me to the pinnacles of success'.

In 1965, after the general elections, he became the President of his country. Ironically, he won on an anti-corruption platform. Throughout his twenty years in office, his salary never varied. He received £3,300 a year, yet he lived in great opulence. He rode in armoured plated

Rolls-Royces, channeled millions of aid dollars to secret bank accounts in Rome and Switzerland, while his financial advisers purchased, on his behalf, properties all over Europe and in New York. As his own greed increased, his patience with democracy wore ever thinner. He won re-election in 1969 in a campaign tainted by allegations that he had practised vote rigging, intimidation and corruption. Three years later, in 1972, Marcos dispensed with democracy in the Philippines and imposed martial law on the country.

HAND-MADE LAVATORY PAPER

The attempted assassination of a senior military figure was the excuse for suspending democracy, though it has been claimed that the assassination was only a pretence, something Marcos set up so that he could justify his political move. Under the new martial rules, thousands of political enemies and dissenting journalists were thrown into jail, tortured and murdered. Then Marcos lifted martial law in 1981 to hold another election. However, his political opponents boycotted these elections, saying that to participate in the farce would only give Marcos a credibility he did not deserve. So the man held on to his immense political power. His power was unchallenged but he became increasingly paranoid. His secret police continued to fill the prisons with rivals, while all political parties were kept under surveillance or infiltrated by Marcos informers.

During these dark days, the Steel Butterfly lived in bizarre luxury. Every detail of her style was richly excessive. Every roll of loo paper was hand-made, silk-screen printed in Thailand and cost seven pounds. There was a storeroom of them in Manila's Malacanang Palace, and each of the building's fourteen bathrooms was graced by two rolls of this exquisite tissue. When she fled her homeland in 1986, she took her collection of pearls that, when it was spread out, covered thirty-eight square feet. She even coined a word for her own excesses – 'Imeldific'.

Guests at the palace were treated lavishly. They got to keep the contents of the wardrobes in the rooms where they stayed as visitors. These wardrobes were stashed with furs, clothes and jewellery. In

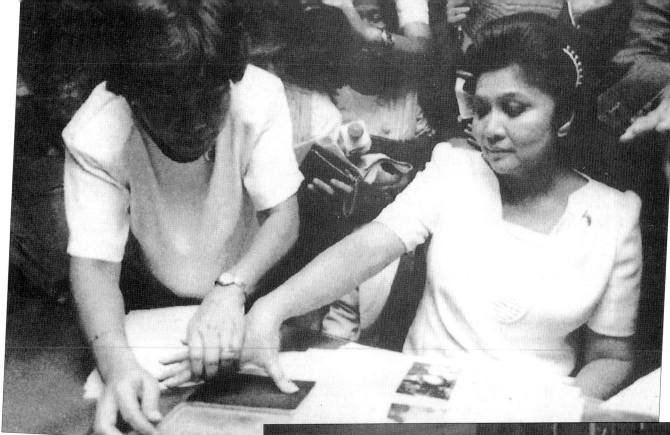

the main dining room, in a silver tureen, Imelda kept a great mound of Beluga caviar, renewed every day. And when she felt very generous, she would airlift a planeload of pals to New York for a little shopping. She could afford it. She headed thirty lucrative government corporations and she used the money for her own purposes. According to Filipino government investigators, Imelda, at one stage, was sending so many suitcases stuffed with cash to a bank in Geneva, that the bank cabled her and asked her to stop because she was overloading the staff with work.

THE YOUNG IMELDA
SANG FOR CANDY

If Imelda ever noticed her fellow citizens, if she did take a trip to the seamy side of town, to the barrios where people lived next door to open sewerage ditches and had no running water, she behaved as if she were royalty and she expected people to bow. But Imelda understood poverty. She came from a poor family, and as a child, had sung to American GIs for gifts of candy. She earned a living as a singer when she was a young woman. Her big break came in 1954, when she won a beauty contest and was introduced to the politician who would make her his Pacific empress.

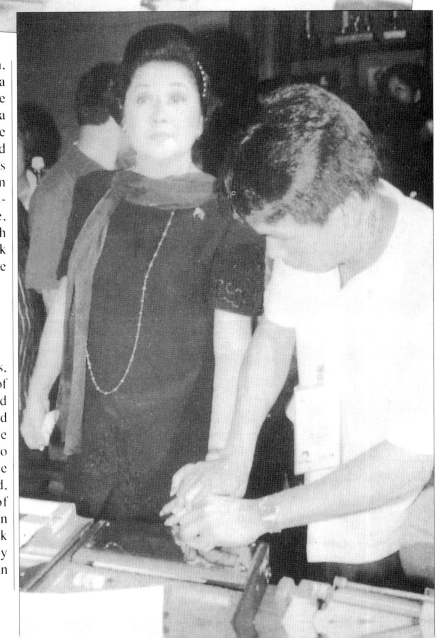

Imelda preferred – naturally – to forget her poor youth. She banned a book called 'The Untold Story of Imelda Marcos', written by Filipino journalist, Carmen Pedrosa. Pedrosa's book revealed that Imelda was once as poor as the people she now ruled over, and had been obliged to sleep on milk crates in the garage of a relative's house after her mother pushed her out of the family home. 'She did not want her poor origins ever to be known,' said Pedrosa. 'She conveyed a completely different image of herself, that she had been born with a silver spoon in her mouth. And that was important to them – because if the Marcoses had been born with wealth, there would be no questioning of that wealth. When she went into the barrio, she was regarded as a celebrity. She would wear a gown in places where people didn't even have a toilet. She was just living a fantasy life in a very poor country.'

THE CIA VERDICT

The fantasy was almost shattered in 1972, when an assassin stabbed her with a foot-long dagger as she was handing out awards at a beauty contest, but she only received a flesh wound. This incident re-inforced Imelda's strange belief that 'God has great things planned for me and is watching carefully over me at all times.'

The CIA had their own impressions of Imelda Marcos. During the Seventies, the agency prepared a character analysis of the woman that was not flattering, but accurate It read as follows: 'Mrs Marcos is ambitious and ruthless. Born a poor cousin of landed aristocracy, she has a thirst for wealth, power and public acclaim, and her boundless ego makes her easy prey for flatterers. Although she has little formal education, she is cunning.'

Imelda's relatives prospered with her. Her brother, Benjamin Romualdez, master-minded the take-over of the Manila Electric Company. Brother Alfredo ran the national government-controlled gambling industry. Initially Marcos outlawed gambling, but legalised it when he realised that huge profits could be made from this form of entertainment. William Sullivan, the US Ambassador to Manila from 1973 to 1977 said: 'When I was there foreign investors did not come into the Philippines without

> 'GOD HAS GREAT THINGS PLANNED FOR ME AND IS WATCHING CAREFULLY OVER ME AT ALL TIMES.'

distributing shares to Imelda or some of her cronies. That was the way business was done.' American officials described the country as being run by two factions – the FM factions loyal to Ferdinand Marcos and the FL faction, loyal to the first lady of excess, his wife, Imelda.

Imee, her beloved daughter, got in on the act too. A vice-chairman of a Filipino bank tells a story about four business people who had fallen behind with their kickbacks to the Marcos gang. The four were summoned to the palace in 1985, where they were

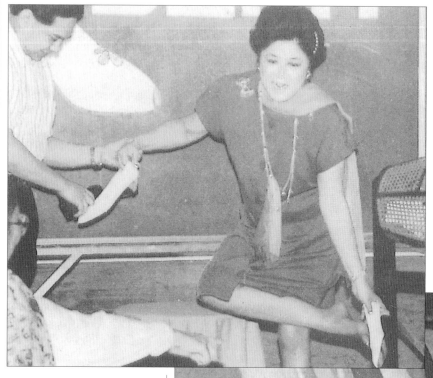

Above: *Imelda Marcos removes her shoes to offer them as a prize in a Filipino radio competition.*

Right and opposite: *Imelda was incredibly greedy. She became notorious for her huge shoe collection, but her numerous homes were filled with vast amounts of valuable objects and furnishings.*

confronted by Imee. She had become her mother's bookkeeper, and she sat in front of the four, with a notebook on her lap and armed secret servicemen at her side. Rather than face the niceties of a torture chamber, they promptly paid the illicit funds to Imee.

> IMELDA SPENT £9 MILLION DURING A SHOPPING SPREE ON DIAMONDS, RUBIES AND PEARLS.

The first lady preferred to spend her money on jewellery and clothes and she lavished gems and couture collections on herself whenever she felt depressed or sad. Documents drawn up by the Aquino government list some of Imelda's treasures: diamond bracelets, brooches and earrings valued at £1 million; one hundred and sixty-seven racks of designer dresses valued at £2 million; five fur coats, four hundred Gucci handbags and a mere sixty-eight pairs of handmade gloves.

But other documents were to make that lot seem like the remnants of a jumble sale.

MULTI-MILLION SPENDING SPREE

On one day in Switzerland in the late Seventies, Mrs Marcos spent £9 million during a shopping spree. She gobbled up diamonds, rubies and pearls, along with a diamond-and-garnet encrusted watch for her husband. Another US customs document proved that in seven days in May and the beginning of June, 1983, she squandered £4 million on a shopping orgy in New York. Imelda also spent a great deal of money on diamonds, shopping at Cartier, Van Clef & Arpels and Tiffany. She then splashed out a further £21,000 on towels and bedsheets. Finance for these spending sprees came from the New York

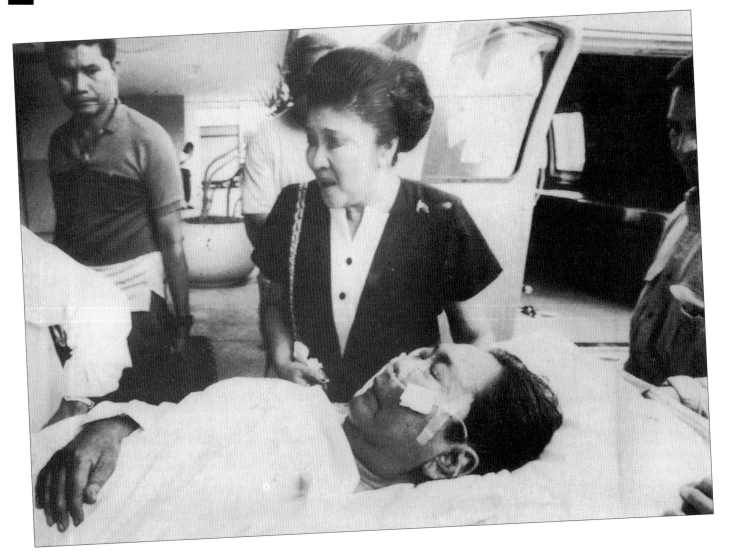

Above: *No one could doubt the very real love the Steel Butterfly felt for her husband. She was desolate when he died in exile and has campaigned ceaselessly to have his body flown home for burial.*

TWENTY-FOUR-CARAT GOLD-PLATED TAPS WERE TARNISHED AND DRIPPING IN EVERY BATHROOM.

branch of the Phillipine National Bank. Bank official, Willie Fernandez, testified at Imelda's trial that between 1973 and 1986 he personally authorised transactions of £24 million for Mrs Marcos.

'The call would come in: "Ma'am needs two hundred and fifty thousand cash," ' said a bank official who was granted anonymity at her trial. 'The money was carried to her in a big over-sized attaché case.' The prosecution called the bank: 'Mrs Marcos' private piggy bank.'

The goodies inside of her Manhattan townhouse made one angry customs official declare: 'Such opulence made me feel sick to the pit of my stomach.'

VALUABLE ITEMS JUST TOSSED ASIDE

Alan Ehrlichman, the auctioneer hired to sell the contents of this house for the Phillipine government, described valuable crystal glasses found hidden in an oven; rare Biblical manuscripts from the twelfth century were stuffed under an old boiler; two gilt mirrors which belonged to Marie Antoinette's husband, King Louis of France, were found broken and mysteriously lying in water in the bath; hand-embroidered bedlinen had been left lying in damp piles which attracted mildew; twenty-four-carat gold-plated taps were tarnished and dripping in every bathroom.

Ehrlichman said: 'It broke my heart. Many collectors aspire to work of that calibre but never attain it. Here's somebody who owned it who had no respect for it. It's a sacrilege. If two words summed up what I felt about it those words would be opulence and waste.' The house also had Jacuzzis in every bathroom and a discotheque where Imelda would gyrate while her bodyguards would sidle up to her to ask her for a dance.

A stitched pillow on one of the many sofas in the room bore the inscription: 'To be rich is no longer a sin. It's a miracle.' Another read: 'I love champagne, caviar and cash.' And then, there were also three baby grand pianos in her New York house.

Yet Imelda rarely stayed in this house, valued at £7 million. She preferred the comfort of a suite at New York's Waldorf-Astoria Hotel. But Ehrlichman said that while she wallowed in opulence, the servants were treated disdainfully, and lived, five beds to a room, in the basement.

Between 1980 and 1986, Imelda drew on another account in New York. This was held in the name of her secretary and was credited with a whopping £19 million. She also used her wealth to commission expensive portraits of herself and her family from New York artists. One of them is a version of the Renaissance artist Botticelli's 'Birth of Venus'. His painting shows the goddess rising from a shell. In her version, Imelda is shown rising from the shell with her arms extending to embrace the world. She commissioned portraits of Nancy and Ronald Reagan, her husband, Ferdinand Marcos and General MacArthur – the wartime leader who liberated the Philippines from the Japanese occupation.

THE TIDE TURNED AGAINST THE MARCOSES

But the politics of the Philippines were changing. On 21 August, 1983, Senator Begnigno Aquino, who had been imprisoned and then exiled by Marcos, returned to Manila. He was shot dead by a Marcos assassin as he stepped from the plane at the airport in Manila. Marcos claimed that the murderer was a Communist agitator, himself shot by government forces just after he had shot the returning exile. No one believed this story. Marcos sought to quieten the growing unrest of his people by calling for an election in 1986. After the votes were counted, Marcos declared himself the elected winner. However, Cory Aquino, the widow of the murdered exile, had won the support of the Phillipine army and had convinced the United States that Marcos was a corrupt and unworthy figure.

Finally, confident that she had the full support of the army, Aquino toppled the Marcos regime. The Marcoses, with their entourage, fled their homeland on 26 February, 1986, as, outside the palace gates, the mob bayed for their blood. Only hours after the deposed leader and his wife had left, this mob broke into the palace and were astonished by the excessive consumerism that they now confronted. The opulence which the Steel Butterfly and her husband had enjoyed was photographed for the world's amazement. Pictures of Imelda's shoe collection also showed closets the size of bungalows, built to hold her vast number of acquisitions.

The Filipino people wanted their money back and an international treasure hunt was launched. Jovito Salonga, the Filipino lawyer charged by his government to find the loot, said: 'They stole and stole and stole. And then they stole some more. Not only did they take what was not theirs, they also seized businesses and created monopolies, granted exclusive import licences and guaranteed bank loans for associates and relatives, loans that they never paid back. As new businesses rose the first payments were delivered to the boss, Marcos, and it got so crazy that I would estimate that even

'THEY STOLE AND STOLE AND STOLE. AND THEN THEY STOLE SOME MORE.'

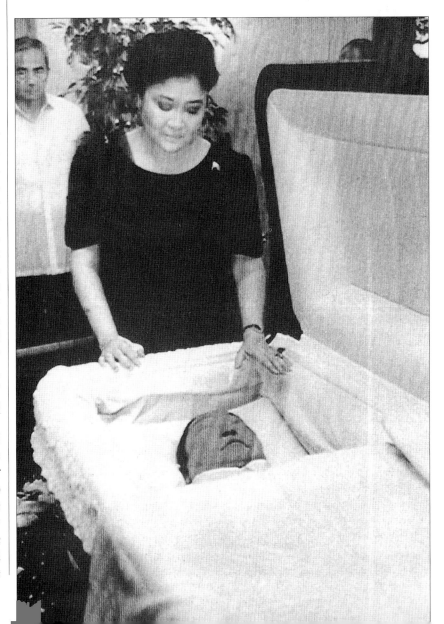

Below: *Ferdinand Marcos died in Honolulu. His wife says her last farewells.*

he doesn't know how much he was worth. The time has come to return their ill-gotten gains to the Filipino people.' Salonga maintained that between them, they ran off with something in the order of £7-9 billion.

Imelda remained proud and arrogant and revealed herself as rather stupid, if cunning. When she arrived in Hawaii, seeking a refuge after fleeing Manila, she declared shamelessly; 'They call me corrupt, frivolous. I am not at all privileged. Maybe the only privileged thing is my face. And corrupt? God! I would not look like this if I was corrupt. Some ugliness would settle down on my system. My people will judge me innocent.'

FAIRY-TALE OF JAPANESE TREASURE

The Marcoses called it a 'despicable act' when the USA government slapped racketeering charges on them. The CIA and FBI had built up an enourmous list of crimes with which to charge the pair. They were charged with, among other things, fraudulent use of foreign aid, with the connivance of members of their family who controlled major western-funded public works projects in the Philippines. 'There wasn't one pie, one cash register, one scam going that this duo didn't have their sticky fingers in,' said international money expert, John Stapleford. 'They were rotten to the core but blessed with a supreme arrogance which made them think that they really could get away with anything.'

Marcos was horrifed that America turned against him. Imelda said they had been 'shamed' by their old ally. Shortly before his death in September 1989, Marcos came up with a novel explanation for his wealth, 'I discovered the treasure of Yamashita,' he said. 'That is the key to it all.' Lt General Tomoyuki Yamashita was the Japanese commanding officer of the occupying forces in the Philippines during wartime. He is said to have stashed priceless works of art and gold bullion in secret caves. However, he was hanged in 1946 as a war criminal and he died without revealing the whereabouts of his hoard. But investigators on the trail of the treasure say it was just one more lie from Yamashita, a man who had spent his life evading the truth and destroying those who tried to tell

it. The treasure is as much myth as reality and there is nothing to prove that Ferdinand Marcos ever laid his hands on anything other than all the money he stole from his own impoverished countrymen.

In July 1987, two US lawyers posing as Marcos allies, telephoned the exiled despot and claimed to be interested in representing him. They taped a telephone conversation in which he claimed to have £7 billion worth of gold bullion lying in secret vaults on the island of Mindanao. He didn't make any claim at this time that this gold was part of the fabled wartime booty of the Japanese general, Yamashita.

THE AMERICANS ARE UNKIND

Before she stood trial, Imelda,whose tears flowed freely during numerous press conferences, said: 'I have only one dream now. I am not asking for justice anymore, I am asking for a divine human right to die, to be buried in my own country. I am shocked by all this inhumanity shown by America, they have not been nice to us – us

Above: *In 1991, Imelda and her son, Ferdinand Jnr., spoke at a political rally in Manila. There is bitter rivalry between the 'reformist' Aquino faction and those who favour the Marcos family.*

Opposite, top: *Attending church, Imelda Marcos is comforted by other church-goers. Despite her years of misrule, she has enthusiastic followers in the Philippines.*

Opposite, bottom: *Imelda Marcos with her attorney, Antonio Coronel, when she faced charges in a Manila court.*

who were such good friends to them.' She believed this statement.

Imelda was left alone to face the music when Marcos, suffering from a disease of the kidneys, died. 'He settled with a higher authority,' one embittered State Department official said. 'She faced earthly justice – and won.' The secrecy of banking laws protected her from detection, but there is no one in the Philippines or in the American intelligence agencies who believes that justice was done.

IMELDAS 'DIVINE' MISSION

The Steel Butterfly has returned to the land she looted, where she risks facing further criminal charges. She has lost none of the arrogance that was her chief characteristic. Recently she has taken to calling herself a goddess, a deity who has confronted mortal challenges and troubles and won. She explains: 'I must be a deity because I was given a divine mission, to return to my homeland, which I did. An ordinary mortal would not be able to stand what I did.'

MA BARKER
Machine-Gun Mama

She was a rare person – a woman who was a leader of men and dangerous gangs; a woman who bred criminals, deliberately teaching her sons to be wicked delinquents. Ma Barker has secured her place in the annals of crime, for her story is that of a truly evil person.

Ma Barker was a mother who taught her children the three 'Rs' – reading, writing and revolvers. She had been brought up in the same rural area that Jesse James used to roam, and she was steeped in criminal lore. She taught her four sons – who became, under her tutelage, one of the most feared and ruthless criminal gangs in American history – to despise authority and follow the maxim that all laws were made to be broken. Unlike their contemporaries such as Pretty Boy Floyd and John Dillinger, who, although notorious, did not make much money from their crimes, the Barker boys did steal vast amounts of money, and were very careful about publicity. They acted with stealth and skill, as they roamed across the United States, from the mid-west to Texas in the far south. And they had no qualms about killing. They were social misfits, encouraged by their own mother to live as habitual criminals.

Ma Barker was born Arizona Donnie Clark in Springfield, Missouri, in 1872, the daughter of a hard-drinking, illiterate ranch hand and a God-fearing mother who taught her to read the Bible and play the fiddle. She left school when she was ten, although she never adandoned her habit of reading lurid penny crime sheets which chronicled the exploits of the James gang and other villains of the Old West. Arrie, as she called herself, was particularly excited whenever she caught sight of Jesse, riding tall in his saddle at the head of his gang. In 1892, when she was twenty years old, she went into a kind of mourning when the evil Dalton Gang were riddled with police bullets during their last vicious bank robbery in Coffeyville, Kansas.

TRAINED IN VIOLENCE

By the end of the year, her grief was mitigated by her marriage to George Barker, a common labourer every bit as coarse as she was. Weak and ineffectual, he winced under the savagery of his wife's tongue – particularly vicious after she had been drinking whiskey. He was a hag-ridden husband, dominated by his wife. But they managed to produce four healthy sons – Herman in 1894, Lloyd two years later, Arthur in 1899 and Fred in 1902. Every single one of them was trained in violence... and they were all to die by the gun, just as their mother did. They started life in Aurora, Missouri, and were known as 'The Four Horsemen of the Apocalypse' by their Sunday school teachers.

In 1908, perhaps driven out by the neighbours who believed that she had given birth to sons of the Devil, Ma moved her brood and her milksop spouse to Webb City, Missouri.

Above: *Jesse James, the outlaw who was Ma Barker's girlhood hero.*

Opposite: *Kate 'Ma' Barker who was the leader of men, and hardened criminal.*

Below: *Another role model for the young Ma Barker was Pretty Boy Floyd.*

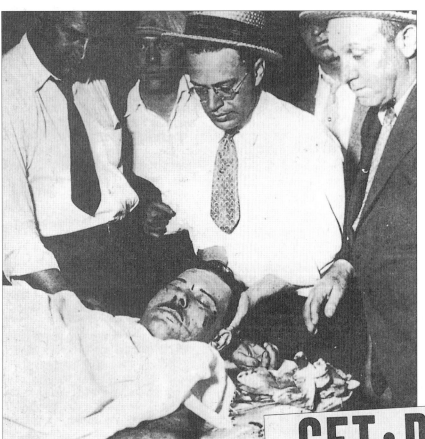

burn in hell before you lay another filthy pig hand on a Barker boy!'

In 1915, after more run-ins with the law, the family upped and left for Tulsa, Oklahoma, where her husband had found a job as a railway worker. They still lived in soul-destroying poverty, and her sons continued to confront the law. These boys went through the whole catalogue of juvenile crime – from breaking and entering, to stealing cars and mugging.

NEW AND DEADLY FRIENDS

Ma Barker herself developed friendships with a motley assortment of bums, heels, con-men, robbers and murderers. She became very attached to an ex-con, called Herb Farmer, who ran a hideout for villains on the run in nearby Joplin, Missouri, and she met many big-name criminals of her day, men like bank robber Al Spencer,

There was money in this town where recently gold had been discovered in the surrounding hills.

But Ma's dream of wealth was sadly at odds with the reality of their impoverished life; the Barkers continued to live in grinding poverty, in a shack made of tar and paper with no running water or electricity. It was the perfect breeding ground for the kind of resentment that turns a dissatisfied young person to crime.

'MY BOYS ARE MARKED'

Ma had a pathological hatred of authority and to those who preferred the slightest criticism of her crooked brood. Policemen, in particular, were regarded as prime suspects in a universal conspiracy against her sons. In 1910, when Herman Barker became her first son to get arrested for stealing, she astonished the neighbourhood policemen at the Webb City police station when, instead of berating her delinquent young son, she turned on the officers of the law with a tirade against them; 'My boys are marked,' she screamed at them. 'You'll

GET·DILLINGER!
$15,000 Reward
A PROCLAMATION

WHEREAS, One John Dillinger stands charged officially with numerous felonies including murder in several states and his banditry and depredation stamp him as an outlaw, a fugitive from justice and a vicious menace to life and property;

NOW, THEREFORE, We, Paul McNutt, Governor of Indiana; George White, Governor of Ohio; F. B. Olson, Governor of Minnesota; William A. Comstock, Governor of Michigan; and Henry Horner, Governor of Illinois, do hereby proclaim and offer a reward of Five Thousand Dollars ($5,000.00) to be paid to the person or persons who apprehend and deliver the said John Dillinger into the custody of any sheriff of any of the above-mentioned states or his duly authorized agent.

THIS IS IN ADDITION TO THE $10,000.00 OFFERED BY THE FEDERAL GOVERNMENT FOR THE ARREST OF JOHN DILLINGER.

HERE IS HIS FINGERPRINT CLASSIFICATION and DESCRIPTION.——— FILE THIS FOR IDENTIFICATION PURPOSES.

John Dillinger. (w) age 30 yrs., 5-8½. 170½ lbs., gray eyes, med. chest, hair, med. comp., med. build. Dayton. O., P. D. No. 10587. O. S. E. No. 559-646.

F.P.C. (12)

	M	9	R	O	O	
	S	14	U	OO	8
13	10	O	O	O	
u	R	w	w	w	
5	11	15	I	8	
u	U	u	w	u	

FRONT VIEW

Be on the lookout for this desperado. He is heavily armed and usually is protected with bullet-proof vest. Take no unnecessary chances in getting this man. He is thoroughly prepared to shoot his way out of any situation.

GET HIM

DEAD

OR ALIVE

Notify any Sheriff or Chief of Police of Indiana, Ohio, Minnesota, Michigan, Illinois.

or THIS BUREAU

SIDE VIEW

ILLINOIS STATE BUREAU OF CRIMINAL IDENTIFICATION

EMMETT

TIM EVANS   BOB DALTON   GROT DALTON   DICK BROADWEL

ANK ROBBERY OGFEEVILLE KANG

Frank Nash, Ray Terrill and Chicago hold-up men Francis Keating and Thomas Holden. Soon it was her house where numerous shifty criminals sought refuge, and these visitors regaled the impressionable boys with tales of murder, robbery and general mayhem. Psychiatrist James Allen, who has made a study of Ma Barker, said: 'This woman saw in the hoodlums and robbers that hung out at her home a reincarnation of the bandits that she idolised as a child. She was incapable of instilling in her offspring a respect for the natural laws and rules of society; she portrayed the underside of life as a kind of romantic, Robin Hood affair, which of course, to wayward young boys with limited education and even shorter attention spans, was exactly what they wanted to hear.'

The Barker boys, by the time they reached adolesence, were carrying guns and were deeply involved in the under-

Above: *The Dalton Gang, laid out like big game safari trophies, were shot by the police during a bank raid.*

Right: *Brothers Bob and Grat Dalton, held up, even as they are dying, for the benefit of photographers. Ma Barker mourned the passing of this notorious gang.*

Opposite: *Ma Barker copied the murderous methods of John Dillinger and taught her sons to do the same. The police eventually killed Dillinger on 22 July, 1934.*

world. Ma Barker took great delight in hearing of the boys' exploits at the family-dinner table, and was happy to dispense advice on how they could best become stick-up men or jewel-store robbers.

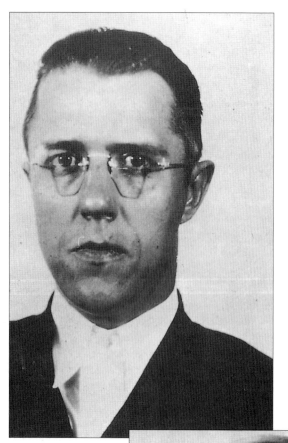

In 1917 the Barkers were members of the Tulsa Central Gang, a loose-knit consortium of teenage hoods who robbed banks, post offices and country gas stations. Ray Terrill, who spent many hours with Ma plotting bank raids, took Herman with him on a number of minor robberies. After these outings, Ma would turn her son's pockets out to make sure he was not holding back her share of the spoil. Once she found a fifty-dollar bill in the top of his sock, and laid into him with the butt-end of a .38 police issue revolver.

inconsolable when he was sentenced to twenty-five years hard labour in Leavenworth Jail, the state's penitentiary. Arthur was next in line for justice when, in 1922, he was convicted of murdering a night watchman in a Tulsa hospital. Arthur was trying to steal a supply of drugs to satisfy his morphine addiction. He got twenty years in jail, despite an attempt by Ma Barker to bribe another man to plead guilty to Arthur's murder charge.

After Arthur went to jail, Ma Barker abandoned her husband, George, and descended into deviant sexual practices with young girls. 'Hell, when Freddie and the others weren't knocking off banks, they were running around trying to find young girls for Ma,' said James Audett, a reformed bank robber who had once been part of the Barker gang and was an expert on the family. 'The boys would bring the girls, all under-aged, to Ma and when the old lady was through with them, she would tell Freddie and Alvin Karpis, an associate of the gang, to get rid of them. Those two crackpots would just up and kill these poor girls and dump their bodies in lakes nearby. God, there were bodies of young girls floating all over those lakes because of crazy old Ma Barker. Disgusting. The whole bunch of them made me so sick that I only went on two jobs with them. They couldn't keep regulars in the gang because of the way they lived.

'THEY WERE ALL KILL-CRAZY LOVERS'

'That was the key to them. Ma became a lesbian, and all the boys – with the exception of Arthur – were homosexuals, and there ain't nothing worse than a homosexual bank robber and killer. You see, if one of them saw a cop coming at them with a weapon they would shoot to kill because they thought their lover might be bumped off. They were protecting their lovers as well as themselves. Freddie killed a lot of people to save his sweetheart Karpis. They were all kill-crazy lovers.'

In 1926, Freddie drew a fifteen-year sentence for the armed robbery of the main bank in Windfield, Kansas – a raid that had been organised by Ma. The only son not in jail was Herman. Ma, saddened by the loss of her sons, was never tempted to make

In 1922 she kissed goodbye to the first of her crooked brood when Lloyd was caught during a raid on a post office, when he shot and wounded a guard. Nothing she could say or do would persuade the court that her boy was innocent and she was

Herman go straight in order to keep him free; instead she encouraged him to join the Kimes-Terrill gang, a mid-western mob who specialised in stealing entire safes from banks. They would drag the safe out with a pulley and a truck, then blow it open. This method worked successfully on many raids but, in 1926, Herman was shot when a posse of policemen surrounded the gang during a raid on a Missouri bank. He scuttled home to Ma's hideout in Tulsa where, even as she tended to his wounds, she plotted new methods of robbing banks and stores. On 18 September, 1927, Herman held-up a grocery store in Newton, Kansas, before fleeing town at the wheel of his getaway car with an unknown accomplice. On the outskirts of town, SherifF John Marshall raised his gun to fire at the speeding vehicle, but was cut down by a hail of Thompson sub-machine-gun fire from Herman. Marshall died instantly.

The next day in Wichita, Herman was alone when he drove his car into a police trap. He emptied his machine gun and pistol at the law officers – then he withdrew a bullet he called his 'lucky piece' from his waistcoat pocket. It was his last round and, although he was wounded by return fire from his cop pursuers, he chose to blow his own brains out.

SHE DEVOTED HER LIFE TO FREEING HER SONS

Ma Barker was convinced that Herman had been executed by police, claiming: 'A Barker don't do things like that. Barkers weren't raised to kill themselves for pigs.' But an autopsy proved that he had, indeed, ended his short, violent life.

She maintained her lust for young girls, but knew that she needed a man to look after her while her boys were in jail. She took up with a penniless alcoholic, Arthur Dunlop, saying: 'A drinking man's better 'n no man at all.' Now, Ma Barker divided her time between writing petitions to governors and prison wardens, asking for clemency for her sons, and maintaining a safe haven for villains on the run. She also began 'fencing' – selling stolen goods – for the rabble who stayed with her. Edgar J. Hoover, the legendary head of the FBI, would later say of her: 'It was the suicide of Herman, and the imprisonment of her

other three sons, which changed her from an animal mother of the she-wolf variety to a veritable beast of prey. She slipped deeper into depravity and villainy.'

The money she received from the desperadoes she was hiding, plus her take from the sale of stolen gems and other valuables, soon meant that she no longer needed the spurious protection of Arthur Dunlop, although she continued to live with him. She ignored his presence, however, as she devoted her life to freeing her sons. Ma said: 'I gotta have at least one of my poor babies free. At least one... it's all I ask. Who would deny a poor woman at least one of her brood?' In 1931, her pleas for clemency finally paid off when Freddie was released from jail. He brought with him his cell-mate and partner-in-crime, Alvin Karpis, who, by a freak quirk, had also wangled his way out of hard time. It was about the worst mistake the authorities could have made.

Now admitted lovers, the duo embarked on a Ma-inspired wave of terror. Karpis later explained: 'What I wanted was big automobiles like rich people had and everything like that. I didn't see how I was going to get them by making a fool of myself and

FREDDIE AND KARPIS WERE RELEASED FROM JAIL TOGETHER. IT WAS ABOUT THE WORST MISTAKE THE AUTHORITIES COULD HAVE MADE.

Opposite: *The morose features of Alvin 'Creepy' Karpis with whom Ma threw in her lot. The lower picture reveals the scar left by a botched plastic surgery job. Karpis hoped to change his looks and evade the law.*

Below: *Fred Barker, the beloved son who died on 16 January, 1935, after a four-hour gun battle with FBI agents in Florida.*

FRED BARKER

- MEMBER OF BARKER-KARPIS GANG.

- HIS CRIMINAL CAREER DATING FROM 1922 INCLUDES ARRESTS FOR LARCENY, BURGLARY, BANK ROBBERY AND KIDNAPING.

- BARKER WAS KILLED ON THE MORNING OF JANUARY 16, 1935, AT OKLAWAHA, FLORIDA, IN A FOUR HOUR GUN BATTLE WITH FBI AGENTS.

Above: *J.Edgar Hoover, crime buster extraordinaire, who ruled the FBI with an iron fist for fifty years. He went to war against the mobsters with astonishing success.*

working all my life.' Such an attitude delighted Ma Barker, so it was no surprise that Karpis became a surrogate son, replacing Herman in her affections.

Freddie had fallen deeply in love with Karpis and, in jail, they made a pact that they would never bluff their way past lawmen after doing a job, nor risk a high speed chase. They would simply kill and take their chances.

In the summer of 1931, with the Great Depression ravaging the lives of millions of ordinary Americans, the pair embarked on a crime wave, robbing several jewellery and clothing stores. Captured twice and confined in small-town jails, they escaped easily and continued their spree. They often returned home to Ma with details of their exploits, and to give her a share of the spoils. They persuaded Ma to move with them from Tulsa to set up their crime HQ in a farmhouse in Koskonong, Missouri. Karpis – a skilled electrician, thanks to his years in the federal slammer – rigged the house with an elaborate alarm system to

> IT WAS TIME FOR THE BARKERS TO HIT THE ROAD, AND FIND SOMEPLACE SAFE UNTIL THE HEAT DIED DOWN.

keep cops at bay. Under the aliases of Dunn and Hamilton, the two lovers roamed the mid-west states. In July of that year they successfully held-up a hardware store and took $1000 before making their getaway. Two days later, however, Sheriff Charles Kelley spotted them sitting in a car, dividing up the loot. He pulled his gun to arrest them, but they fired first and he fell dead on the road. It was time for the Barkers to hit the road, and find someplace safe until the heat died down.

Ma cleared out of the Missouri farmhouse, and headed for St Paul, Minnesota, well-known as a place where gangsters could hide from the law. Once more, she set-up a refuge for gunmen, while she became closely associated with the well-known hi-jackers Jack Pfeifer and Harry Sawyer. Ma planned the hi-jackings of long distance trucks and Freddie and Karpis carried them out. The goods were fenced through Pfeifer and Sawyer, and Ma used her share to pay lawyers in her fight to free her other sons from prison.

Now poor Arthur Dunlop, overshadowed and detested by the criminal family into which he had married, was no longer wanted. His bullet-riddled body was found floating in the icy waters of Lake Freasted, in Wisconsin, towards the end of 1931. It was Freddie Barker who pulled the trigger on his own stepfather.

Freddie and Karpis had, by now, acquired some criminal clout of their own, and no longer relied on Pfeifer and Sawyer. Many hoodlums and gunslingers were prepared to work for Freddie and Karpis, and the pair began to run their own gang. Between 1931 and 1933, they knocked off dozens of banks, killing numerous people along the way, including a marshall called Manley Jackson. Several armed guards and policemen were also killed. Ma Barker and Freddie were now among the most-wanted criminals in America, for they had stolen an incredible $500,000 in cash and had murdered many people.

In October 1932, Arthur Barker was released after being paroled. Now Ma had two sons to run her business in crime. In May, 1933, Ma had a brainwave. She had tired of bank robberies and plotted a kidnapping. She reasoned in her warped brain that, just as she herself would pay any amount of money and pull any string to get a loved one out of jail, so a wealthy family would hand over any amount of cash to get one of their brood back. Teaming up with Fred Goetz, a member of the old Al Capone gang, wily Ma Barker hatched a plan to seize William Hamm, the head of a wealthy brewing dynasty.

MA'S FIRST KIDNAPPING

On 15 June, 1933, after Hamm left his brewery in St Paul, he was snatched by Freddie and Karpis. He was ordered to sign a ransom note, was fitted with a pair of goggles stuffed with cotton wool, and

MA BARKER AND FREDDIE WERE NOW AMONG THE MOST-WANTED CRIMINALS IN AMERICA.

Below: *The most famous inter-gang killing of them all – the St Valentine's Day Massacre, masterminded by Al Capone. But Fred Goetz, the close friend of Ma Barker, was rumoured to have played the role of executioner at this grisly event.*

Below: *Sent by Ma to live in Chicago, Arthur Barker was arrested as he left his apartment. He was killed when he tried to escape from Alcatraz prison in California.*

driven for several hours to the Ma Barker hide-out, where he was placed under the machine-gun guard of Goetz. For three days the brewer's family consulted with police, and their own consciences, before deciding to pay the ransom. On 17 June, the ransom was thrown from a car speeding along a dark road on the outskirts of St Paul; the plot hatched by Ma Barker had worked perfectly and William Hamm was returned safely to his family.

ARTHUR BARKER
ALIAS "DOC" BARKER

- MEMBER OF BARKER-KARPIS GANG.

- CRIMINAL CAREER DATING FROM 1918 INCLUDES ARRESTS FOR LARCENY, JAIL BREAKING, BANK ROBBERY, MURDER, AND KIDNAPING.

- APPREHENDED BY FBI AGENTS IN CHICAGO, ILLINOIS, ON JANUARY 8, 1935.

- CONVICTED AND SENTENCED TO LIFE IN PRISON.

- HE WAS KILLED IN AN ATTEMPT TO ESCAPE FROM ALCATRAZ PENITENTIARY ON JANUARY 13, 1939.

The Barker brothers, with Ma as the mastermind, then resumed their old trade of robbing banks. In August, 1933, they hit a payroll truck in St Paul, and stole $30,000. But in the subsequent shootout with cops, one policeman died and another was seriously wounded. Another cop was killed in a botched Chicago raid a month later.

MA AS MASTERMIND

Ma decided to go back to kidnapping, believing that the ease with which they ransomed Hamm was proof that this was a lucrative, and relatively safe, criminal pursuit. Feeling the heat after their numerous killings, with the Barker names on

KARPIS AND FREDDIE BARKER, TOGETHER WITH MA, NOW CHOSE TO HAVE PLASTIC SURGERY TO ALTER THEIR APPEARANCES.

thousands of FBI wanted posters, Ma proposed the kidnapping of Edward Bremer, a wealthy Minneapolis banker.

Ma masterminded the snatch meticulously, spending several months on the crucial planning stages before unleashing her boys to do the dirty work on 17 January, 1934. Bremer dropped his eight-year-old girl off at school that morning and began driving to his office. He was ambushed at a traffic light by Arthur, who held a gun to the victim's head.

Bremer was forced to sign a ransom demand for $200,000. The Bremer family did not contact the police, but their attempts to pay the ransom were botched on several occasions. Meanwhile, the psychopathic Arthur Barker tried to kill Bremer but his brother Freddie stopped him with the words: 'Sure, blow his brains out, but you know what Ma will think about that!' The mere mention of the one and only person Arthur feared was enough to make him put his twin revolvers down. Edward Bremer lived to be re-united with his family after the ransom cash was delivered on 17 February, 1934.

PLASTIC SURGERY FOR MA BARKER AND HER BOYS

Karpis and Freddie Barker, together with Ma, now chose to have plastic surgery to alter their appearances and so elude the law. They selected a doctor called Joseph Moran, who was also an alcoholic. Moran drugged them with morphine before setting about his crude surgery. Ma was about to undergo her operation when she saw the results that Moran had achieved on Freddie. Moran was murdered by Freddie and Arthur on Ma's orders.

Ma insisted that the gang should split up, so she sent Arthur to live in Chicago. She rented a house in the rural backwater of Oklawaha, in Florida, where Karpis and other gang members were regular visitors. In 1935, following an underworld tip-off, Arthur was arrested outside his Chicago apartment by FBI agents. In normal circumstances he would have reached for his gun and started blasting away – but he had left his weapon indoors and was captured without a struggle.

A search of his apartment revealed a detailed map and directions to the hideout in Florida, used by Ma and Freddie. This was a welcome breakthrough for the police who alerted FBI agents. An armed siege of the hideout was carefully planned.

THE END OF MA BARKER AND HER SONS

On 16 January, 1935, agents surrounded the house and one inspector, wearing a bullet-proof jacket, drew the short straw: he actually had to approach the house and tell Ma to surrender. She opened the door the merest crack and hissed through yellowing teeth; 'To hell with you, all of you.' As she closed the door the quaking law enforcer heard her say: 'Let the damned Feds have it – shoot!' Ma, the cool brains behind the murderous brawn of her thieving sons, went to an upstairs window to begin firing a gas-powered automatic rifle at the men ringing her lair. While Freddie opened up with a sub-machine gun, the FBI returned automatic fire and poured tear gas shells into the house. For forty-five minutes, the air crackled and hissed with the sound of gunfire and splintering wood.

Finally, when the return fire from the house quietened and stopped, a handyman, who worked for the Barkers, volunteered to go check on the outlaws. He found Ma Barker with three bullets in her heart, Freddie dead from fourteen machine gun bullets. Ma Barker's reign as the berserk gangland matriarch was over.

Her two remaining sons were to die violently. Arthur was killed by guards in the Alcatraz fortress jail in San Francisco Bay on 13 June, 1939, when he tried to escape the prison. Lloyd served his full twenty-five-year stretch for murder and was freed in 1947. He married soon after his release and his wife stabbed him to death in 1949. It was a fitting end to the story of the Barker boys who did everything for a wicked woman, their own Ma.

SHE OPENED THE DOOR THE MEREST CRACK AND HISSED THROUGH YELLOW-ING TEETH; 'TO HELL WITH YOU, ALL OF YOU.'

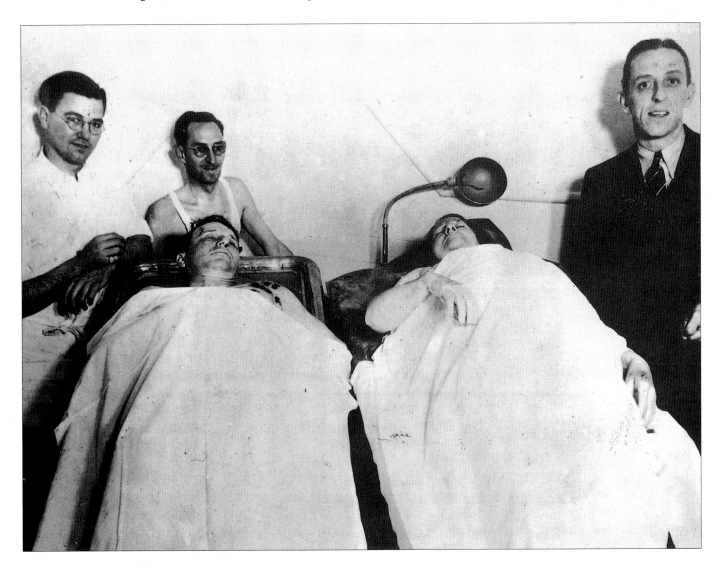

Below: *Side by side for all eternity – Ma Barker, right, and her son, Fred, after they died resisting FBI agents. Few mourned their passing.*

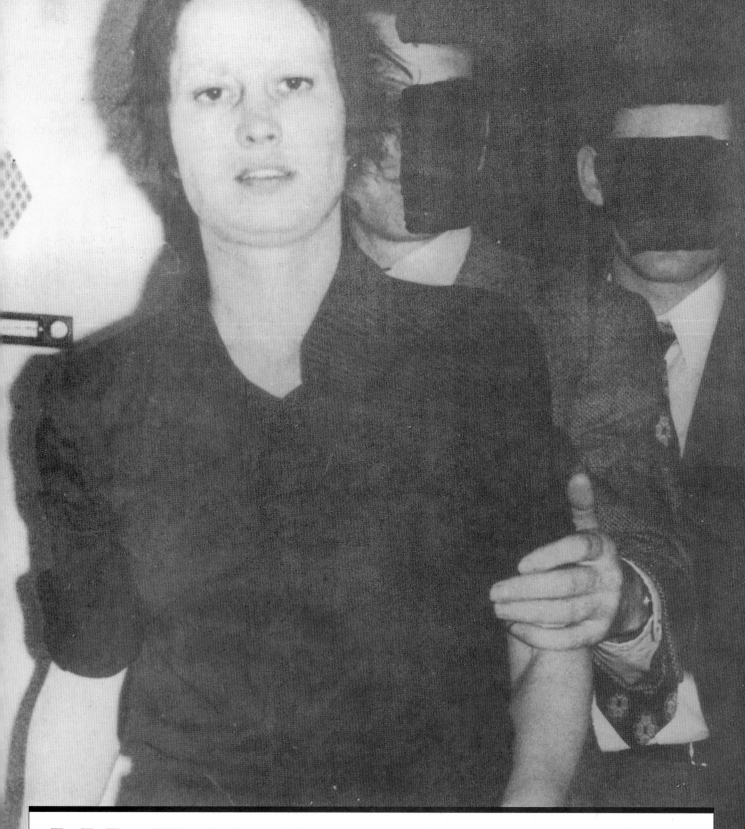

ULRIKE MEINHOF
Queen of Terror

This woman is one of the most enigmatic poltical figures of our time. Ulrike Meinhof was well-educated, bright and the radical darling of the national media. But she chose to become an outcast, a fanatic and a ruthless killer. Hers is a very mysterious tale.

Not all of Germany's post-war children shared in the vision of the economic miracle, the rebuilding of their shattered industries and bombed-out cities to heights greater than that which the Third Reich achieved. Nestling in the schools and universities, in certain stratas of the intelligentsia and the academics, the seeds of a new revolution were being nurtured by a breed who looked to the east and, particularly, the German Democratic Republic, hiding behind its wall and its wire, as the model state of the future.

These coffee-bar radicals and middle-class Communists believed that capitalism was a dead concept and that the time for the true proletarian revolution had arrived. But their vision held no hope for such a Utopia to be achieved by peaceful means – the new Jerusalem was to be forged with guns and blood. Into such a maelstrom of fury and fire fell Ulrike Marie Meinhof to be indelibly linked in history with Andreas Baader when they formed the Baader-Meinhof gang which scorched its way across Germany to become one of the most successful terror groups the world has ever known.

A QUICK WIT AND READY CHARM

She was born in Lower Saxony on 7 October 1934, a child of the misfit generation called 'Hitler's Children'. Spawned in his rise to power, old enough to see him

bring her country to its knees, she lived through the conflagration and came out of it an orphan. Her father died from cancer at the outbreak of war and her mother in 1948. A foster mother took care of her during her high-school years – a period when she matured into an intelligent, thoughtful young woman, highly gifted in classes, polite to all she met and possessed of a quick wit and ready charm. She was also a pacifist who devoured works by Bertrand Russell and Vera Brittain. Her views were shaped by her mother; but also by the turbulence of the era which left its stamp on her young mind.

By the time she was twenty-three and studying for her post-graduate doctorate at the University of Münster she had embraced many ecological, left-wing and

Above: *The brooding good looks of Andreas Baarder helped attract many women to his violent cause.*

Opposite: *Ulrike Meinhof, darling of the left, brilliant scholar, gifted teacher, loving mother and urban terrorist par excellence.*

pacifist causes, including ban-the-bomb campaigns and calls for Germany to resist growing militarism from the right. It was mainstream stuff – even Willy Brandt, the anti-Nazi socialist who went on to become Chancellor of the Federal Republic, was a supporter of similar trends. In 1959, her reputation as a chic radical and avant garde academic was established. And Ulricke knew how to keep an audience interested, so she was asked to speak at an anti-bomb conference in the capital, Bonn. It was there that she met Klaus Rainer Rohl, the Marxist editor of the student newspaper 'Konkret'. They fell in love and were married in 1962, and Ulrike gave birth to twins the following year.

> SHE DIVORCED HER HUSBAND – A COMMITTED WOMANISER WHO FINALLY INDULGED IN ONE AFFAIR TOO MANY.

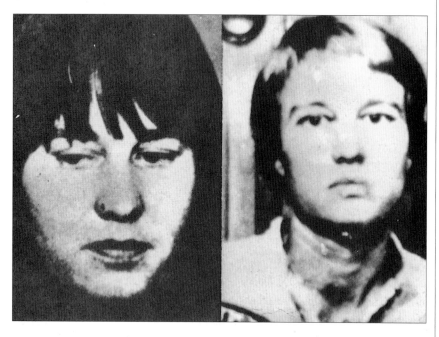

Above: *The changing of Ulrike. She became a master of disguise and this talent helped her evade the law for some time.*

> THE COMMITTED PACIFIST HAD TAKEN THE FIRST STEP TOWARDS BECOMING AN URBAN TERRORIST.

Although committed to her domestic life, her husband and family, Ulrike's infatuation with the politics of the Left began to deepen. In the permissive Sixties, as England swung to a beatnik sound and 'free love' were the two words on everyone's lips, the old order of capitalism and class seemed worthy to her of destruction. But even as she steeped herself more and more in left-wing ideology she prospered within the system she was one day to despise.

She and Rohl led comfortable lives. Rohl began to translate some pornographic Swedish books into German at a considerable profit while Ulrike's income expanded as she took on the editorship of 'Konret' and increased its sales. In their avant-garde world they attracted an eclectic mix of friends – some rich, some poor, but all imbued with a passion to change the world. She became a successful talk-show host and a radio personality, wheeled out to give the 'alternative' viewpoint whenever an issue of the day was being dissected by the media. And not once, during these years of comfortable affluence, with a white Mercedes parked outside her door and her cellar stocked with fine Rhine wine, did Ulrike Meinhof for a moment consider that violent upheaval was the only answer to all the ills of society.

Towards the end of the Sixties, two events occured which went a long way to derailing her peaceful and ordered world. The first occurred in 1968 when she divorced her husband – a committed womaniser who finally indulged in one affair too many. The second was the trial of a young revolutionary – Andreas Baader.

Baader, born in Munich on 6 May, 1943, was a believer in a violent solution to the class struggle which he saw confronting modern German society. Work-shy, handsome, appealing to women, he drifted in his twenties to Berlin where he was a regular in the agitprop demonstrations that happened daily in the old imperial capital against everything from squatters' rights to increased students' fees. In 1967 Gudrun Ennslin, a committed Communist, left her husband with her young child to live with Baader, whom she had met at a student demo. It was during this period that Andreas Baader began to evolve his philosophy of anger and class hatred, leading him to call for an armed guerilla war against the state – his so-called 'People's War'.

ULRIKE'S FIRST STEP TOWARDS TERRORISM

However, their very first act of armed resistance went badly wrong. He and Ennslin planted incendiary bombs in Frankfurt department stores in a protest at the Vietnam War. They were seen escaping, soon tracked down and put on trial. It was while the trial was going on that Ulrike Meinhof began to speak out for him and for the action he had taken. The committed pacifist had taken the first step towards becoming an urban terrorist – absorbing the atitudethat any human life is worth taking if the cause is worthy enough.

Baader, Ennslin and two other guerillas who were caught torching the department stores were sentenced to three years each for arson. In June 1969, after serving fourteen months each, they were released pending the outcome of an appeal, but Baader, his lover and one other militant fled to France. When they were re-captured on an Interpol warrant in 1970 and sent back to jail in Germany, the flame of righteous indignation burned deep within Ulrike Meinhof. Now living in Berlin and her credentials with the the Left firmly established, her apartment became a meeting place for political sympathisers. In 1970, Ulrike committed herself to the path of terrorism when she plotted with Baader cohorts to spring him from jail.

There was a group in sympathy with Baader and his cause. It was known as the Red Army Faction, a Marxist cadre founded by Horst Mahler, a lawyer who defended Baader at his trial, and was committed to the violent overthrow of the

MAHLER, A LAWYER WHO DEFENDED BAADER AT HIS TRIAL, AND WAS COMMITTED TO THE VIOLENT OVERTHROW OF THE WEST GERMAN STATE.

Below: *The scene of devastation at Frankfurt Airport after a bomb was planted by terrorists. Three people were killed and twenty-eight injured.*

West German state. Linked to an underground network of revolutionaries via university and Communist party contacts, the Red Army Faction also had contact with Middle Eastern terror groups.

On 14 May, 1970, Baader was freed in an audacious escape from the Institute of Social Studies in Dahlem. The prison authorities had allowed him to further his academic studies at the institute, although he was kept under guard. After the getaway Mahler, Meinhof, Baader and Ennslin fled to a terrorist training camp in Jordan where they hoped to learn advanced terrorism.

STUDYING WITH THE PLO

Under the tutelage of the Palestinian Popular Liberation, Meinhof was an adept pupil. She learned how to roll out of a fast-moving car without seriously injuring herself and how to aim accurately with a recoiless pistol. But the relationship between the Arab hosts and their German

guests was a frosty one; each side accused the other of behaving arrogantly. Apparantly the Arabs were particularly annoyed by Baader, who refused to take part in commando exercises saying they were 'unnecessary' for the kind of war he was planning back in Europe.

On 9 August, tension between the two groups reached breaking point and the Germans were asked to leave the training camp. Ulrike wanted to stay longer – she was particularly interested in bombs and how to fuse them correctly and she was reluctant to depart before she had completed her bomb-making course. But the Palestinians insisted and the gang slipped back into Germany, where they were hidden in the flats and houses of the radical friends whom Ulrike had cultivated during her political activities with the left.

ULRIKE SENT HER SONS TO THE TERRORIST CAMP

Ulrike was so convinced by the cause of the Red Army faction that she arranged for her seven-year-old twins to be packed off to the terror camp in Jordan that she had just left. She wanted them to become fighters in the Palestinian conflict with Israel. This ambition was, she explained, the ultimate expression of her love for them. The children travelled no further than Palermo, Sicily, on their journey to the Middle East when they were stopped by police who promptly arrested the terrorist who was acting as their escort. Weeks later

Top: *A bomb planted outside the gates of the Munich Oktoberfest in 1980 killed nine people. These random attacks on the public were a legacy of the Baader-Meinhof reign of terror.*

Klaus Croissant (above) and Christoph Hackernagel (right) are the terrorists suspected of the murder of industrialist, Hans Martin Schleyer.

the camp their mother had chosen as their new home was reduced to rubble in an air strike by King Hussein's forces.

Ensconced in their safe houses and apartments, Ulrike and her colleagues set about planning the 'People's War'. First, they needed that essential tool – money. Mahler co-ordinated a series of bank raids intended to provide the loot needed to buy explosives, false papers, arms and the places needed to store these goods. In one day, they hit three banks, but Ulrike was disappointed because she netted just £1,500. There were more robberies and a mixture of bravado with clinical planning ensured their repeated successes.

Karl-Heinz Ruhland, a working class car mechanic, was brought into the gang because he was able to supply them with a constant stream of getaway cars. The elitist, intellectual fighters looked down on this lowly working-class recruit, but he was to be the first of two lovers Ulrike chose from the men of the Red Army Faction. Gossips said her sexual choice demonstrated her belief that the class system was dying and that she did not recognise it anyway.

However, Ruhland had his view. 'I am a worker she has studied,' he said later. 'But although she is intellectually far above me, she never reminded me of that.'

Ulrike became the quartermaster for the group, securing weapons from Palestinian contacts and planning raids on government offices for official paperwork and stamps. These latter were used to forge documents that would give the gang access to places like army camps and government research facilities. The raids on the banks continued and the money – some £100,000 in 1970 – mounted up. But while the institutions of capitalism were being hit, the pillars of the system were not. The People's War had yet to define its targets clearly .

In October of that year Mahler was arrested when he blundered into a police trap, and leadership of the gang fell to Baader. Slightly unbalanced, prone to erratic mood swings, Baader needed the intellectual and analytical mind of Ulrike to help him keep his guerilla army together.

THE CRAZY GANG JOINS THE RED ARMY FACTION

In 1971, after the gang robbed two banks in Kassel and escaped with £15,000, police pressure to capture them became intense. Germany's Kriminalpolizei – known as the Kripo and the equivalent to the CID – formed a task-force assigned to eradicate

> BAADER NEEDED THE INTELLECTUAL AND ANALYTICAL MIND OF ULRIKE TO HELP HIM KEEP HIS GUERILLA ARMY TOGETHER.

Christian Stroebele (above right) Kurt Groenwald (centre) and Rolf Clemens Wagner (left) were drawn to the Baader-Meinhof cause. They deliberately cultivated an 'ordinary' appearance to avoid suspicion from both neighbours and police but Wagner is believed to have played a major role in the killing of Hans Schleyer.

them. One by one, the members of the Red Army Faction were arrested. At one stage just Baader, Meinhof and six others remained free, but there was no lack of willing recruits to their twisted cause. Some of these came from a revolutionary group calling itself the SPK. Soon the blood would start flowing, as the gang switched from knocking off banks to wiping out human lives.

The SPK – Socialist Patient's Collective – was the warped brainchild of Dr Wolfgang Huber of Heidelberg University, who taught that mental illness was created by the state; change the political system and psychiatric illnesses would disappear. He schooled his patients in explosives, in surveillance techniques, in judo and other forms of unarmed combat. His wife Ursula assisted him. By mid-1971 the SPK, a bunch of psycopathic killers, believed that they had found their spiritual home with the Red Army Faction. The Kripo gumshoes trailing this network of misfits called them the Crazy Gang.

On 22 October, 1971, a patrol car in Hamburg spotted Margrit Schiller, an SPK

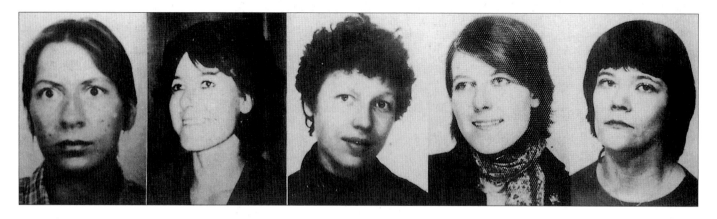

Above: *The chilling faces of evil. These are some of the women warriors enlisted in the Red Army. From the left they are: Gudrun Hoffman, Ingrid Barabass, then an unknown woman, Regina Niclait and another unidentified woman.*

> BUT MEINHOF DECREED A POLICY OF 'LIQUIDATION' FOR ANY MEMBER OF THE RED ARMY WHO WANTED TO DESERT... ULRIKE DROVE INGEBORG TO A REMOTE GRAVEL PIT NEAR AACHEN, WHERE BAADER EXECUTED THE GIRL.

Right: *The cold, hard stare of the fanatic. Irmgard Moëller worshipped Baader and, on his death, tried to kill herself in jail. Her suicide attempt failed.*

member, walking out of a train station. She met two comrades. The patrol officers, Helmut Schmid and Heinrich Lemke, chased them into a park. But the trio were heavily armed, and the policemen presented just the kind of target these crazies favoured. Schmid died with six bullets in him, Lemke was lucky to escape with only a leg wound.

A NEW RECRUIT LIQUIDATED

The killing of the policeman gave added impetus to the police in the determination to capture the Red Army Faction. Margrit Schiller was arrested two days after the killings. She carried a considerable amount of weaponry and a book written by Meinhof called 'The Church Black Book Volume 1'. It contained a list of pastors, doctors, journalists and lawyers who could

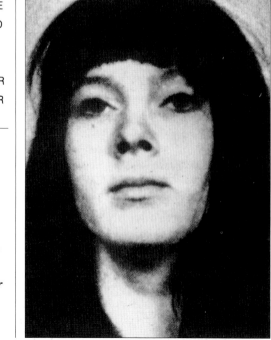

be relied upon to give aid and succour to the Red Army. This book, with its damning list, caused an outrage in a Germany that was disgusted by the ruthless violence of these urban guerillas.

Nevertheless, the killing continued. On 22 December, 1971, Herbert Schoener, a policeman, was shot dead as the gang robbed a bank in the Rhineland town of Kaiserslautern. Aged thirty-two, with a wife and small children, Schoener was shot three times and was severely wounded by flying glass before he died. The robbers seized £33,000 in loot, but the bloodshed and the screams were too much for Ingeborg Barz, a nineteen-year-old girl who had recently joined the gang. She wanted to go home to her mother in Berlin, perhaps resume her job as a typist in a small clerical firm and try to forget her life as a revolutionary and forget the screams of the children frightened in that bank raid. But Meinhof decreed a policy of 'liquidation' for any member of the Red Army who wanted to desert. Gerhart Muller, a gang member who would later turn state's evidence against his former comrades, said Meinhof flew into a rage when she heard Ingeborg say she wanted to leave. Muller said that Ulrike Meinhof drove Ingeborg to a remote gravel pit near Aachen, where Andreas Baader executed the girl.

ULRIKE'S 'BABY BOMB'

More policemen were killed – one of them with dum-dum bullets fired by a Crazy Gang member. Meinhof, meanwhile, perfected a series of pipe bombs, and a device called a 'baby bomb'. This consisted of an explosive device slung from shoulder straps, so that it lay on a woman's belly and gave her the appearance of being pregnant.

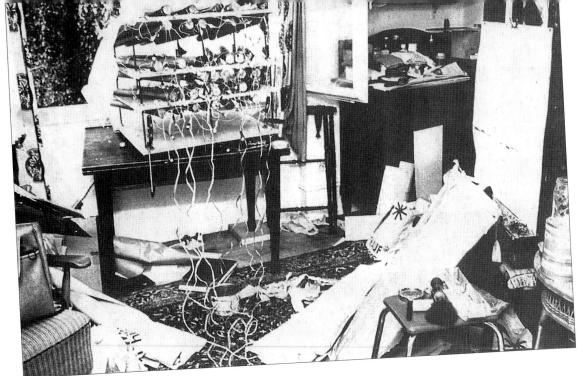

Left: *A 42 barrel home-made rocket launcher. The Red Army held a couple hostage in their own flat, then aimed this weapon across the street to the home of Germany's chief prosecutor but the police apprehended the gang before they launched the rocket.*

Meinhof, the brains of the bombing campaign, mapped out targets at government offices near Hamburg, Heidelberg, Augsburg, Munich and Frankfurt.

At Frankfurt, on 11 May, 1972, Jan-Carl Raspe, now Ulrike's lover and a leader in the group, Baader and Ennslin, planted several pipe bombs in the American Army's 5 Corps HQ. The explosion was devastating, killing a Lt Colonel and wounding thirteen other civilians and military personnel. The US army was deemed a target by Ulrike because she said America 'pulled the strings' in Europe, and also for its involvement in the Vietnam War, a conflict that the Red Army was opposed to for obvious idealogical reasons.

The following year the campaign was stepped up. Five policemen were injured in Munich's CID offices when time bombs left in suitcases exploded. In May, the wife of a judge who had signed arrest warrants for the terrorists, was seriously wounded by a bomb that went off as she turned the key in her car ignition. On 19 May, 1972, Ulrike personally planted the bombs which ripped through the offices of the right-wing publisher Axel Springer in Frankfurt. Three more Americans died a week later in a bombing at a barracks in Heidelberg. Ulrike's bombs were perfected in their design by Dierk Hoff, a mechanical genius who swopped his occupation as a sculptor to become a political terrorist. He manufactured timers so sensitive that armaments manufacturers would later ask for the

designs so that they could be applied to commercially-manufactured ordnance.

The police were frustrated that they could not find the core of the gang, even though several lesser members had been captured and several more killed in shootouts on motorways and outside banks. At the height of their terror campaign, the Red Army could still count on some thirty-five safe houses and a fleet of forty cars with false number plates to ferry them around Germany with ease and privacy.

THE DEADLY AMBUSH

The ease with which they operated and the carnage they left behind caused acute embarrassment and concern to the West German government. They knew that often Meinhof slipped across the border to East Germany to replenish arms supplies, but it was extremely difficult to trace her because of the multitude of aliases under which the gang-leaders operated. Ulrike Meinhof was the brains behind the entire operation, even though much of the blood was spilled by Baader and Raspe.

Seven days after the Red Army committed the murders in Heidelberg, people leaving their homes in a Frankfurt suburb to go to work, did not give a second glance to the corporation workers unloading turf outside a row of garages in a neat suburb. There was a patch of scrubland nearby and observers thought that the council labourers were at long last going to lay grass on it. In

Above: *The wife of Johann Heinrich von Rauch abuses a photographer outside the court where her husband, a Red Army member, was facing charges of murder.*

fact, the labourers were Kripo marksmen, and the turf was to be used as a barricade if they needed such protection. The Kripo had received a tip-off that in one of the garages was a Red Army weapons cache. After a lengthy wait, the police swooped on the site and found a formidable weapons dump – but none of the gang. They replaced the explosives and guns with harmless substitutes and waited for their quarry to show.

At 5.50am on 1 June, a Porsche drew up in the street where the police marksmen waited, and three men got out. Two walked to the garage while the third, Raspe, the lover of Ulrike Meinhof, waited nervously as he scanned the gardens nearby. Years as a criminal fugitive had taught him well; he smelled something was up and decided to flee. He let off a hail of bullets, but he was brought down by a rugby tackling lawman.

Andreas Baader and Holger Meins, were in the garage when tear gas bombs were hurled at them. The two terrorists fought back, but Baader took a bullet in his right leg. Eight minutes after the first tear gas bomb was released, Meins appeared with his arms in the air. Moments later, police stormed the garage where Baader lay with blood pumping from his wound.

THE LAST REFUGE

A week later, Gudrun Ennslin was seized in a Hamburg boutique. She was picking out sweaters to try on and carelessly threw her leather jacket on to a chair, while she went into the changing room. An assistant, who picked it up to fold it neatly, felt the unmistakeable coldness of a gun barrel. She told the manageress who feared that the woman might be a robber, and she in turn called the police. When they arrived Ennslin went for the weapon but after a fierce fight the female terrorist was overpowered.

Only Ulrike remained at large. And because she was the ideological force behind the Red Army Faction, she was the most wanted member of the group. Ulrike knew the organisation was badly-damaged by the police activity. Her lover was arrested, her co-leader arrested, her 'family' dead, dispersed or incarcerated. Even her friends in the political left had deserted her, for they were now thoroughly frightened and disgusted by the violence and robbery that she and her group had practised.

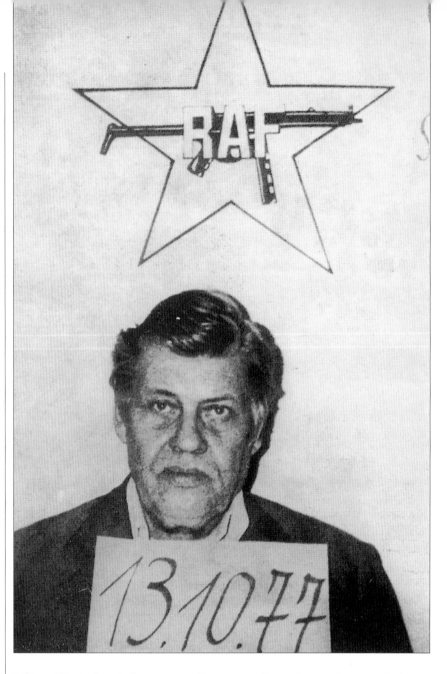

Above: *The industrialist, Hans Martin Schleyer, was kidnapped on 13 October, 1977. He was photographed beneath the Red Army emblem before the Baader-Meinhof gang killed him.*

> YEARS AS A CRIMINAL FUGITIVE HAD TAUGHT HIM WELL; HE SMELLED SOMETHING WAS UP AND DECIDED TO FLEE.

Desperate for refuge, after a safe house in Berlin fell under police suspicion, Ulrike and Gerhard Muller turned up at the home of Fritz Rodewald, a left-wing schoolteacher who, initially, had been sympathetic to her cause. But Rodewald was a socialist, not a terrorist. He was a respected president of a teacher's union, a man with a family and a position in the society she wished to destroy. He took the advice of friends and called the police.

When Kripo squads swooped on the apartment, Ulrike was unpacking her luggage. Nestling among her clothes were three 9mm pistols, two hand grenades, one sub-machine gun and one of her beloved bombs. Gerhard Muller was to become the state's witness against her. But she struggled like a wildcat when the police seized her and eventually had to be sedated. Her face looked puffy when the mug-shots were taken at the police station but, in fact, life on the run had been unkind to her; Ulrike had lost three stone and now weighed less than seven stone.

The capture of Ulrike Meinhof was the final nail in the Red Army coffin. She had been the driving force behind the whole operation; she was much admired by her kind, and many guerilla groups sprang up to committ numerous terrorist acts, including bombing the West German embassy in Sweden in an effort to free her. On 21 May, 1975, in the ultra-secure £5 million Stammheim Prison, the trial of Meinhof, Baader, Ensslin and Raspe opened – Meins would have joined them but he had starved himself to death in captivity.

FOUR THOUSAND MARCHED AT HER FUNERAL

For a year the trial dragged on, a litany of bank robberies, murders, arsons and explosions. The defendants said nothing, save that they did not recognise the court. Finally, Ensslin broke in May 1976 and admitted that the gang had carried out a series of murder-bombings. Four days later Ulrike tore her yellow prison towel into strips, tied it to the bars of her cell, and slowly strangled herself to death.

The agit-prop brigades that she had once so proudly led poured into the streets of several European capitals, claiming that she had been murdered by her guards during the night, although independent examinations of her corpse proved that she had ended her own life. It was an unexpected end to the woman who intellectualised terrorism, who once wrote in a training manual for her fellow guerillas: 'We women can do many things better than the men. We are stronger and much less anxious. This is our People's War and we must all fight it alongside the men. Violent revolution is the only answer to society's ills.' When this misguided follower of the left was buried in Berlin, four thousand sympathisers, many of them masked, marched to her grave.

Her death unleashed new waves of terror, that, culminated in the murder of industrialist Hanns Martin Schleyer and the seizure of a Lufthansa airliner bound from Majorca to Frankfurt in October 1977.

Eventually the plane landed at Mogadishu after a five-day ordeal in which the captain was murdered and the eighty-six passengers terrorised. A German commando team, under the guidance of British SAS officers, stormed the plane. Three of the four terrorists were killed outright, one wounded, but no passengers were hurt.

The news caused Raspe, Baader and Ensslin, now all serving life sentences after being Found Guilty of the kidnappings and murder, to kill themselves – the men with smuggled pistols, Ensslin by hanging.

When police issued the list of wanted terrorists in connection with the killing of Schleyer – murdered in the hours after the failure of the Mogadishu hi-jacking – it was significant that half of them were women from the same background and class as Ulrike Meinhof.

> ULRIKE TORE HER YELLOW PRISON TOWEL INTO STRIPS, TIED IT TO THE BARS OF HER CELL, AND SLOWLY STRANGLED HERSELF TO DEATH.

Jillian Becker, who chronicled Meinhof's life, said: 'She was an ambitious love-hungry child. Her education bred both a puritan and a rebel in her, the one never reconciled to the other. She was drawn to Utopian Communism.'

But those who fought her would say that somewhere within her was a bitter hatred, and not a longing for love or the need for affection, that turned Ulrike into the terror queen of Europe.

Above: *A US Army personnel office after a Red Army firebomb attack in 1981.*

CHARLOTTE BRYANT
Killing Killarney Katey

Kate was an Irish beauty who was generous with her charms and beauty. The soldiers loved her. But her obsession with sex drove her into a bizarre marriage and the dreadful role of poisoner.

Her real name was Charlotte McHugh but to scores of British troops garrisoned in her native Ireland she was Killarney Kate. A native of Londonderry, Charlotte was a woman of ill-repute who dispensed her favours to the hated troops then stationed in her homeland. The time was the early Twenties, and sections of Dublin were still in ruins after the abortive Easter Rising by the Irish Republican Army.

Kate's was a dangerous profession made doubly risky by the clientele she sought out. The nationalist militants seeking to overturn Westminster rule to establish an Irish free state did not take kindly to one of their own indulging men whom they regarded as the enemy. But Kate was a free-spirited, determined young woman who brooked no advice and slept with whomsover she chose – and she chose British troops, for the simple reason that they had money to spare.

A SPECIAL QUALITY

She had hair as black as coal, a milky white complexion, full breasts and bright green flashing eyes, and she provoked, not exactly love, but certainly lust in the occupying army. Killarney Kate captured the imagination of many a man and long, long after she swung from a gibbet for her crime, the memory of her lived on in many a soldier's head and heart. She braved the

SHE PROVOKED, NOT EXACTLY LOVE, BUT CERTAINLY LUST IN THE OCCUPYING ARMY.

Opposite: *Killarney Kate as she appeared at the trial for her life.*

Below: *The last home that Kate shared with her husband, Frederick Bryant. The cottage was near the Dorset village of Dover Compton.*

Above: *The kitchen of the cottage where Kate, her husband, her gypsy lover, Bill Moss and Kate's five children lived.*

'BILL WAS MORE OF A MAN THAN ALL THE REST OF THEM PUT TOGETHER. THERE WAS A MAGIC BETWEEN US.'

threats of tar and featherings from her countrymen, as she boldly flaunted her profession. It could, murmured the Irish sages and righteous gossips who watched her grow up, only end in tragedy.

Regiment after regiment, platoon after platoon, soldier after soldier visited Killarney Kate for her services. But Kate was bored and restless in her native land, fearful that her future offered only more of the same for the rest of her life, and she was searching for that one special soldier who would one day take her to England, where she would bury her past and live happily ever after.

OVER THE WATER

She thought she had realised her dream when she met Frederick Bryant, an easy-going military policeman in the Dorset Regiment. Bryant had served in the last great battle of the First World War when he was shot in the legs during the closing days of the campaign. His wounds were to cause him pain throughout his life. But all physical and mental pain were forgotten when he met the beautiful Kate, who stole his heart. In him, she saw the passport across the water to the land she dreamed about, the cities like London and Manchester.

In 1925 he was discharged from the army and married Kate in Wells, Somerset. They started their life together on a local farm where he was employed as the head cowman. All went well for the first few months, but rural life in England turned out to be every bit as hard as country living back in Ireland. They lived in a rented cottage with neither electricity nor running water, ate poor food and barely had enough money for the necessities, let alone any of the luxuries that Kate had dreamed about.

Kate turned once again to prostitution while her husband toiled twelve hours a day, often in remote areas of the farm. Her 'gentleman callers' brought her luxury gifts like sides of beef and bottles of champagne

declared her love for the gypsy wanderer and Fred was consigned to the couch. They were evicted from their cottage when Fred's employer heard the village tittle-tattle about the strange arrangement. The three-some were to be evicted from other homes. Once, Fred walked out on Kate, but he soon returned, to live with Kate and Moss in the bizarre three-way relationship.

However, in May 1935, Fred began to suffer from a mysterious illness. He thought, at first, that the shrapnel inside his body was affecting him. Several times that month, and in subsequent months, he was doubled up in agony, unable to move, and was seized by the most excruciating cramps. Doctors diagnosed an acute case of gastro-enteritis, brought on by his rugged

while, with the money she earned, she became one of the best customers at the little village shop in the hamlet of Over Compton. Even though she bore five children for poor cuckolded Fred, she never let her motherly duties interfere with her profession. Local legend has it that she enjoyed sex every bit as much as the men who pleased themselves with her. Her neighbours, of course, painted a black picture of her, but she was never troubled by their wagging tongues. Indeed her motto was: 'To hell with fishwives – and their simpering menfolk too!' Fred, who knew about his wife's activities, appreciated the money she brought to the domestic budget.

But this sweet, if strange, life came to an end when Kate fell madly in love with one of her callers. On 11 December, 1933, she entertained a gypsy called Bill Moss. She believed that she had met a man as darkly mysterious, as sensual as herself. Moss was classically handsome and very charming. She said of him: 'Bill was more of a man than all the rest of them put together. There was a magic between us. It was like trying to hold back the sea at high tide; I couldn't deny what was passing between us even if I had wanted to.' The high-tide washed over them – and caught in its backwash was Fred, who, perhaps wanting to please his wanton wife, invited the swarthy ne'er-do-well to stay in their home.

When Fred went to work in the mornings Moss jumped from his place on the settee into the marital bed. Pretty soon this arrangement came to an end; Kate

Top: *The back of the house with a view of the wash-house where Kate tried to destroy a tin of poison.*

Below: *The bedroom that Kate shared first with her husband, then with her lover, Moss.*

outdoor life and poor diet. Fred began to suspect that Bill Moss was the cause of the illness but then gypsy Moss suddenly moved out, apparently no longer in love with Kate. However, Fred's home was soon occupied by another intruder.

A LADY FRIEND

Kate had struck up an intense friendship with a woman called Lucy Ostler, a widow with six children. Fred suspected that his wife's sexual urges had taken a lesbian turn. He was determined that this new 'friend' would not take over where the gypsy left off. But on 21 December, 1935, Mrs Ostler spent the night in his cottage.

Kate and her children were placed in the care of the local authorities, while the police searched the cottage and questioned neighbours about Fred and Kate's marriage. The investigation went on for many weeks, but there was no evidence to reveal the poisoner. However, after both Kate and her new friend, Mrs. Ostler, were hauled off to an identity parade to be scrutinised by a pharmacist, who had reported selling arsenic to a woman several weeks before Fred's death, Mrs Ostler broke.

THE GREEN TIN

Although neither she nor Kate were picked out in the line-up, Ostler went to police and blurted out her story: 'There was a green tin in her [Kate's] cupboards. She pointed at it and said: "Don't touch that. I must get rid of it." I asked her what was inside it but she refused to tell me. A few days later I was cleaning under the boiler, raking out the old ashes, and I saw the tin, all burned and charred. I threw it into the yard because the ashes were to go on to the compost heap. It's probably still there now.'

Luckily for the police it was – and, even in its charred state, clearly recognisable as the container which the pharmacist claimed he had sold to a woman. The tin was sent for scientific analysis to University College, London where it was confirmed that the tin contained traces of arsenic.

Kate was arrested, charged with wilful murder and told that, if found guilty, she could expect the maximum penalty as prescribed under the legal system – death by hanging. The prosecution built its case

Fred, however, was too ill to argue. That night the excruciating cramps returned and he was rushed to hospital but died the next morning. The surgeon at the hospital could not diagnose the cause of the abdominal pain that brought death. Fred had been a healthy, well–built man, burdened by hard work but nevertheless fit. The surgeon ordered an autopsy; the results revealed that the old soldier, who had survived the bombs and bullets of the Western Front, had been poisoned with arsenic.

Above: *Frederick Bryant in his Dorset Regiment uniform. He was to suffer all his life from wounds sustained in the First World War.*

Below: *The burnt tin of poison that proved to be damning evidence at Kate's trial. It is flanked by undamaged tins of the same brand.*

on the bizarre lifestyle that Kate enjoyed with her husband, Fred Bryant, and Bill Moss, and then with Mrs Ostler. Both these lovers appeared as chief prosecution witnesses, perhaps for fear that otherwise they would be linked with the crime. Moss, whose real name was Leonard Edward Parsons, had tangled with the police previously on account of some petty crimes he had committed, and perhaps he did not wish to incur their displeasure once more. When the trial began on 27 May, 1936, Kate found Ostler and Moss arraigned against her, as were her two eldest children, Lily aged ten and Ernest, twelve. Both had been deeply fond of their father and were extremely aggrieved by their mother.

It seemed that no one would support poor Killarney Kate. Sir Terence O'Connor, the Attorney General, led the prosecution and set the trial's tone when he announced: 'The prosecution contends that the prisoner destroyed her husband in order that her marriage might be at an end… crime for which there can only be one penalty and one we heartily endorse: death.'

THE POISON STORY

Ostler's testimony came first. She said on the night that Fred died, she heard him coughing in the main bedroom. Kate was sleeping on a chair in the sitting room, the same room that Ostler was occupying. Later, she claimed, she heard Kate trying to get Fred to drink some beef extract. 'A few minutes later I heard him vomiting,' she said. 'Later he was taken so queer he had to go to hospital.' She said that Kate wept when she learned her husband had died. But Ostler told the court that she found this strange, claiming that Kate once confided that she hated Fred. Ostler said: 'In that case, I said to her, why didn't she go away and she said she couldn't provide for the children and didn't want to leave them behind.' Perhaps Ostler's most damning evidence was her testimony that she used to read aloud murder accounts from 'penny dreadful' magazines to Kate, who was illiterate. She told the court that she read the story of how a woman in America had poisoned her husband. According to Ostler, Kate's ears had pricked up at this story and she had turned to her friend to ask: 'How do you think I would get rid of someone?'

However, outrage was expressed in court and in the press about the prosecution's use of Kate's children to testify against her. But called they were, although their evidence was of limited use; it centred on a small blue bottle with which they alleged Moss used to threaten their mother.

Kate's passionate eyes burned into her former lover as he was led into the witness box, yet Moss' testimony centred on his affections for her, though he repeated a conversation he had with her concerning a tin of weedkiller. 'It was one day in 1935,' he said. 'I was standing outside the kitchen door when I heard Mr. Bryant say to his

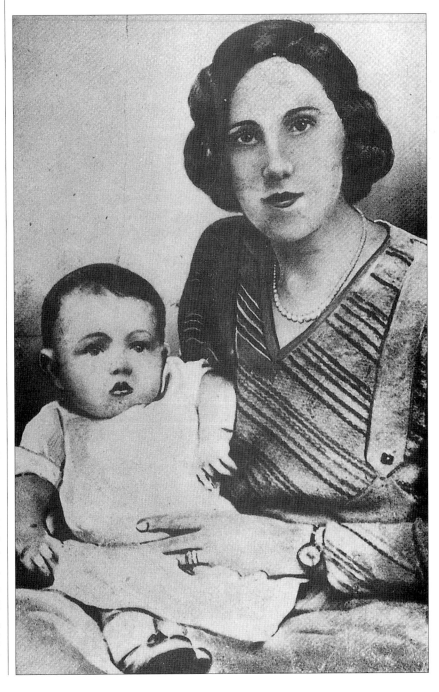

Below: *Kate pictured with Ernest, one of the five children she bore Frederick Bryant. She was, by all accounts, a loving if carefree, mother.*

harm to his wife and, indeed, had gone out of his way to accommodate her special needs and desires, slowly dying in agony from a malady that he could not fight and that he could not understand.

A QUICK JUDGEMENT

In all, there were thirty witnesses against Kate and not one in her defence. She presented a pathetic figure in the dock, a lost case who, unable to read and write, seemed baffled by the weighty and majestic court proceedings unfolding before her. She denied, as best she could in her simple terms, that she had murdered her husband in order to win back Moss. Under further questioning, she said that her relationship with Mrs Ostler was merely a friendship, and did not elaborate upon it.

All Kate could do was refute the suggestion that she had murdered her husband. But the others had no motive to kill him. Moss had returned to his wife, Mrs Ostler had been in Fred's cottage for only one night and was not around him to administer poison over a prolonged period. The trial at

*Above: **The majesty of the law, as represented by Mr Justice MacKinnon, frightened the accused, an illiterate country woman.***

*Right: **Dr Roche Lynch gave damning testimony on the poison.***

wife, "What's this?." "It's weedkiller," she replied.' With these words, Moss managed to suggest to the court that Killarney Kate had contemplated weedkiller as a means of killing her husband before she switched to the more lethal poison, arsenic.

Expert Home Office testimony seemed to confirm Kate's long, premeditated campaign against her husband. Dr Gerald Lynch, the department's senior analyst, said samples taken from Bryant's corpse showed that he had been slowly and systematically fed the poison over many months. He painted a picture of a man, who had done no

Dorchester Assizes took two weeks, and the jury were out for an hour. When the jury foreman appeared, he pronounced the word 'Guilty'. Kate took this calmly but became hysterical when, moments later, Mr Justice MacKinnon donned the black cap and solemnly announced that she would die upon the scaffold at Exeter jail. In a state of collapse, the frightened prisoner was led by prison warders into the condemned cells beneath the court.

An appeal was lodged and the defence introduced testimony from a professor in London who was an expert on the effects of arsenic. Unfortunately, it was evidence that fell on deaf ears. Lord Chief Justice, Lord Hewart, said: 'This court sets its face like flint against attempts to call evidence which could have been made available at the trial. Moreover, in this case, it is clear that there has been no mistake. The court will not listen to the opinion of scientific

Above: *The local papers gave full coverage to the trial of a murderess. It was unusual to have a woman accused of this crime, and the fact that a mother of five children was sentenced to death caused a horrified reaction throughout the country.*

Above: *The grim and unpitying features of Lord Chief Justice Lord Hewart who turned down Kate's appeal. He announced that the court 'set its face like flint' against new evidence.*

Right: *J.D.Casswell, the defence barrister who fought for Kate's innocence and her life.*

gentlemen bringing their minds on evidence that they have not heard.' But even though the appeal was dismissed, the public conscience had been aroused by the proceedings. Questions were raised in parliament, and there was a public call for a re–trial. There were press articles about the fate of her children, and of how Kate, in her condemned cell at Exeter jail, had turned to God. Her repeated assertions of her innocence were also widely reported. So vociferous was she in protesting against the wrongful judgement that a leading member of the campaign against the death penalty pledged £50,000 in the poor woman's defence.

DON'T LET THEM KILL ME

Kate was learning to read and write and composed a moving, if simple letter to King Edward VIII in which she stated: 'Mighty King. Have pity on your lowly afflicted subject. Don't let them kill me on Wednesday. From the brink of the cold, dark grave, I, a poor helpless woman, ask you not to let them kill me. I am innocent.' This sad appeal brought no personal response from the king. Did His Majesty even see the letter?

At 8am on 15 July, 1936, Killarney Kate saw dawn come up for the last time. She was led to the scaffold by two warders and the condemned woman listened as a chaplain read the service for the dead. Five minutes later she was pronounced dead.

Was she guilty? The question has echoed down the years. There was no motive to drive the lover, Moss alias Parsons, to murder Fred and as the poison was apparently administered over a long period, no time for the new acquaintance Mrs Ostler to have been the culprit. Criminal historians have looked back time and again on the case of Charlotte McHugh, the girl known to soldiers as 'Killarney Kate'. Charles Skipple, a criminologist in the United States, who specialises in studying doubtful verdicts, said: 'I think she did it. Her's was the classic defence that echoes in jails around the world. "I'm innocent." And yet she couldn't prove that innocence while the jury obviously believed the proof of the guilt. It's the way of the world, the system we live by. Imperfect, of course, but all we have and all we shall probably ever have.'

MURDEROUS MEN

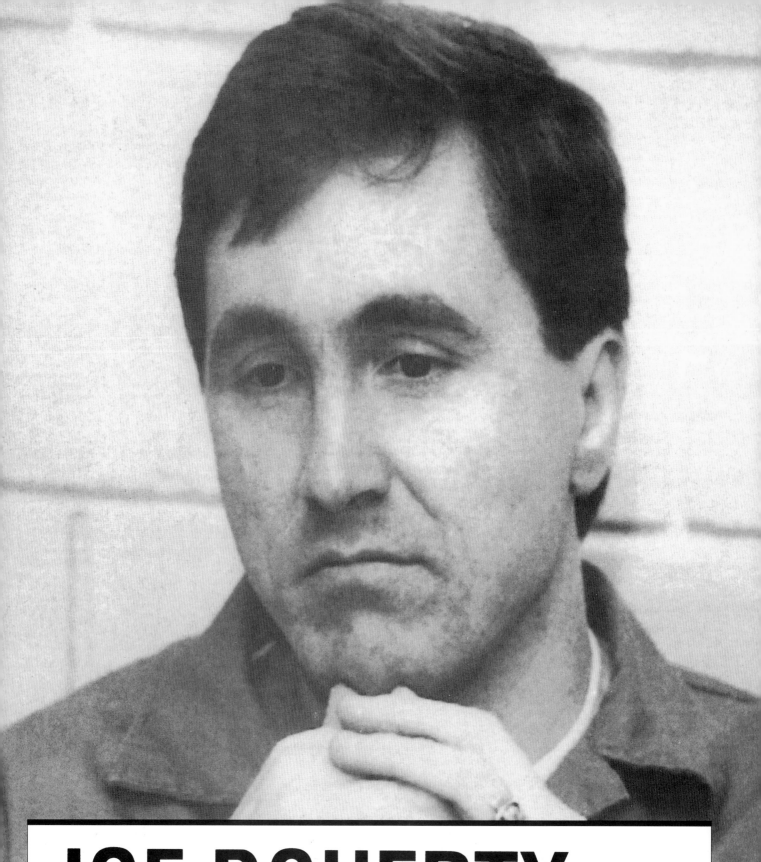

JOE DOHERTY
IRA Hitman

He grew up in bitterness and with a strong sense that he was a victim. Joe Doherty took his revenge with evil acts of killing and maiming the innocent – all in the name of patriotism.

The murder of a Special Air Services officer in a grubby Belfast street in 1980 would, on the surface, have little connection with the 1986 bombing of Libya's deranged dictator Colonel Gaddafi in Tripoli. One was carried out by a psychopathic Irish Republican Army terrorist called Joe Doherty who dressed up his murderous outrage in the guise of freedom fighter. The other was carried out by trained pilots on the orders of Ronald Reagan, US president, as a warning to Ghaddafi to desist from his global sponsorship of terrorist causes.

Not until 1992, when the fugitive gunman Doherty was finally brought back in chains from America to serve a life sentence for his killing of Captain Herbert Richard Westmacott did the correlation between his murder and the Tripoli bombing raid become clear. For it was Mrs Thatcher, as much as any police officer, intelligence operative and FBI agent whose long arm stretched across the Atlantic to bring Doherty home from America – where he sought political sanctuary – to face justice. Doherty was 'payback' for Tripoli because Mrs Thatcher had allowed US warplanes to take off from British bases on their mission. She weathered a great deal of criticism at the time over the decision and made it plain to her American opposite numbers that, one day, a favour might have to be returned. That favour came in the form of thirty-seven-year-old Joseph Patrick Doherty, the killer that Mrs Thatcher would not let get away.

The story of Joseph Doherty – street-thug, rioter, ambusher, political assassin and propaganda pawn – is an odyssey from the breeding ground of hatred through to the highest levels of international intrigue and diplomacy. If he had chosen another path as a youngster, one away from the gun and the hard men who rule his ghetto area of West Belfast, he might now be a father with a secure job and a bright future. Instead, he will be almost a pensioner when he is finally released. The only value he has to the IRA now is to embellish the memories of 'the cause' when the stories are told around pub fires and in meeting halls where the Republican ethos is worshipped like a religion.

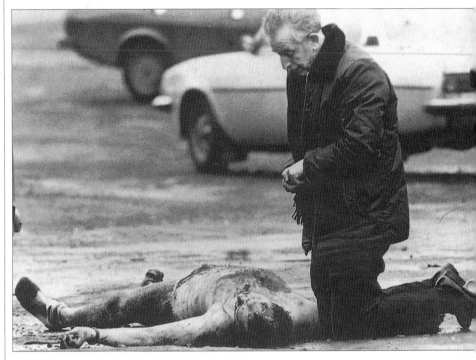

Below: *A priest kneels by the body of David Howe, killed when he inadvertently blundered into an IRA funeral procession.*

Before he became infamous, Joe Doherty was born into a system that preached and practised unfairness towards the Catholic minority in Northern Ireland. Artificial electoral boundaries, discrimination towards Catholics in schools, housing, jobs and civil rights and terror in the form of the police 'B Specials' combined to fuel the resurgence of the Republican movement that was dormant, if not dying, by the time Doherty was born in 1955, to a family that celebrated Irish rebel heroes in the uprising with Britain in the early part of the century that won the south its independence. Doherty says when he was five he felt the first stirrings of a grave injustice being committed in his country. He said: 'I remember going to school and being taught English instead of our national language. You take the history classes we went to. It

Opposite: *Joe Doherty, the IRA man who murdered in cold blood, then sought sanctuary in the United States by claiming he was a political refugee.*

The glamour of the gun soon lured Doherty into the clutches of the IRA, the illegal but best guerilla operation in the world. Involved with petty crime from the age of fourteen – offences like housebreaking and thieving – he joined the organization Na Fianna Eireann, the junior wing of the Provisional IRA. In these early days, with the burning resentment against British troops in his land growing inside him, he was a willing recruit. In the far-flung, remote regions of County Donegal and on the west coast of Ireland, he attended the indoctrination and training sessions that would give him both the spirit and the practical tools to become an effective IRA operative. In this role he became an intelligence scout for the IRA killers on the streets of Belfast; warning of the approach of a police or army patrol,

Above: *On the right, the then-Mayor of New York, David Dinkins, his political antennae keenly aware of the massive Irish-American vote in his city, woos the Irish murderer, Joe Doherty. Dinkins was not heard to give sympathy to Irish – or other – victims of Doherty's killing habits.*

Right: *The reality of the IRA's actions was seen yet again in London when nine soldiers and seven cavalry horses were blown apart by terrorist bombs in Hyde Park in 1982.*

THE GLAMOUR OF THE GUN SOON LURED DOHERTY INTO THE CLUTCHES OF THE IRA.

was mostly on the Tudors and royal heads, kings and queens of England. We were told nothing about our own country. When we took geography we were given the map of England, Scotland and Wales, Europe, the United States, but we were never given a map of our own country. So it was resented by a young person at my age that I couldn't learn where the hell I am living. I knew more about Birmingham and Manchester than I knew about my own city and the beautiful countryside that was around it.' Bitter words from one of the oppressed.

luring soldiers into ambushes and assisting in diversions when terrorists or arms had to be removed from an area rapidly.

He also became a member of the notorious knee-capping squads. These vigilantes were an important factor in IRA rule in the early days of the troubles – patrolling dances and drinking halls, dispensing rough and ready justice to those who they deemed were either drunkards, drug pushers or potential enemies of the IRA. Doherty would later claim that he was little more than a concerned citizen when he carried out these vigilante duties – but he had shown himself, to his IRA superiors, ruthless and efficient – two qualities which they prized very highly indeed.

PRISON LESSONS IN TERRORISM

Doherty's pathological loathing of the British continued to rise as army attempts to root out and contain terrorism spilled over into his own neighbourhood. He witnessed his family being pulled from their beds at midnight by soldiers and was continually quizzed by intelligence officers about his membership of the junior IRA. On 22 January 1972, a day after his seventeenth birthday, he found himself interned without trial at one of the several British camps. He claimed he was tortured in Girdwood camp. While human rights investigators have determined that some terrorists were subjected to cruel and inhuman treatement while in internment camps, not a shred of evidence exists to say that Doherty was mistreated, and certainly he never suffered the use of electric shock apparatus which he claimed was in common use in the camp.

Later he was interned on the prison ship Maidstone and in Long Kesh where IRA cell leaders marked him down as a zealot who would soon be ready for active service in the field – namely, killing people. Inside the camps was a well-organized IRA network that kept prisoners indoctrinated with the lectures on the Republican movement and weapons they would be using on their release. Doherty joined the adult arm of the IRA upon his release, swearing his allegiance to the terrorists in the traditional way; placing his hand upon a Bible, a .45 revolver and the Irish tricolour, he thus became a volunteer in C Company, 3rd Battalion of the Irish Republican Army. During the early Seventies, outfits like Doherty's caused tremendous civilian loss of life with indiscriminate bombings, sectarian murders and numerous shootings of security and police personnel, but he was never charged with any specific murders, although security personnel had plenty of suspicion. The only charge they nailed him on came in 1973 when he served three months for being caught in possession of a starting pistol; a tool he used to intimidate neighbourhood youths.

> NOT A SHRED OF EVIDENCE EXISTS TO SAY THAT DOHERTY WAS MISTREATED, AND CERTAINLY NEVER SUFFERED THE USE OF ELECTRIC SHOCK APPARATUS.

Below: *Another view of the bombing in Hyde Park, where men died like animals and animals died like men.*

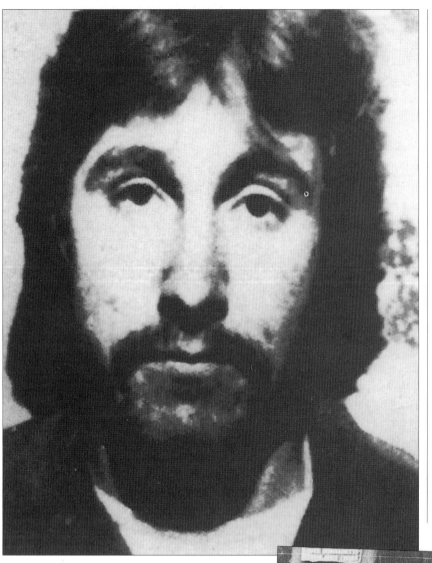

He was released shortly before Christmas 1979 – the last Christmas he would know as a free man. When he was neither a fugitive on the run, or a man held behind bars.

MASTERING A LETHAL WEAPON

After he walked free again Joe Doherty was singled out for special training with the M60 heavy machine gun, a fearsome weapon capable of cutting a man in two with a split-second burst. He later denied ever being trained in the handling of these, but an IRA informer told his Special Branch handlers in Ulster that Doherty was so familiar with every nut and rivet of the weapon, that he could break it down and then re-assemble it wearing a blindfold. This gun, one of a batch stolen from an armoury in America, was to play a major part in his designated IRA 'mission' the following year.

His unit was assigned to kill policemen and soldiers by using the high-powered weaponry acquired from America. Again, Doherty and his cohorts were not charged in this period with any offences and, naturally, he has been at pains to play down any of his activities. The incident which would land him with a life sentence for

Upon his release, shortly before Christmas of that year, he was told to report for active duty to the 3rd Battalion. He was ordered to stay 'on the run', avoiding the homes of friends and family in favour of unknown IRA sympathisers, because the IRA had plans for him. In February 1974 he removed eighty pounds of gelignite from one of the organization's dumps and moved it by car to another unit across town. Unfortunately for him an army spot check found him and his portable, unprimed bomb and both were taken into custody. He was given a three-year sentence, compounded shortly afterwards with another eighteen months after a futile prison escape attempt ended in abject failure. In jail he rose in the IRA ranks and was an officer in charge of other men. His masters on the other side of the wire bided their time for Joe Doherty, because they were nurturing big plans.

murder came towards the middle of 1980. His IRA masters chose to mount an attack on a British army patrol – any patrol, it did not matter which – that passed by a house that his unit would take over on the Antrim Road .Doherty knew that military vehicles from the Girdwood base passed by all the time; there was bound to be a rich target. Almost certainly 'blooded' in IRA actions by this time, Doherty and his gang were chosen for the operation on the direct instructions of the leader of the Belfast Brigade of the terror organisation.

Doherty personally planned the operation, ordering that the M60 heavy machine gun was to be fired from one window while the rifles and revolvers used

by the gang were positioned at another. He ordered his gang to hijack a vehicle the evening before the ambush in order to transport themselves and their weapons to the scene. He gave orders for the family in a house overlooking the spot where they intended to spring the trap to be held hostage. Both were standard IRA procedures for this kind of assassination. But unknown to Doherty and his allies the eyes of army intelligence were already upon them. Members of the 14th Intelligence Company had, through an IRA informer, learned of the operation planned for 2 May, 1980. A unit of the Special Air Services was given careful instruction to tackle them on the day.

Above, right: *Police check vehicles for IRA car bombs after the terrorist attack on military bandsmen in Deal in Kent, 1989.*

Above, left: *The army on full alert during an IRA funeral in Belfast.*

Opposite, above: *Joe Doherty hid behind a beard and long hair when he fled to the USA.*

Opposite, below: *Hooded IRA men patrol in Belfast.*

The night before the ambush, a blue Ford Transit van was hi-jacked by volunteers and handed over to Doherty's team and driven to the rear of house number 371 in the Antrim Road – designated for the take-over the next day and the base for the ambush. The following morning nineteen-year-old Rosemary Comerford and her two-year-old son Gerard were alone in the house.

She recalled: 'At 10.30am a knock came on the door and I opened it. Two men were standing there and one of them said they were Irish Republican Army. The man who spoke had a handgun pointing at me. This man said they were going to take over the house and they were going to hold me and my son as hostages. He then took us into the bedroom at the rear of the house. The other man who did not speak remained in the bedroom with us. I could hear the other man moving about. I think the man who stayed in the bedroom with us brought the handgun with him. At about 12.30pm my sister Theresa called and the man who was in the bedroom with me told me to go and see who it was. He told me to let her in and said she'd have to stay in the bedroom with us. My husband Gerard came home and the same thing happened.'

At 2pm that day, as Doherty and his 'freedom fighters' took up positions in the occupied house that gave them the best view on to the anticipated killing zone, Captain Herbert Westmacott, thirty-four, and his men were on their way to the scene. The SAS career veteran and his men were trained precisely for this kind of urban assault. SAS headquarters in England were equipped with houses such as these which Westmacott and his men had neutralized time and time again in their training missions. But a terrible blunder in trying to determine what was the exact entrance to the house gave the gunmen inside vital seconds. The entrance to the house was actually through 369 and not through the door marked 371. Captain Westmacott fell

would leave no prisoners. But, as if to disappoint the IRA propaganda machine about such atrocities, they gave the killers inside the kind of chance never afforded to Captain Westmacott. A priest was brought in at Doherty's request to oversee their surrender after the SAS had surrounded them for several hours. Forensic tests taken later on his clothing showed that, of the four-man gang, he had the most ballistic

CAPTAIN WESTMACOTT FELL IN A POOL OF BLOOD OUTSIDE THE ENTRANCE TO 371 AFTER THE HITMEN IINSIDE OPENED UP FIRST.

Right: *Airey Neave, on the left, survived the Nazi prisoner-of-war camp at Colditz Castle, only to die in a cowardly IRA killing. They planted a bomb in his car on 30 March, 1979 that killed him the instant he started the vehicle.*

FORENSIC TESTS TAKEN LATER ON HIS CLOTHING SHOWED THAT, OF THE FOUR-MAN GANG, DOHERTY HAD THE MOST BALLISTIC RESIDUE ON HIM.

in a pool of blood outside the entrance to 371 after the hitmen inside opened up first. The British government would later charge Doherty, who as he was led away from the scene of the murder said of the M60 that killed Captain Westmacott said: 'that's my baby', with being the triggerman.

Trapped inside like rats Doherty and his men believed they would endure first smoke, then stun grenades before the SAS mounted a charge on their positions that

residue on him, indicating that it was probably him who fired the M60 which killed Captain Westmacott.

British interrogators were intent on breaking down Doherty when he was in custody; they knew he was a valued IRA operative who had probably killed before. But he was well versed in the cat-and-mouse games that his handlers had taught him. Every question that was not answered with a refusal was answered with a

question. Doherty was a misty-eyed Republican who fondly remembered his grandfather's medals from his time spent fighting the British earlier in the century. He wavered between bravado and mute silence to arrogance and foul language during his interrogation sessions, but he finally cracked when his mother's name was mentioned. He admitted he had tried to get out of the movement but had failed and only wanted a better Ireland to live in. He did not admit to killing Westmacott specifically, only that he had fired a gun.

BACK IN THE BOSOM OF THE IRA

Doherty soon found himself back in the cold familiarity of the Crumlin Road jail after his inquisitors had finished with him. Here he was among familiar faces and old IRA comrades and the bravado that led him to kill easily returned. He was back under the discipline of the IRA where top-level decisions were taken by his masters to turn him into a cross between a martyr and Robin Hood. At the time of the beginning of his trial in April 1987 things were going badly for the IRA leadership; the hunger strike at the Maze prison was claiming lives with five volunteers dead and no sign of the Thatcher government backing down. The leadership of the terror gang badly needed a propaganda break and they saw their opportunity in gaining it with Doherty. He had already refused to recognize the court sitting in justice on him

Above: *In 1988, a girl walked into an army disco in Mill Hill, North London and laid an IRA bomb. A young man lost his life in the blast.*

Below: *British soldiers returning to their barracks after home leave in 1988 were blown apart by the IRA. Eight men lost their lives as the bus in which they travelled exploded.*

and the fact that he had killed a member of Her Majesty's most elite force ensured that his name was already high up in the newspapers. His leaders instructed him to work on escape plans for him and seven of his fellow inmates.

Doherty handed his commanders their much-needed propaganda victory on 10 June, 1981, when he and seven others made a successful break out from the jail. Using guns smuggled in by IRA sympathisers they overpowered guards – clubbing one brutally – and dressed in prison uniforms to pass a series of checkpoints leading to the staff entrance to the jail. Finally out in the street, a gun battle ensued in a car park between the security forces and the IRA units sent to pick up the escapers. Doherty fled through the warren of streets in the Shankhill area of town – a fiercely loyalist enclave, but nothing happened to him and he was able to reach his own turf unscathed. Once there he was kept away from his family and friends – the first target of searches by the army – and sheltered at the homes of sympathisers who had no record of IRA membership or of terrorist offences. Within days he was moved south of the border into the Irish Republic where he was hidden in an even more remote region. As he bided his time for several months he heard the news from Belfast that Lord Justice Hutton had found him Guilty of murder *in absentia*, sentenc-

ing him to life imprisonment with a recommendation to the Home Secretary that he should serve a minimum of thirty years inside. It did much to take the edge from his fame as 'The Great Escaper' as he was now known among Republican sympathisers. His masters in Belfast knew that his pursuers would leave no stone unturned in their hunt for him and so took the decision to give him a new identity and send him off to America where a massive Irish community – which gave literally millions of dollars each year to the war chests of their fighting units – would ensure his safety as a fugitive. He left Ireland under the name of Henry J. O'Reilly in February 1982... ready to bury himself in anonymity until his overlords called him to service once again when the heat was off.

Margaret Thatcher was not prepared to let the killer of a British officer escape so easily. In his authoritative book on Doherty entitled 'Killer in Clowntown' author Martin Dillon wrote: 'Doherty was a prestige target and, little did he know then, to the British prime minister at the time, Margaret Thatcher. The killing of Westmacott and the escape of his killers angered her. Doherty was the only one

Above: *Eighteen soldiers were killed when the IRA ambushed a convoy in Warrenpoint, County Ulster in 1979.*

Right: *Funerals for IRA men are given the importance and ritual suited to matyrs. These men are bearing the coffin of IRA hitman, Brian Mullin.*

HIS MASTERS IN BELFAST KNEW THAT HIS PURSUERS WOULD LEAVE NO STONE UNTURNED AND DECIDED TO GIVE HIM A NEW IDENTITY AND SEND HIM TO AMERICA.

unaccounted for and eventually become so important that she would demand to be personally briefed about him. Thatcher believed that his recapture would enhance relations between Britain and Ireland and repair damage to security in Northern Ireland resulting from the 'Great Escape.' Neither the IRA nor Doherty needed to be convinced of her intentions or her determi-

physical trait of the wanted man together with a profile of his habits and psychological breakdown. Soon questions were being asked around town among a network of IRA informers and it came to the notice of FBI agent Frank Schulte that there was a young man working at Clancy's Bar who fitted the bill. On 18 June 1983, he was seized at work. Margaret Thatcher was informed later that same day and she thought that he would be home in a matter of days to begin his thirty-year sentence. But it would be many years of tortured manouvreings and murky intrigue before Doherty heard the slam of a British cell door clang behind him.

Below: *Joe Doherty, healthy, defiant and fighting against an extradition order requested by the British government. Doherty was detained for eight years in custody in the USA during his determined attempts to appeal against the order. He lost his case and was returned to Britain where he resumed a life sentence for murder.*

nation to see them fulfilled. But they were unaware then of her growing personal interest in him.'

DOHERTY'S NEW LIFE IN NEW YORK

In New York, Doherty got a job with a construction company while lodging with a family sympathetic to the Republican cause in Ulster. He also worked as a shoe-shine boy, a bell-hop in a hotel and, with a fake social security number, managed to get a job as a barman at Clancy's Bar in Manhattan. Here he earned upwards of $120 per day with tips and thought the going was good. He had a girlfriend, a comfortable apartment in New Jersey and had adapted to life outside the strict discipline of the IRA with ease. He thought he had it made.

But the heat was on in Ireland to get him back. Thatcher, receiving almost weekly intelligence briefings on his suspected whereabouts, gave her Royal Ulster Constabulary chiefs and army intelligence officers but one brief: find him. The Federal Bureau of Investigation in America was contacted in 1983 and a full file sent over to officers in New York listing every

Above: *The scene of horror at Enniskillen, Northern Ireland, when the IRA slaughtered worshippers at a Remembrance Day service in 1987. Eleven people were killed.*

JOE DOHERTY FOUND HIMSELF IN THE ENVIABLE POSITION OF BEING A HERO TO A LARGE PART OF THE IRISH-AMERICAN POPULATION IN NEW YORK.

Joe Doherty found himself in the enviable position of being a hero to a large part of the Irish-American population in New York. To these citizens of the Big Apple he was not the common murderer as depicted by Mrs Thatcher and the British establishment; rather he was a freedom fighter, a hero in the armed struggle to rid Ireland of the English 'oppressor'. He soon found himself with the kind of fame usually reserved for a showbusiness celebrity. Everyone wanted to press Doherty's flesh – the American senator Jesse Jackson was among one hundred politicians who petitioned for him to be granted political asylum in America. Eventually Mayor David Dinkins of New York would come to name the block outside the Manhattan Correctional Centre where he was held 'Joe Doherty Corner.' To Mrs Thatcher and all the victims of IRA terrorism it was the equivalent of re-naming a London street after the Boston strangler for Doherty is also a crude killer.

Initially Doherty was charged with illegal entry into the USA – he had, after all, committed no crimes in America. Time after time after time courts ordered his release on bail and a full immigration hearing, only to have the legal process blocked from on high. Clearly, the hand of something or someone much bigger than the usual legal process was being brought into play repeatedly. Ronald Reagan, who enjoyed an unusually cozy relationship with Mrs Thatcher, was, like her, a man dedicated to the opposition of terrorism. She expected him to deliver Doherty up to her, but he was thwarted at every turn by the procedures of the US judicial system. In 1986 came the Libyan bombing when Reagan took his own stand against world terrorism by attempting to kill Colonel Gaddafi. Mrs Thatcher stood alone among western leaders by allowing the American warplanes to take off from British bases on their mission. When Britain continued to be frustrated by the American courts Mrs

Thatcher's emissaires diplomatically reminded America that they 'owed' Britain a favour. The favour was Doherty for Tripoli and it was said so by Sherard Cowper Coles, a senior British diplomat, to Otto Obermaier, US attorney assigned to prosecuting him. He told Obermaier: 'The prime minister believes you owe us this one. She allowed your government to use our territory for your F1-11s when they were on their way to bomb Tripoli.'

But the legal process ground on and on in Doherty's favour. The American court system, examining the statues of the constitution of the United States and every similar case that had gone before, could not find sufficient arguments to warrant the deportation of Doherty. At one bail hearing in September 1990, after he had won over a dozen court cases that kept being referred to higher and higher authorities, Doherty gave a classic terrorist's 'doublespeak' account for his killing of Westmacott. He said: 'It was to bring pressure on the British government, to force them to negotiations. That was the reason I was involved in the operation, to bring to the British government that their presence in the North of Ireland is unworkable, politically and militarily, and that they cannot suppress the IRA, that the IRA can survive and strike back.' This from a man who lied to the American courts that he had left the organization in 1982.

THE SUPREME COURT REJECTED ANY FURTHER HEARINGS

By 1992 he was the longest held political prisoner, held without a charge other than that he had come into the country illegally, in America. There was still intense pressure on the White House – now under the occupancy of the Bush administration – from No.10 Downing Street, whose keys had passed to John Major. By February 1992 Joe Doherty's case reached the highest court in the land, the Supreme Court. He prayed for an immigration hearing, a separate tribunal that might allow him the political sanctuary he craved. But, almost nine years after he had first been arrested and locked up, it ended for him. The Supreme Court rejected any and all further hearings. On 19 February they came for him – as he rightly predicted they

TIME AFTER TIME AFTER TIME COURTS ORDERED HIS RELEASE ON BAIL AND A FULL IMMIGRATION HEARING, ONLY TO HAVE THE LEGAL PROCESS BLOCKED FROM ON HIGH.

Below: *Mrs Thatcher was guarded by a young marine as she went to show her respects to the dead bandsmen in Deal, Kent. She called the IRA terrorists 'monsters' and was relentless in her fight against them.*

would – to, in his own words, 'complete my sentence in the hell of a British prison.' Doherty was taken from a new lock-up in Kentucky and flown to Northern Ireland where IRA men in Belfast's Crumlin Road jail, scene of his great escape, welcomed him with cake and tea.

The saga of Joe Doherty ended in complete victory for Mrs Thatcher and the opponents of terrorism everywhere. Doherty's supporters, and particularly his lawyer in America, Mary Pike, argued that the American judicial system had been bent, perverted to the cause of Britain and not the interests of the Stars and Stripes.

However, one senior British diplomat, who wishes to remain anonymous, said: 'He was a top operative before he got caught and he tried to con the people of America that he had seen the senselesness of violence, that he had reformed.

'He cannot complain of dirty tricks because he formerly employed every one in the book. Yes, America did owe Britain one for Tripoli – and now the debt has been repaid in full.'

CARLOS THE JACKAL
The Supreme Terrorist

As a boy he was trained in hatred; as an adult he has terrorised the entire globe with his murderous acts. Yet Carlos the Jackal has never been caught and the whereabouts of one of the world's most wanted men remains a mystery.

H e has written his name in blood across the world. A master of disguise, an expert urban guerilla, a killer without compunction or compassion, he moves at ease within the terror networks who support him or hire him, with a slush fund of ready cash and an inexhaustible supply of passports. At various times in various places, he has gone under the names of Carlos Andres Martinez-Torres, Hector Lugo Dupont, Cenon Marie Clarke, Adolf Jose Muller Bernal, Flick Ramirez, Glenn Gebhard and Ahmed Adil Fawaz. His real name is Illyich Ramirez Sanchez. But to police forces all over the globe he is known simply as Carlos the Jackal.

This master of global terrorism is as elusive as he is infamous. Interpol dragnets, complex deals within deals of the diplomatic and espionage worlds, and operations masterminded by the world's leading anti-terrorist units have failed to flush him out and bring him to justice for his crimes – crimes that include the attempted assassination of Joseph Sieff, head of Marks and Spencer; the murder of two French counter-espionage agents; the mass kidnap of OPEC delegates in Vienna; car bombings in France that claimed five people; the machine-gun massacre at Israel's Lod Airport which claimed twenty-five lives; and rocket attacks on aircraft at a Paris airport.

This bloody killer, who mocks the combined efforts of the civilized world to capture him, comes from simple roots. Born in 1949 in Venezuala, he was the son of a left-wing lawyer who admired Stalin.

Instead of nursery rhymes and picture books, Carlos grew up on a diet of orthodox Marxist-Leninism. His father believed violent, global revolution was the only lesson worth teaching and by the time he was a teenager, Illyich – named after Vladimir Illyich Ulyanov, Lenin's real name – was a willing disciple of his father's beliefs. Clever, dispassionate, Carlos believed in the overthrow of world capitalism, and he identified with the minorities of the world. The IRA in Ulster, the Palestinians in Israel, the ETA terrorists in the Basque region of Spain – these were the heroes of the young Carlos. When he was seventeen, his father packed him off to a terrorist training camp in Cuba.

THIS BLOODY KILLER, WHO MOCKS THE COMBINED EFFORTS OF THE CIVILIZED WORLD TO CAPTURE HIM, COMES FROM SIMPLE ROOTS.

At the camp near Havana, Carlos learned the rudiments of handling explosives, unarmed combat and weaponry. In the latter field he was particularly adept, proving himself a crack shot with any calibre of weapon from a pistol to an automatic rifle. He also developed a thorough disregard for human life which served him well in his chosen profession. One of his instructors gave an interview to a Paris newspaper several years later: 'He was clinically detached from everything he

Above: *Scene after the 1983 terror bombing of the US Marine base in Beirut which many suspect was masterminded by Carlos.*

Opposite: *Carlos the Jackal, master of disguise and ruthless terrorist.*

did, mechanical, a superb pupil to train. You could tell from the way he pulled a trigger or pulled down an opponent on the judo mat that there was no emotion attached to anything. It was all just business for him.'

After his initial training in terrorism in Cuba, he was shipped to London where he lived briefly with his mother – estranged from his father – at addresses in Wimpole Street and the King's Road, Chelsea. His brother Lenin – his real name – was with him during this time, around 1968, and the two of them spent endless hours with

Opposite, top: *Carlos pictured at a cocktail party in London in the Seventies. He is with his mother and a girlfriend.*

Opposite, bellow: *The collection of arms and ammunition that Carlos left behind when he fled a Paris flat.*

Here he learned about the various guerilla groups who needed help and were willing to pay for it. From the Middle East to the killing fields of Asia, from the back alleys of Belfast to the sun drenched plains of Spain's Basque region, there were wars for 'freedom' by minority groups. Also at Patrice Lumumba, he forged contacts that were to be invaluable to him, and he mastered the intricacies of the world banking system. This latter lesson was to serve him well when he began to procure arms and secure payment for his own terrorist operations.

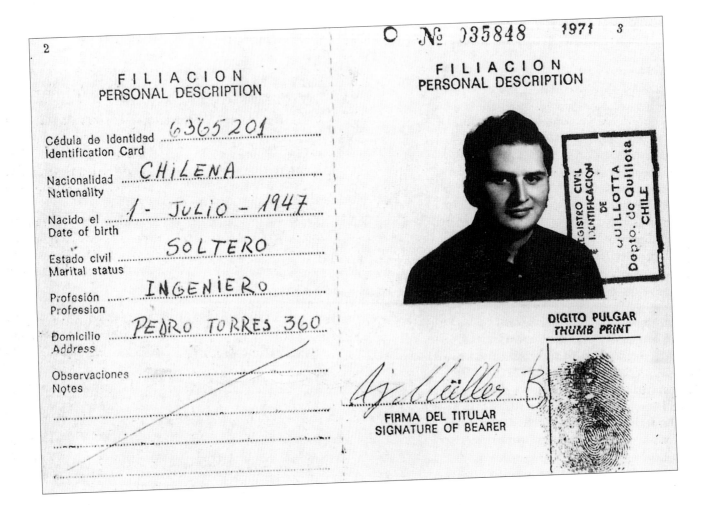

anarchists in bars where they talked about changing the world through violence. In 1969, Carlos moved on again – this time to the 'finishing school' for terrorists, the Patrice Lumumba Friendship University in Moscow. This seat of learning was in reality the world's top terror academy. Within its walls the Soviets trained some of the most diabolical killers in the world, all of them intent on changing society to fit in with the Marxist-Leninist doctrine.

Above: *A false passport found in a Paris flat after French law officers had been shot by Carlos.*

He spent a year here before he was dismissed for 'riotous and dilettante behaviour.' But western intelligence experts regard this cumbersome phrase as a feint dreamed up by the spy lecturers in order to fool the west that Carlos was never going to be part of international terrorism. Equipped with his new, lethal knowledge, he wrote a letter to his father : 'I am ready for what I must do. Thank you for pointing me on the true and correct path.'

Red Army terrorist, Kozo Okamoto, to lead a kamikaze-squad of terrorists in one the most heinous acts of terrorism ever perpetrated against innocent people. Okamoto and two others were flown to Israel on an Air France flight from Rome. In Rome they checked in luggage packed with automatic weapons and grenades – luggage which in those innocent days of air travel was not checked. Upon arrival in Israel, Okamoto and his accomplices, Rakeshi Okudeira and Yoshuyiki Yasuda, opened their luggage and began spraying the crowded terminal with automatic weapons fire, and hurling grenades into the lines of passengers. A defective grenade accounted for one terrorist, a second was shot by a policeman. Okamoto, who had intended to die in the assault, was knocked to the ground by an El Al maintenance worker as he aimed his machine gun at aircraft on the tarmac. On that dark day, 30 May, twenty-four people died, four more died from their wounds in hospital and seventy-six were wounded, many seriously. It was Carlos' grand opening venue on the stage of world terrorism.

He was paid £1 million for organizing the successful killing mission and his name – taken from the title of 'The Day of the Jackal', the Frederick Forsyth novel about

A BLOODTHIRSTY CREW

He spent some time in Paris with a cell of the Popular Front for the Liberation of Palestine, the PFLP, whom he had befriended in Moscow. He would become the leader of this bloodthirsty crew when the Israeli secret service assassinated its head. The first outrage committed by him is believed to be a bomb aboard a Swissair plane bound for Tel Aviv from Zurich on 21 February, 1970. The bomb exploded within minutes of take-off in the baggage hold, causing a massive fire which brought the jetliner down, killing all two hundred people on board. But Carlos revealed his masterly flair for planning when he organized a 'big target' as he referred to the 1972 massacre at Israel's Lod Airport.

Thanks to the contacts he made in Moscow, Carlos employed the Japanese

an assassin stalking Charles de Gaulle – was widely broadcast in terrorist circles as a man who gets things done. Next, Carlos turned his sights on a prominent Jewish figure in Britain: Joseph Sieff, boss of the Marks and Spencer stores and a prominent supporter of Israel. But Carlos botched the assassination and, six years later, he discussed it in a newspaper interview given to a French journalist for the Parisian-based Arabic publication Al Watan Al Arabi. The two men met at a secret hideout in the Middle East and Carlos erroneously referred to Mr Sieff as Lord throughout his interview and said he had been chosen to die 'because he was the most important

> **THE ATTEMPTED MURDER OF SIEFF WAS THE ONLY MISSION THAT CARLOS IS EVER KNOWN TO HAVE BOTCHED.**

opened the bathroom door I fired my old Beretta. He was wounded at the upper lip below the nose. I usually fire three times around the nose. It's sure death. But in Lord Sieff's case only one bullet went off, though I fired three times. When Lord Sieff survived I decided to try again. But by the time I managed to get the necessary weapons two weeks later he had gone off to Bermuda.' The attempted murder of Sieff was the one and only mission that Carlos is ever known to have botched.

In 1974, he struck at the Hague in Holland. He again used Japanese Red Army fanatics for this mission. The terrorists seized the French ambassador and his

Above: *Captives taken from OPEC's headquarters in Vienna by Carlos' terror gang are forced to board an aircraft to Algeria.*

Zionist in Britain.' Carlos elected to carry out the assasination himself because of his expertise with small arms weapons.

His first operation in England started on 30 December, 1973. Here is how Carlos described it: 'I drove to the Lord's home, parked my car, rang the bell and held the butler at gunpoint. It was 6.45 in the evening. I ordered the butler to call out for his master from the bathroom. The butler did so and fainted. When Lord Sieff

staff and held them hostage, while Carlos demanded the release of another Red Army terrorist held in Paris. To prove he was not bluffing, and to stave off any 'cheating' from the governments he was blackmailing, Carlos bombed the Drugstore Publics in St Germain-des-Pres in the heart of Paris, killing two and injuring thirty. In the same interview with the Arab paper in which he boasted of the attempted killing of Sieff he said: 'The French authorities

panicked. A Boeing 707 was sent to Holland along with the freed Red Army terrorist to pick up the embassy assailants in the Hague. The operation succeeded completely.' Carlos was boastful.

ELUSIVE AND EFFICIENT

By now the western intelligence agencies were building up a profile of this master terrorist. They knew he was based in Europe, but he never stayed in one place long. He was as elusive as he was efficient. The French authorities came close to capturing him, when on 27 June, 1975, a Lebanese informer of the PFLP led two agents of the French Direction de la Surveilance du Territoire to Carlos' apartment in the centre of the city. Michel Mourkabel, the informer, had been at one time Carlos' liason man with the PFLP leadership in the Middle East. Carlos described what happened when Mourkabel brought agents Jean Donatini, thirty-four, and Raymond Dous, fifty-five, to his apartment on the third-floor of a block on the Rue Toullier in the Latin quarter of the city. Carlos has always claimed that there were three French agents present, although the authorities have only ever admitted to two agents. Carlos said to the Arabic newspaper journalist: 'It was 8.45 in the evening when they knocked on the door. I was with two Venezualans and a student girlfriend. One of the Venezualans opened the door and shouted "police." '

'We asked the policeman to have a drink with us. They sat for a while and asked for our passports. We produced them and then they started questioning me about Moukarbel. I denied that I had ever met him. But they said he told them that he knew me and that he was waiting outside to identify me. I then challenged them to

Above: *Israelis celebrate their successful raid on terrorists who held an aeroplane and its passengers hostage at Entebbe, Uganda.*

HE NEVER STAYED IN ONE PLACE LONG. HE WAS AS ELUSIVE AS HE WAS EFFICIENT.

bring him in. They consulted among themselves and then one of them went out. Fifteen minutes later Moukarbel was brought in. When he started to point his finger at me I realised I had to shoot it out. I realised I had to execute the death sentence. I whipped out my Russian-made pistol and fired first at Donatini who was going for his gun. He was reputed to be a fast marksman. But I was faster and slugged a bullet into his left temple. Then I shot Dous between his eyes. Then I put a bullet under the ear of the third Frenchman.

Only Michel was left. He moved towards me, covering his face with his hands. He must have realised at that moment that he who cracks in this field of action is bound to be executed. These are the rules of the game. When he was almost at point-blank range I fired between his eyes. He slumped. I fired a second bullet into his left temple and then raced out into the darkness through the neighbouring apartment. The whole operation took six seconds.'

Carlos fled to London where he holed up with beautiful revolutionary, Nydia Tobon,

Below: *Marines lay a dead comrade on a stretcher after the massive Beirut bombing, probably organised by Carlos, that took two hundred American lives.*

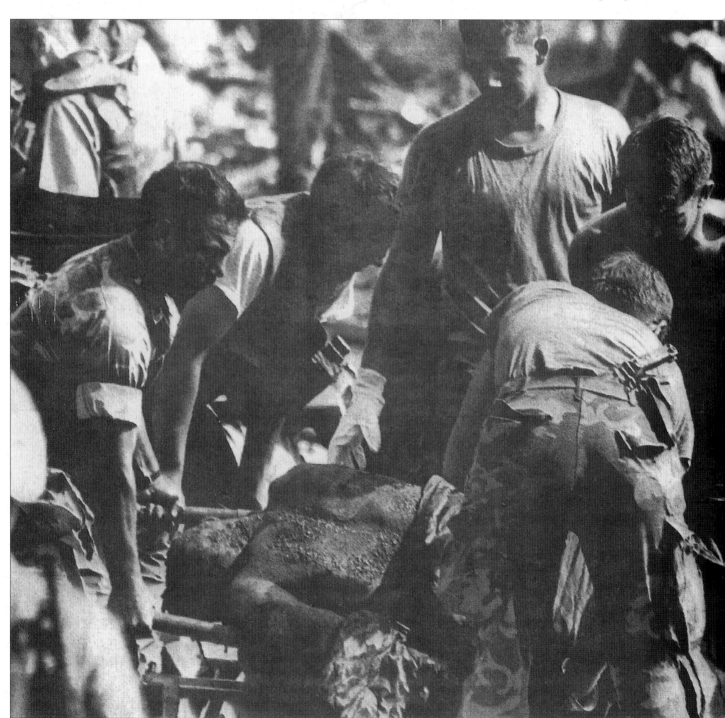

Above: *Rescuers dig through the rubble, looking for survivors, after the US Marine base was blown up during the troubles in the Lebanon.*

'CARLOS WANTED TO KILL THE COP. I TOLD HIM TO USE A BIT OF CHARM INSTEAD.'

when police raided the Hereford Road, Bayswater, apartment he had previously shared with twenty-three-year-old Spanish waitress Angela Otaola. They found a cache of arms and in one of the suitcases stashed with weapons, was a shopping list of death. Among the prominent members of British society on the list were Lord and Lady Sainsbury, Sir Keith Joseph, Sir Bernard Delfont and violinist Yehudi Menuhin. Later, Carlos was stopped on the M4 motorway near Reading by Thames Valley police. Tobon, who was expelled from Britain two years after the incident, returned to her native Columbia where she said: 'He had been driving way too fast and we were stopped. The policeman came over and he reached for his pistol. He wanted to kill the cop. I told him to use a bit of charm instead and he let him go with a warning. In the back of the car he had several more weapons and at least eight passports.' Carlos had luck on his side.

In December of the same year Carlos pulled off his most daring exploit.

Working for the PFLP, Carlos masterminded and led a team of daring guerillas in an assault on the OPEC delegates, assembled in Vienna for a conference on world petroleum pricing. Eighty-one delegates of rich Middle Eastern states were present on 21 December when Carlos and his fanatics struck. The PFLP were angry at what they regarded as an Arabic 'sell-out' by states to the 'imperialist' Americans who gave so much support to their arch-enemy Israel. There was an element of that to it, but the main purpose of the mission was to raise funds for future operations – and to line the Swiss bank account of Carlos, Illyich Ramirez Sanchez.

The OPEC meeting was in its second day when Carlos, accompanied by two West German terrorists linked with the Baader-Meinhof gang, two Palestinians and a Lebanese burst into the meeting hall after a shootout with Austrian security guards. They killed three people, including the Libyan delegate to the conference, a bad move, as Libya was one of Carlos' main weapons suppliers, a policeman and an Iraqi employee of that nation's delegation and they wounded seven.

THE MEN WERE RELEASED INTO THE DESERT AFTER AN ESTIMATED 50 MILLION DOLLARS WAS PAID IN RANSOM.

Below: *One of Carlos' men was wounded in the OPEC seige in Vienna. He was furious that the authorities removed the man to give him medical care.*

A SAFE PASSAGE OUT OF AUSTRIA

The terrorist gang then seized dozens of hostages, among them Sheik Yamini and Jamshid Amouzegar, Iranian Minister of the Interior. Responsibility for this attack was claimed by the Arm of the Arab Revolution, but it was in reality a PFLP operation. Carlos demanded massive amounts of ransom cash for several of the wealthier delegates and a safe passage for his gang out of Austria. One of the gang members who was wounded by return fire in the initial storming of the conference was treated at a city hospital and returned to Carlos. In return for the freedom of forty-one Austrian hostages the government allowed Carlos to fly out with his hostages from Iraq, Saudi Arabia, Gabon, Ecuador, Venezuala, Nigeria and Indonesia. They flew to Algiers and from there to Libya and the men were eventually released into the desert after an estimated $50 million was paid in ransom by the hostages' nations. It was a stunningly

brilliant terrorist operation thanks to the masterful cunning of Carlos.

In the following months he committed a string of assassinations across the world, including the murders of a dissident Syrian exile, a Palestinian rival guerilla leader and several PFLP commanders who needed to be 'purged' from the movement. After resting in a guerilla training camp in Libya, he masterminded, in 1976, the hijacking of an Air France jet en route from Tel Aviv to Paris with two hundred and fifty–eight passengers on board. The plane was diverted and hi-jacked in order to obtain the release of imprisoned terrorists, among them the crazed Okamoto who had caused such carnage at Lod Airport. The hijacked plane landed at Entebbe in Uganda, where Israeli commandos stormed the parked aircraft and released the hostages in a brilliant display of anti-terror tactics. Carlos was said to be angry that the terrorists he sub-contracted for the operation were 'not up to the task'.

After the Entebbe fiasco, Carlos faded into some obscurity. He began training guerillas for Gaddafi in Libya and was said by intelligence agencies to be, at various times, in East Berlin, in Syria, in Czechoslovakia, Iraq, South Yemen and Hungary. He was a man admired for his cool skill but derided by his fellow murderers as a vain, egotistical urban warrior who spent hours on personal grooming. Hans Joachim-Klein, the terrorist badly injured in the OPEC operation, gave an interview to a German newspaper in 1978: 'He was mocked, certainly by his German accomplices, for his vanity. He was always taking showers and powdering himself from head to foot. But no-one could fault him professionally although he did upset

Opposite, left: Carlos as he appeared in a 'wanted' poster after he killed two lawmen in Paris.

Opposite, right: Sheik Yamani, the Saudi Arabian oil minister who was furious that Carlos had sabotaged his meeting in Vienna.

Above: *Terrorist Hans-Joachim Klein, wanted in connection with the OPEC assault, in a car with the French philosopher, Jean-Paul Sartre (front of car) and left wing lawyer, Klaus Croissant. The urban terrorists attracted some unexpected support.*

HIS MURDERS WERE PLANNED TO COINCIDE WITH THE THIRTIETH ANNIVERSARY OF THE FOUNDING OF THE STATE OF ISRAEL.

---

several with his constant attempts to take over German revolutionay groups that had nothing to do with him. He was very cool during the whole OPEC operation – he even rode the tram to the hall with all his weapons.' And always well-groomed.

In May 1978 Carlos surfaced in London where he was spotted in Notting Hill by a man working for a foreign embassy in London. Scotland Yard's anti-terrorist branch was put on full alert and the Notting Hill area of the city, where he was seen, was combed, but he was not found. There is speculation that he came to fulfill the contracts on several of the people on the death list drawn up years earlier, and his murders were planned to coincide with the thirtieth anniversary of the founding of the state of Israel.

A WORLDWIDE TERROR CAMPAIGN

When Israel launched the 1982 invasion of Beirut for a full and final reckoning with the Palestine Liberation Organization Carlos hired himself out to Hezbollah fanatics. He is credited with numerous assassinations committed at this time, including the killing of fifty-eight people at the French military headquarters in Beirut.

His last known mission happened just before the outbreak of the Gulf War in 1991. Intelligence sources say Carlos was summoned to Bagdhad by Saddam Hussein and asked to organize a world-wide terror campaign if the West resorted to military action to free Kuwait from the Iraqi invasion. Carlos was alledgedly offered $10 million to organize the terror squads, but pressure was put on him by Syrian and other Arab governments to stay out of this one. Many Arab nations that he had worked for in the past were actually allied with the West against Saddam. Carlos backed out, reputedly with a million-dollar 'consultancy fee' in his back pocket.

Apart from the crimes he is known to have masterminded and committed, he is wanted for questioning on many, many more. His bloody handprints are seen in the murder of Swedish premier Olaf Palme and in the murder of more than two hundred US Marines in Beirut. But with the ruthlessness and cunning he displays, and the number of nations in the world willing to give terrorists refuge, it is highly unlikely that Carlos the Jackal will ever be brought to justice.

His nest is nicely feathered with booty from his bloody games and he may find retirement easier to enjoy than the danger of his terrorist existence. He is reported to have travelled in November 1991, on a Yemeni passport, to Yemen after a falling out with Colonel Gaddafi over the political direction of terrorism. It is believed that Carlos is living with Magdalene Kopp, a Baader-Meinhoff terrorist that he somehow found time to marry at some point during his bizarre international odyssey of death and mayhem.

But perhaps there is a kind of justice waiting for Carlos – the same kind of justice that he himself has dispensed without mercy. According to America's CIA, there is a group of wealthy Arab businessmen which has put out a contract on his head. Aware that fanatics like Carlos pose a threat to everyone in any society, these men are said to have pooled millions of dollars that will go as a reward to the person who assassinates Carlos. But international terror expert, David Funnel, said in Washington: 'It will take a killer of very high calibre indeed to catch Carlos. He has been schooled for too long and is too wily to allow himself to become vulnerable. If his antennae sense danger, he will uproot from one spot and move to another. He is that clever and that cunning.'

'IT WILL TAKE A KILLER OF VERY HIGH CALIBRE INDEED TO CATCH CARLOS.'

Below: *Red Army guerilla, Kozo Okamoto, the killer who opened fire on the crowds at Lod Airport, Israel, in 1980. He was freed for an exchange of Israeli prisoners in a deal between the Palestinians and Israel.*

JEFFREY DAHMER
The Cannibal Killer

He seemed to be just another quiet worker at the chocolate factory but there have been few monsters to equal Jeffrey Dahmer – sadist, sodomite, killer and cannibal.

It was a balmy Milwaukee night in July 1991 when horrified police uncovered the secret life of America's most twisted serial killer, Jeffrey Dahmer. His one-bedroomed flat had been turned into a slaughterhouse for his hapless victims and, as the case unfolded, revelations of cannibalism, perverted sex, brutal murder and other unspeakable horrors shocked the whole world.

Photos of police forensic experts carting out vats of acid filled with bones and decomposing body parts, filled television screens around the world and ensured that Milwaukee would forever be known for something other than its beer.

Even though thirty-one year-old Dahmer pleaded Guilty to the murders of fifteen young men he still had to go to trial because he claimed that he was insane – and only a jury could decide whether his acts were the work of a twisted madman or of a cold, calculating, killing machine. The trial itself was one of the most disturbing America had ever witnessed and a national audience of millions of television viewers were to hear tales of human carnage, bizarre sex, sick killings and grisly fantasies that would have ensured a XXX rating had it been a movie.

The strange case of Jeffrey Dahmer ended with a verdict of Guilty and sane. The judge was forced to sentence Dahmer to mandatory, consecutive life terms in prison with no chance of parole for 930 years. The jury disregarded the testimony of psychiatric experts who said that Dahmer was 'psychotic' and suffered from unstoppable sexual urges caused by the mental disease of necrophilia. Dahmer himself appeared to undergo a physical change when he was in prison for the six months before the trial. Expressing remorse and asking to be put to death, the Milwaukee Monster had lost the mad, staring eyes that he had when he was first arrested. But experts still could not agree about his thought processes.

Like the capture of many serial killers, the arrest of Jeffrey Dahmer happened

almost by accident. It had been a routine night for Milwaukee police patrolmen Robert Rauth and Rolf Mueller on 22 July 1991 when they spotted a black man running towards their car with a pair of handcuffs dangling from his wrist.

HE HAD FLED FOR HIS LIFE

The man with the handcuffs was Tracy Edwards and he told them a wild story about a man in the Oxford Apartments who had threatened to cut out Tracy's heart and eat it. He had fled for his life. It would turn out that Edwards had narrowly avoided becoming victim number eighteen for America's most bizarre and warped serial killer, Jeffrey Dahmer.

The two veteran policemen, used to responding to trouble in the rundown section of Milwaukee that had become their beat, took Edwards back to the ordinary looking block of flats and rang the buzzer of one of Dahmer's neighbours. 'Open up, this is the police,' they told John Batchelor through the intercom. He let them in and looked at his watch – it was 11:25pm.

Opposite: Jeffrey Dahmer, the man who shocked the world when his depravity was revealed in a criminal court.

Above: Carolyn Smith weeps as court testimony describes the horrible death that her son, Eddie, suffered in the hands of Dahmer.

THEY SPOTTED A BLACK MAN RUNNING TOWARDS THEIR CAR WITH A PAIR OF HANDCUFFS DANGLING FROM HIS WRISTS.

Nothing had prepared the two cops for what they would find after they rapped on the door of apartment number 213 as Tracy Edwards stayed a safe distance away down the corridor. A slight man with dirty-blonde hair and wearing a blue T-shirt and jeans opened the door. As they entered the dingy flat the policemen smelled a foul stench. A hi-tech electronic lock on Dahmer's front door further heightened their suspicions and they started to ask what had been going on. Mueller spotted some pots on top of the stove, some of them filled with a gooey substance and lots of dirty dishes.

Edwards had told the policemen that he had met Dahmer at a downtown shopping mall and agreed to come back to his flat to drink some beer. When he said he wanted to leave Dahmer threatened him with a knife and put the handcuffs on one of his wrists, holding the other end in his hand. When Edwards later recounted his incredibly lucky escape from the Milwaukee Monster to a packed courtroom, he was too frightened to even look across at the

Above: *In 1978, Jeffrey Dahmer was normal enough to go to the high school prom with a girl, Bridget Geiger. In 1982, he was photographed by the police when he was arrested for disorderly conduct.(Below)*

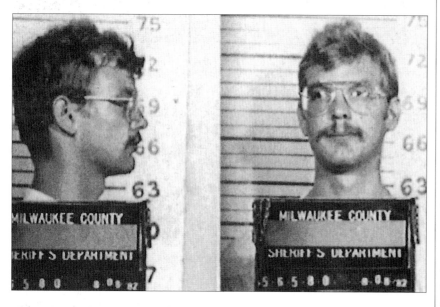

defendant. We must assume that Jeffrey Dahmer had wielded a similar dread power over most of his victims.

After several hours inside the Dahmer lair, during which time Dahmer lay on top of Edwards' chest and listened to his heart, the killer began to get restless. Edwards testified that Dahmer began going in and out of a trance, chanting and swaying back and forth. This gave Edwards the opportunity to escape. Officer Mueller radioed back to police headquarters to 'run a make'

'OH MY GOD! THERE'S A GODDAMN HEAD IN THERE. HE'S ONE SICK SON OF A BITCH.'

on Dahmer. When they replied that the man was still on probation for a second degree sexual assault charge against a thirteen-year-old boy, the officers instructed Dahmer to lie face down on the floor so they could handcuff him and take him in. It was then that Officer Mueller wandered over to the refrigerator and opened it. 'Oh my God! There's a goddamn head in there. He's one sick son of a bitch.'

Jeffrey Dahmer had been found out and his killing spree had been brought to an abrupt end, but as the gory details of his murderous orgy began to emerge it became clear that for more than a year, he had been killing people and chopping them up.

A COLLECTION OF POLAROIDS SHOWING DAHMER'S VICTIMS

As forensic specialists began to pour into the apartment building to catalogue the series of horrors, neighbours, awakened by all the commotion, started filing out into the streets. Police found a barrel drum filled with acid and the remains of three human torsos. Decomposed hands and genitals were kept in a lobster pot in one of his cupboards along with human skulls, hands and fingers. A collection of Polaroids was found showing each of Dahmer's fifteen victims in various states of undress and then, according to the forensic report 'in different degrees of surgical excision'. They had been slaughtered, butchered and then dissolved.

Photographs from gay magazines hung on Dahmer's bedroom walls and a collection of pornographic videos, heavy metal records and a tape of 'The Exorcist II' littered the living room. The only normal foodstuffs police found in Dahmer's flat were packets of crisps, a jar of mustard, and some beer. Not only had he been murdering and butchering his prey, he had been eating their flesh as well. He would later tell police how he fried one of his victim's biceps in oil and had it for dinner. In his freezer, police found human hamburgers made up of strips of muscle and flesh. Horrified neighbours watched as police in protective anti-toxic suits carried the evidence out of the building.

Dahmer grew up in a normal American family. His father Lionel worked as a research chemist in Bath, Ohio where he married Joyce Flint in 1959. Jeffrey was born exactly nine months after his parents got married, and doesn't seem to have had a terribly traumatic childhood. His parents divorced when he was eighteen and he was left to fend for himself. He was just about to graduate from the Revere High School and he moved into a motel to be by himself while his mother and father sorted out custody of his eleven-year-old brother. By this time, however, Dahmer was beginning to show signs of being 'a little odd'. He had trouble having relationships with girls, he was considered 'weird' by many of his classmates, and his favourite pastime was imitating mentally retarded people. 'He was a class clown but not in a wholesome sense,' recalled Dave Borsvold. 'He was only amused by the bizarre. He used to trace outlines of bodies out on the floor with chalk. He was definitely a little bit different.' But he did not seem dangerous.

His high school guidance counsellor George Kungle said: 'Jeff was never a discipline problem – he was a quiet but not necessarily introverted guy. He never let anyone get to know him well. I would try and talk to him, like you would any kid, hoping to get some insights. He just never said a whole lot about himself.'

A FATHER'S SENSE OF SHAME

During a bitter divorce Jeffrey's father accused his wife of 'extreme cruelty and gross neglect' and he made references to her 'mental illness' and the medical treatment she was receiving. Even the experts do not know what causes a serial killer to develop, but in Dahmer's case an hereditary mental illness might not be too far from the mark. 'In retrospect I wish I had done more in terms of keeping in touch of what he was doing and visiting him more often,' said Dahmer's father when he discovered what his son had been doing. 'I don't know about feeling guilty for what he did, but I feel guilty that I didn't do more. I feel a deep sense of shame. I think any father who has some sense of responsiblity feels the transfer of shame or the responsibility somehow for this. When I first heard about it I could not associate him with what I was hearing was done. Absolutely not. I didn't think in my wildest dreams he was capable of something like that,' added

'JEFF WAS NEVER A DISCIPLINE PROBLEM – HE WAS A QUIET BUT NOT NECESSARILY INTROVERTED GUY.'

Above: *Jeffrey Dahmer, was at last, in 1991, unmasked for the monster he is. Here he is led into court to face charges of murder and cannibalism*.

Dahmer Sr. who paid for an expensive criminal defence lawyer, Gerald Boyle, to act for his son.

'I didn't look at him and see a monster. He acts – under most conditions – polite, kind, courteous. I can only imagine in my mind those occasions when he attacked the victims that was the monster who was out of control.' In Revere High School's yearbook Dahmer is described as a 'very valuable' member of the tennis team. He also played in the school band. In the space reserved for what he would like to do with his life, he said he wanted to attend Ohio State University and then pursue a career in business. It would later emerge that Dahmer had already committed his first murder the year he left school. He often killed and mutilated animals in the woods behind his home, before he killed a young male hitch hiker, Stephen Hicks, who was on his way to a rock concert. Dahmer did indeed go to Ohio State in September of 1978 but he dropped out in January the next year to join the army. Friends who remember him say he was set on the idea of becoming a military policeman.

Instead, Dahmer ended up becoming a medical orderly and was sent to Germany to the Baumholder base in Rhineland-Palatinate state. The army has not revealed why he was discharged before his commis-

THE YEAR WAS 1988 AND, UNKNOWN TO THE LAW, HE HAD ALREADY KILLED FOUR TIMES...

Right: *His defence team pleaded insanity on Dahmer's behalf, but the jury were to hear that he had planned his crimes with cunning forethought and in full awareness of his dreadful acts.*

sion was up, but members of Dahmer's family say it was because of alcoholism. His time in the forces equipped him with a rudimentary knowledge of anatomy. When Dahmer returned to America he started drifting into casual, blue collar jobs that paid little and afforded little respect from anyone. After six months in Miami he moved to Bath, Ohio, where he received a disorderly conduct charge for having an open container of alcohol on the street. In January 1982 he moved to Milwaukee to live with his grandmother, where he dispalyed a pattern of bizarre sexual activity by exposing himself to young

and was told to report regularly to a probation officer.

For almost two years probation officer Donna Chester sat across a table from Dahmer every first Tuesday of each month for fifteen minutes. Never in a million years did she dream that he could be capable of the brutal butchery of the eleven young men. Thirty-five-year-old Chester, who still works for the Wisconsin State Probation Service, was assigned to Dahmer's case in March 1990 after he was released from prison. To Chester, Jeffrey Dahmer was no different from most of the one hundred and twenty-one criminals that

children until he was charged with sexual abuse of a thirteen-year-old boy. The young boy's brother was to be a murder victim.

Shortly before he was due to be sentenced for the abuse of the boy, Dahmer wrote a lucid letter to the judge in the case asking for leniency and promising never to do it again. 'The world has enough misery in it without my adding more to it,' he wrote. 'That is why I am requesting a sentence modification. So that I may be allowed to continue my life as a productive member of our society.'

The year was 1988 and, unknown to the law, he had already killed four times. Regardless of his letter Dahmer was sentenced to eight years in jail, though he was released after serving just ten months because he proved to be a model prisoner

were part of her caseload. He was trying to make his way back into society with the help of counselling and supervision after a bout in jail time that he said he regretted.

As he sat in her room in the district office he would tell Donna how his counselling sessions were going, he would talk about his hobbies, his personal life and the things he did in his spare time. What she did not realise was that this was no ordinary sex offender working his way diligently through rehabilitation. Jeffrey Dahmer held a dark secret close to him. And he was so good at it that Donna even cancelled a home visit to his apartment. A spokesman for the Department of Corrections, Joe Scislowicz, said it was unfair to blame Donna Chester for what happened. He remembered Dahmer as

FOR ALMOST TWO YEARS THE PROBABTION OFFICER SAT ACROSS A TABLE FROM DAHMER EVERY FIRST TUESDAY OF EACH MONTH. NEVER IN A MILLION YEARS DID SHE DREAM THAT HE COULD BE CAPABLE OF THE BRUTAL BUTCHERY OF THE ELEVEN YOUNG MEN.

polite, punctual and reliable. 'He was only unable to report on two occasions in two years, otherwise he was here at the same time every month,' said Scislowicz. 'Both times he called ahead and said he wouldn't be able to make it and gave a good reason. He was excused from appearing both times. He was very meticulous about reporting to his probation officer once a month. I'm told he was like that in his work, too.'

NAKED AND BLEEDING, HE RAN FROM DAHMER

Scislowicz would not elaborate on the kind of rehabilitation treatment Dahmer was going through – saying it was a breach of privacy – he said his case file shows that Dahmer felt he was making some progress at working towards his goal of becoming a 'useful contributor to society'. Chester's inability to see through Dahmer's tissue of lies brought criticism from Milwaukee police chief Philip Arreola who spoke out about how the system failed its people and its policemen. 'We try to put these people away for a long time and they get let back out on to the streets,' he said. 'Now we can see the tragic results of a system that has simply ceased to function.'

It was a hard pill for the probation department, and Chester to swallow. They felt they had done all they needed to keep tabs on Dahmer. As Scislowicz said: 'There was a lot of evidence he was doing alright. Most people who have a residence and a good paying job tend to stay out of trouble. This is such an exception, it's not fair to blame it on any individual.'

Arreola got a taste of his own medicine just a few days later when it emerged that a tragic, careless act by three bigoted policemen allowed Dahmer to continue with his killing spree unabated. Choking back tears of embarassment the police chief had to admit that he was bringing in the Internal Affairs Division to investigate reports that three officers actually came face to face with Dahmer on the night of 27 May. One even went inside his flat – and not one of them thought anything was wrong.

The incident involved Konerak Sinthasomphone, a fourteen-year-old Laotian refugee who was seen running out of Dahmer's apartment apparently bleeding. Neighbours, mostly black people,

called in the police but were more or less told to 'stop bothering the white guy' according to witnesses. Not only was Sinthasomphone naked and bleeding, but he had been drugged with a heavy dose of sleeping pills – Dahmer's favourite form of rendering his victims unconscious before strangling them – and there were tiny drill marks in his head. Dahmer had fantasised about creating zombie-like lovers that could be his sex slaves and he began to experiment on some of them by doing crude lobotomies with an electric drill and some acid. One poor victim stayed awake for an entire day before finally dying. As soon as the police left the building Dahmer, who told them the boy was his lover, strangled Sinthasomphone, and dismembered his body – all the while taking polaroid pictures. The three policemen responsible have been fired.

Within hours of his arrest Dahmer admitted to killing seventeen people, twelve of them inside his Milwaukee flat and two in a different state. He identified photographs of missing persons for detectives. Forensic psychologists and other experts all testified at his trial, which drew large crowds for three weeks at the Milwaukee County Safety Building. But they could not agree on whether he was able to stop his urge to kill, a crucial aspect of his insanity defence. Dahmer sat emotionless, occasionally stifling yawns, as he listened to detectives and psychiatrists recount hundreds of hours of interviews they conducted with him to trying to understand his vile and terrible acts.

> DAHMER HAD FANTASISED ABOUT CREATING ZOMBIE-LIKE LOVERS WHO WOULD BE HIS SEX SLAVES.

Below: *This young boy, Konarak Sinthaomphona, ran screaming from Dahmer's flat but passing policemen were convinced by Dahmer that he and the boy were playing a 'homosexual game'. They let the boy go. Dahmer killed him*

Below, left: *Konarak's brother and sister are haunted by their brother's desperate death.*

Relatives of his victims, who were almost all black, listened intently to the gruesome testimony. They hugged each other and cried as they heard for the first time what really happened to their loved ones. At the end of the trial, after a jury found that Dahmer was sane, the relatives gave voice to their horror and grief.

For one young woman, seeing Dahmer face to face was too much. Rita Isbell stared into the eyes of the Milwaukee Monster as Judge Laurence Gram invited her to make a statement before sentence was to be imposed. Rita became hysterical

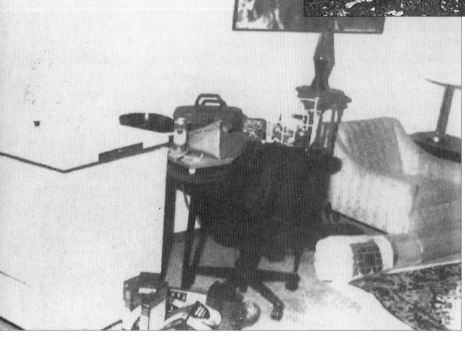

when she started talking about her dead brother, Errol Lindsey, who was just nineteen when he was butchered and dismembered by Dahmer in his Milwaukee apartment in 1991. Dahmer had satisfied his twisted fantasies by having sex with the corpse.'I never want to see my mother go through what she went through because of you,' said Isbell. 'Do you understand Jeffrey? Jeffrey, I hate you,' she shouted. Isbell, wearing a sweatshirt that read '100 per cent black', then ran around the outside of the witness box and towards the table where Dahmer was sitting with his lawyers. 'You Mother ****er, I'll kill you Jeffrey,' she screamed hysterically as five court officers held her back.

After other families called him 'a devil' and asked the judge to ensure that he never

Top: *A Milwaukee police-man is obliged to photograph human bones found in the alley behind Dahmer's apartment.*

Above: *The freezer where Dahmer kept his nasty store of human flesh.*

saw daylight again, Dahmer surprised and stunned everyone by asking to make his own statement – an articulate and far reaching apology he had composed himself in his prison cell. Asking for 'no consideration' in his sentencing and declaring that he would have rather had the death penalty – something the state of Wisconsin does not have – Dahmer said: 'It is over now. This has never been a case of trying to get free. I really wanted death for myself. I hope God can forgive me. I know society and the families can never forgive me. I promise to pray every day for their forgiveness. I have seen their tears. If I could give my life right now to bring their loved ones back I would. This was not about hate. I never hated anyone. I knew I was sick or evil or both. Now I have some peace. I know the harm I have caused. I can't undo the terrible harm I have caused but I cooperated as best I could. I am very sorry.

'I understand their rightful hate,' he said of the victims' families, some of whom said they wished he would go to hell. 'I know I will be in prison for the rest of my life. I will turn back to God. I should have stayed with God. I tried and failed and created a holocaust. Only the Lord Jesus Christ can save me from my sins.' Dahmer promised to devote his time behind bars as a study for doctors and psychologists. He said he would to turn himself into a human guinea pig so that they can further examine his bizarre mind to try and find out what would make a human being turn into such a monster. The killer vowed to help psychia-trists to understand what made him do the ghastly things that he did on his killing, mutilation and cannibalistic spree.

'I pledge to talk to the doctors to help find some answers,' Dahmer said in a prepared statement. 'I know my time in jail will be terrible but I deserve whatever I get because of what I did.' Dahmer – who admitted to detectives that he studied the Satanic scripts – read a passage from the Bible and declared: 'Jesus Christ came to the world to save the sinners, of whom I am the worst. Dahmer apologised to the victims' families, his probation officer, and even the policemen who were fired. Dahmer also apologised to his father Lionel and step-mother Shari, who both sat quietly and listened intently every day of the court proceedings.

'I regret that the policemen lost their jobs,' said Dahmer. 'I know they did their best. I have hurt my mother, father, step-mother and family. I love them all so much. I only hope they find the same peace I have. I take all the blame for what I did. I hurt many people. I decided to go through with this trial for a number of reasons. I wanted to show these were not hate crimes. I wanted the world to know the truth. I didn't want any unanswered questions. I wanted to find out what it was that caused me to be bad or evil. Perhaps if there are others out there, this all might have helped them.'

ROUND-THE-CLOCK SURVEILLANCE IN ISOLATION

Dahmer was sentenced to a total of one thousand and seventy years in prison on fifteen consecutive counts of murder plus extra sentences for habitual criminality with no possibility of parole for nine hundred and thirty years. Just one day after the sentence he was taken to Wisconsin's toughest jail – the maximum security Columbia Correctional Institution where he is held in a segregated cell. The Portage prison houses five hundred and seventy-five of the worst criminals in the state – sex offenders, murderers, drug dealers and now Jeffrey Dahmer. There is a chance that he could be absorbed into the main prison population but for now he will be under round-the-clock surveillance in isolation. 'At the beginning we will be observing him twenty-four hours a day to ensure that he is not a danger to himself,' said Columbia's warden Jeffrey Endicott. 'The best way for us to do that is to have him in that section of the prison. It is safest for all concerned.'

Endicott added that many inmates are moved out of the isolation block after a few days, but that Dahmer may be kept there longer than others. Many of the one hundred and fifty sex offenders in the prison never leave their single cells or mingle with other prisoners. Fellow serial killer Henry Lee Lucas, who is on death row in a Texas prison said that life in jail for him was 'pure hell'. Lucas, who was convicted of eleven murders and suspected of committing one hundred and forty more, says Dahmer will have a rough time of it. 'He'll be lucky to stay alive in prison. There's a thing in prison about kids, you know,' he said. 'If somebody kills a kid like that he'll have a hard way to go.'

Dahmer will have no contact with other prisoners at first and even though he says he no longer wants to kill, guards have been told to take every precaution when dealing with him. All of his food is passed to him through a drawer in a wall to avoid contact and he will be kept under constant surveillance twenty-four hours a day by guards who sit inside a protected 'control bubble'. Columbia Correctional Institution is a large complex, with five watchtowers, razor wire topped high security fences and electronic surveillance of its nineteen-acre perimeter. There is no chance that Dahmer could escape. He is allowed to exercise once a day but is always accompanied by several guards. And he must wear the bright orange jumpsuit uniform he was given when he walked in the front door of the prison.

DAHMER WAS SENTENCED TO A TOTAL OF ONE THOUSAND AND SEVENTY YEARS IN PRISON ON FIFTEEN CONSECUTIVE COUNTS OF MURDER.

Above: *The freezer, vital evidence to support the charge that Dahmer was a cannibal, is loaded on a police van.*

Right: *Another mother grieves for her son during a candlelit vigil held in Milwaukee for the murdered boys. Her son was Tony Hughes, and he was dismembered by the monster.*

Below: *Oliver Lacy, one of the many victims. Dahmer decapitated the corpse and kept the head.*

HE IS SIMILAR TO MANY OF AMERICA'S WORST MASS MURDERERS IN THAT HE CAN BE PERFECTLY NORMAL WHILE HE IS NOT IN HIS 'KILLING MODE'.

Dahmer will not be allowed any more than six books, four magazines, ten pictures and fifteen letters. Each week he receives more than two dozen letters – some from women who want to meet him and fall in love. Dahmer came from a middle-class family, but was affected in early life by a trauma or rejection which sent him over the edge.

He is similar to many of America's worst mass murderers, in that he can be perfectly normal while he is not in his 'killing mode', and that may work to his advantage in jail. Ed Gein was working as a babysitter while he was spending his nights digging up graves; Ted Bundy worked at a Samaritans' hotline in Seattle in between killings; John Wayne Gacy performed as a clown at childrens' parties; amd David Berkowitz now spends much of his time counselling other inmates at a New York state high security prison.

He helps them with their problems, reads their mail to them and cleans floors. He is considered a model prisoner and will be elligible for parole in ten years. 'Many of these killers are frequently glib and superficially charming, helpful, sweet and kind,' said Helen Morrison, a Chicago psychiatrist and serial killer expert. 'I'm sure Dahmer falls into that same category.' Judith Becker, who testified at the Dahmer trial for the defence, says it is too soon to tell how the prison term will affect Dahmer's personality or his mind. 'He did indicate to me that he hated what he had been doing and he talked about a 'nuclear explosion' that had happened within him since he had been caught,' she said. 'He's talked about killing himself, but obviously he won't be able to do that in prison. He says he is sorry for what he did and that he feels pain for the relatives of the victims. He has already had a lot of time on his own to think about that, and he seems to be coping with it now. The fantasies have stopped, he says. But there is no way of really knowing if they will start up again.'

THE CHANCES ARE THAT HE COULD BECOME A MODEL PRISONER

'The prosecution made a strong case by identifying that Dahmer was able to make definite decisions not to do things at certain times,' said David Barlow, an assistant professor of criminal justice at the University of Wisconsin. Richard Kling, who defended serial killer John Wayne Gacy, added: 'I don't think there is a person in the world who would come in and say Dahmer isn't abnormal. The problem is that abnormal doesn't add up to insanity.' How he deals with being in prison is something that will fascinate psychiatric experts for years to come. The chances are that he could become a model prisoner, with the ability to be outwardly friendly to both fellow inmates and guards.

During the trial McCann pointed out Dahmer's ability to manipulate doctors and psychiatrists for his own ends. His supply of prescription sleeping pills – which he used for drugging his victims before he strangled them – came from doctors who thought he was having trouble sleeping.

Dahmer also deliberately misled court appointed therapists who were trying to help him after he was convicted of sexual assault. He rejected the hand that could have helped him,' said McCann. 'He knew what he was doing.' No matter what happens the files of Jeffrey Dahmer will provide endless hours of research material for the FBI's academy in Quantico, Virginia – where special agents are trained to produce profiles of serial killers. Although the project is temporarily dormant after the departure of its director, Robert Ressler, Dahmer's court files will be entered into the FBI's extensive databanks on serial killers.

'SILENCE OF THE LAMBS'

Ressler, who has interviewed such killers as Charles Manson, Sirhan Sirhan, Ted Bundy, John Wayne Gacy, and 'Son of Sam' killer David Berkowitz will attempt to see Dahmer so that he can include his files in his rogue's gallery.'How can a person be sane and do these horrendous acts ?'. He would be a fascinating study for me,' said Ressler, who now runs his own investigating company. 'Any information we can collect on individuals like Dahmer is like gold dust in tracking down others out there who might be doing the same thing.'

In the film 'Silence of the Lambs' Jodie Foster played a young FBI agent who had to befriend the demented Hopkins character – Hannibal the Cannibal – so that she could help catch another serial killer, a murderer based on Wisconsin's other famous maniac, Ed Gein. Gein killed women and then skinned them to satisfy his twisted transvestite fantasies. He also dug up freshly buried bodies so that he could use their skin to build himself a body. He was found mentally incompetent to stand trial in 1957 and so never had the opportunity to

> DAHMER DELIBERATELY MISLED COURT-APPOINTED THERAPISTS WHO WERE TRYING TO HELP HIM AFTER HE WAS CONVICTED OF SEXUAL ASSAULT.

plead guilty. He died at the Mendota Mental Health Institute in Madison in 1984. Other psychiatric experts have pointed out that a thorough investigation of Dahmer would be invaluable as research material into sexual perversion.

Judith Becker said: 'We could learn a tremendous amount from studying Dahmer because necrophiliacs are extremely rare. I have not seen anywhere in the literature the sucessful treatment of this disorder.' Even the most highly qualified experts cannot agree on what kind of demons live inside the mind of Jeffrey Dahmer. He showed early on in his life a twisted fascination with the macabre and the bizarre. Some psychiatrists claim that the emotional distance between him and his parents might have contributed to his feelings of abandonment. Those feelings fuelled his

Above: *Jeffrey Dahmer claimed to feel 'remorse' for his acts. But it needed a police investigation to provoke these feelings in him.*

ghastly killing spree – he told doctors that he killed his victims because he didn't want them to leave him. Some experts say being locked up for life with other criminals who won't be leaving might actually appeal to the perverse needs of Jeffrey Dahmer.

'One great myth about serial killers is that they secretly want to get caught,' said James Fox, a professor of criminal justice at Boston's Northeastern University and author of 'Mass Murder: The Growing Menace'. 'That's just not true, these guys enjoy what they do. They might get a little guilty afterwards for a while, but the fantasies that drive them are so powerful that they have to do it again soon. Dahmer will not be able to do it again now that he's in jail and I'm sure he won't be happy about that. He doesn't even have any of his souvenirs – the photos or even the body parts – to look at anymore. That may be why he has asked for the death penalty, he has nothing else to live for. Souvenirs are very important to the disorganised serial killers because they remind them of the best times they had. Dahmer's murders were driven by his fantasies of destruction, tied up with a sexual desire.'

Prosecutor E. Michael McCann said that Dahmer has always managed to control his violent tendencies when he has been in closely controlled situations and some feel that prison life will do him a lot of good.

DAHMER LONGS FOR DEATH

Worst of all for Dahmer will be the long hours of contemplation he will have to spend alone. He told detectives after his arrest that he wished Wisconsin or Ohio had the death penalty. Now he will have to spend the next forty years thinking about what he did. 'It will probably tear him apart,' said one expert. 'If the court didn't think he was insane when he killed, just wait a few years and see what the torture of his acts does to his mind.'

Dahmer may have to go through the trial process all over again in Ohio where he killed his first victim in 1978. But Ohio, like Wisconsin, has no death penalty – the one thing that Dahmer has wished for.

The world will be a safer place without Jeffrey Dahmer. But the world might never know what it was that drove him to commit some of the worst crimes in American history. One thing is certain, inmates at Columbia will not be jumping over each other for a chance to share a cell with him.

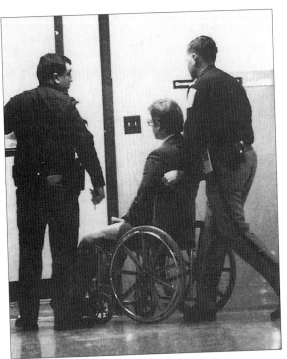

Above: *The Milwaukee Monster is wheeled into court. His hands and legs were shackled in irons as befits a dangerous beast.*

Right: *Lionel and Shane Dahmer, Jeffrey's father and stepmother, sat in court throughout his trial.*

VICTIMS AS NAMED BY PROSECUTOR'S OFFICE:

1 January 1988 – James Doxtator
Killed at age fifteen at Dahmer's grandmother's house. Strangled after drinking sleeping potion. Dismembered, bones smashed with a sledgehammer.

2 March 1988 – Richard Guerrero
Killed at age twenty-three at grandmother's house. Drugged him and then dismembered the body.

3 March 1989 – Anthony Sears
Killed at age twenty-four at grandmother's house. Strangled and dismembered. Dahmer kept his skull, boiled off the skin and then painted the skull as a souvenir.

4 May 1990 – Raymond Smith, aka Ricky Beeks
Killed at age thirty in Apartment 213. Strangled after being drugged. Dahmer had sex with the dead body. Dismembered him but kept the skull and painted it.

5 July 1990 – Edward Smith
Killed at age twenty-eight. Dismembered and disposed of in rubbish bags.

6 September 1990 – Ernest Miller
Killed at age twenty-three. Dahmer slit his throat, dismembered him and kept his biceps in the freezer to eat later. Also kept the skull and skeleton which he bleached.

7 October 1990 – David Thomas
Killed at age twenty-three. Killed even though he was not Dahmer's 'type' for fear that he would tell police he had been drugged. Body disposed of.

8 February 1991 – Curtis Straughter
Killed at age seventeen. Strangled with a strap after being drugged. Dismembered him but kept the skull.

9 April 1991 – Errol Lindsey
Killed at age nineteen. Strangled him and then had sex. Dismembered the body and kept the skull.

10 May 1991 – Anthony Hughes
Killed at age thirty-two. Strangled and dismembered him but kept the skull.

11 May 1991 – Konerak Sinthasomphone
Killed at age fifteen. Murdered after police left Dahmer's apartment following telephone call from neighbours. Strangled, dismembered but kept the skull.

12 June 1991 – Matt Turner aka Donald Montrell
Killed at age twenty-one. Strangled with a strap. Kept his head in the freezer and put his body in the acid-filled barrel.

13 July 1991 – Jeremiah Weinberger
Killed at age twenty-four. Strangled with his hands. Put his head in the freezer and his body in the barrel.

14 July 1991 – Oliver Lacy
Killed at age twenty-five. Strangled him and then had sex. Placed head in the bottom of the fridge and kept his heart in the freezer to eat later. Also kept his body in the freezer.

15 July 1991 – Joseph Bradehoft
Killed at age twenty-five. Strangled with a strap while he slept. Dismembered, head put in the freezer and body in the barrel.

Two additional victims Dahmer has admitted killing were not in the Milwaukee charges. They were:

Stephen Hicks was killed in Dahmer's parents' home in Bath, Ohio. Dahmer killed him with a barbell, then disposed of the body in the woods.

Stephen Tuomi killed in Milwaukee hotel room in September 1987. Dahmer says he doesn't remember how he killed the man, but he took his body back to his grandmother's house in a trunk and dismembered him.

Above: *Investigators were sent to Dahmer's boyhood home to look for the remains of the Monster's first victim, killed in 1978.*

HE DOESN'T REMEMBER HOW HE KILLED, BUT HE TOOK THE BODY BACK TO HIS GRANDMOTHER'S HOUSE AND DISMEMBERED IT.

PETER SUTCLIFFE
The Yorkshire Ripper

In the 1970s Yorkshire women were terrorized by a serial killer who, like the notorious Jack the Ripper, inflicted hideous mutilations on his victims. Was Peter Sutcliffe a paranoid schizophrenic, or just 'a wilfully evil bastard'?

Late on the afternoon of 22 May 1981, a dark-haired, bearded, scruffy little man rose to his feet in the dock beneath the dome of Number One Court at the Old Bailey to hear judgement passed upon him.

Found guilty of murdering thirteen women, and attempting to murder seven others, thirty-five-year-old Peter William Sutcliffe, 'The Yorkshire Ripper', was sentenced to life imprisonment with a recommendation that he should serve at least thirty years.

AN ORDINARY MURDER

The Ripper murders began in 1975 in the rundown Chapeltown area of Leeds. A milkman spotted a frosted bundle of what appeared to be rags on the white-rimmed grass. He went and peered at it. It was a woman's body.

She lay on her back, her dyed blonde hair dark and spiky with dried blood. Her jacket and blouse had been torn open and her bra pulled up, revealing breasts and abdomen, and her trousers were round her knees, though her pants were still in position. Her torso had been stabbed and slashed fourteen times, after her death from two crushing hammer blows to the back of the skull.

The dead woman's name was Wilma McCann. She was twenty-eight years old, and what the police classed as a 'good time girl'. Because Mrs McCann's purse was missing, West Yorkshire Metropolitan Police treated the case as murder in the pursuance of robbery. Despite the brutality of the attack there seemed no other motive. Yet, when another murder was committed just over two and half months later, the similarities convinced the police that they were dealing with a double murderer.

ANOTHER GOOD TIME GIRL

Emily Jackson, like Wilma McCann, came to Chapeltown only once or twice a week to sell herself on a casual basis.

Her body was discovered in the early

THE MILKMAN THOUGHT THE PILE OF RAGS WAS AN ABANDONED GUY FAWKES FIGURE – WHEN HE LOOKED, HE SAW IT WAS A WOMAN'S BODY

morning of 21 January 1976. She had also been killed from behind by two blows from a heavy hammer. Her breasts were exposed and her trousers pulled down, though again her pants were in place. On her right thigh was stamped the impression of a heavily ribbed wellington boot. The only solid clue the police had so far was that the perpetrator took size seven in shoes.

SERIAL KILLER ON THE LOOSE

No progress was made on either case, and a year passed by. Then, on 5 February, 1977, the killer struck again. Another 'good-time girl', twenty-eight-year-old Irene Richardson, was discovered by a jogger on Soldiers' Field, not far from Chapeltown. She was lying on her face and had died from three hammer blows to the back of her skull. Her killer had stripped her from the waist downwards. Her neck and chest had been subjected to a frenzied knife attack. The pattern of wounds now left no doubt that the police were dealing with a serial killer.

This alarmed the street-girl population, and their numbers in Chapeltown declined. Not so, however, in the red light district of Bradford, some ten miles away, where 'Tina' Atkinson lived and worked. On Sunday, 24 April, Tina's friends called for her at her flat, but got no answer. She had been out boozing the night before, and the door was ajar so they went in. Tina lay naked on her bed, the back of her head crushed by four hammer blows. Seven knife wounds had lacerated her stomach, and her side had been slashed open.

Any doubts about the killer's identity were dispelled by a clue found imprinted on the bottom bedsheet. It was the mark of a size seven wellington boot, identical with the imprint found on Emily Jackson's thigh.

The police believed that the killer was specifically targeting prostitutes and so began touring the red light districts, questioning street girls about any regulars who might have acted suspiciously. But, it soon became clear

Above: *Police examine the scene where Emily Jackson was murdered.*

IT WAS WOUNDED MALE PRIDE THAT HAD LED SUTCLIFFE TO CARRY OUT HIS FIRST 'REVENGE' ATTACK ON A PROSTITUTE

Below: *Assistant Chief Constable George Oldfield and Superintendent Richard Holland at a 'Ripper' press conference.*

that the Yorkshire Ripper regarded any woman out alone at night as fair game.

THE RIPPER SPREADS HIS NET

On Sunday, 26 June 1977, a sixteen-year-old girl named Jayne MacDonald was found slumped and dead in a street on the fringes of Chapeltown. She had sustained at least three hammer blows to the head. She had been stabbed once in the back and several times through the chest. But she was no prostitute or good-time girl. A fortnight later, a Bradford housewife, Maureen Long, was struck down near her home but miraculously survived.

The police stepped up their enquiries. Three hundred and four officers were assigned to the case. And to hear them, veteran detective George Oldfield, Assistant Chief Constable (Crime), came out from behind his desk at administrative HQ in Wakefield.

The next time the Ripper struck he changed his location and killing pattern, but left a vital clue.

On 1 October 1977, Jean Bernadette Jordan, was picked up near her home in Moss Side, Manchester and driven by her murderer to the Southern Cemetery two miles away. She demanded £5 in advance and was paid with a crisp new note, which she stored in her purse.

As she climbed from the Ripper's car on to allotment land adjoining the large cemetery, Mrs Jordan was knocked to the ground with a hammer blow and beaten eleven times more. Then she was pulled into a clump of bushes. Disturbed by a car, the killer then fled.

The £5 note had been given to Sutcliffe in his wage packet two days before the attack. He realized that it might be a valuable clue, so eight days later returned to the scene. He searched in vain for the handbag, then attacked the decaying body with a shard of glass.

Below: *Police search the alley where the body of Barbara Leach was discovered.*

Bottom: *Police search for clues in their hunt for the Yorkshire Ripper.*

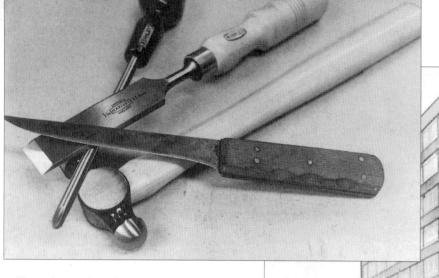

Two days after the second attack, Mrs Jordan's remains were discovered along with the missing handbag which had fallen among the bushes. The £5 note, serial number AW51 121565, was traced to the wage packets of the road haulage firm T. and W. H. Clark. One of their drivers was Peter Sutcliffe, who had worked there since October 1976.

LIVING VICTIMS

Detectives visited Sutcliffe at his home. He seemed a steady, quiet man, and the officers left, satisfied that he was not the Ripper.

But had they had time and reason to do so, they would have discovered from old Bradford City Police files that Peter Sutcliffe had once been questioned by police regarding an attack back in August 1969. This first attack was not quite motiveless. Earlier that summer he had suspected his girlfriend Sonia of seeing another man. To 'get even', he had approached a Bradford prostitute, but had been unable to maintain an erection. The woman had laughed at him, taken his £10, and got her pimp to chase him away.

In August he had seen her in the St Paul's red light district, crept after her, and hit her violently on the back of the head with a stone in a sock. The woman had noted the number of his van, and Sutcliffe had been traced. But because he had no record, he had been let off with a caution.

Since then he had left five women damaged but alive. Each of these living victims had tried to describe their attacker. One described him as thirtyish,

Above left: *Peter Sutcliffe's murder weapons could have been bought at any local hardware store.*

Above: *The bus stop at Leeds' Arndale Shopping Centre where Jacqueline Hill was accosted and murdered by the Yorkshire Ripper.*

about 5 ft 10 ins tall, and bearded. Another had described him accurately as having a black, crinkly beard.

On the evening of 21 January 1978, a twenty-two-year-old 'career' prostitute named Yvonne Pearson was seen in Bradford, climbing into a car driven by a man described as having a dark beard and black, piercing eyes - it was Sutcliffe. He took her to waste ground in Arthington Street, killed her with a club hammer and jumped on her chest until her ribs cracked. He then piled an old abandoned horsehair sofa on top of her. About a month later, when the body remained undiscovered, Sutcliffe returned and placed a current copy of

The Daily Mirror under one of her mouldering arms. Between this killing and the newspaper incident he had also paid a visit to Huddersfield.

On the snowy night of Tuesday, 31 January 1978, Sutcliffe picked up Helen Rytka. They went into a timber yard under railway arches near the centre of the town and, uncharacteristically, Sutcliffe managed to have intercourse with her before killing her in his usual fashion.

Immediately after this murder, the police were optimistic. Helen's abduction had taken place in the early evening on a busy street. But despite tracing a hundred passers by, and with all but three cars and one man eliminated, there was no real result.

The police were convinced that the Ripper lived in the locality of Leeds or Bradford, but they little realized that, by the end of 1978, they had interviewed him no fewer than four times. Apart from two visits concerning the £5 note clue, they had called at his home because routine checks had turned up Sutcliffe's car registration in red light areas. They also called to check on tyre tracks to compare them with some found near the scene of Irene Richardson's murder.

But they did not check two vital clues they knew about the Ripper against Sutcliffe. The Ripper was a B secretor – a rare blood type. And he took size seven boots – very small for a man.

On the night of 16 May 1978, two months after Yvonne Pearson's body was found, Sutcliffe killed Vera Millward, a forty-one-year-old prostitute. He then waited eleven months before he killed again. His next victim was nineteen-year-old Josephine Whittaker, a clerk in the Halifax Building Society headquarters. She was attacked and killed with sickeningly familiar ferocity.

TAUNTS AND HOAXES

Between Josephine's death and September of the same year there was another lull. This time it was filled by a brutal hoax which almost certainly cost three women their lives.

Since March 1978 George Oldfield had received two letters supposedly

Above: *Peter and Sonia Sutcliffe's house in Garden Lane, Heston, Bradford.*

OBSESSED WITH THE 'SUNDERLAND CONNECTION', THE POLICE DISREGARDED ONE OFFICER'S DEEP SUSPICIONS OF SUTCLIFFE

Left: *Police dig up Peter Sutcliffe's garden shortly after his arrest on suspicion of being the Yorkshire Ripper.*

from the Ripper. Shortly before the Whittaker murder a third letter came, mentioning Vera Millward's death. All three letters were postmarked from Sunderland. On the third, traces of engineering oil, similar to traces found on Josephine Whittaker's body, were discovered. This seemed to confirm that the letters were written by the Ripper.

When, on 18 June 1979, a tape recording addressed in the same handwriting as the letters was received, West Yorkshire police were convinced that this was their man. The tape, a taunting message to Oldfield, was in a broad Geordie accent. Therefore, the West Yorkshire police became convinced that anyone without a Geordie accent could be eliminated from their enquiry. This, of course, put Sutcliffe temporarily in the clear.

In July Sutcliffe was visited by Detective Constable Laptew, who had noticed that his car had been spotted in one red light area on thirty-six separate occasions. Laptew was deeply suspicious of Sutcliffe but he went unheeded by his superiors who were convinced their killer was a Geordie. As a result, Sutcliffe went on to kill three more times.

On 1 September 1979 Sutcliffe ambushed and killed a social sciences student named Barbara Leach.

On 18 August 1980 his victim was forty-seven-year-old civil servant Margaret Walls. Because she had been bludgeoned and strangled, but not mutilated further, the Ripper Squad were reluctant to add her to their list of victims. But there was no question of the authenticity of his thirteenth and final slaying.

Below: *There was tight security as a crowd assembled to watch the arrival of Peter Sutcliffe at Dewsbury Magistrates' Court.*

Left: *Police help Sonia Sutcliffe as she enters Dewsbury Court for her husband's hearing.*

SUTCLIFFE CLAIMED THAT A VOICE IN A GRAVEYARD HAD ORDERED HIM TO GO OUT AND KILL PROSTITUTES

Below: *Peter Sutcliffe after being attacked in prison.*

Twenty-year-old Jacqueline Hill, a language student at Leeds University, was walking home when she was dragged by Sutcliffe on to waste land and savaged with a hammer, a knife and a screwdriver. This brutal death caused a backlash of frustration among the public and police.

The Home Office set up a 'super squad' of four outside detectives and a forensic scientist. The idea was that this team should review the evidence. They did make some progress, but eventually, it was by chance that Peter Sutcliffe was caught. On 2 January 1981, two police officers were cruising along Melbourne Avenue, Sheffield – a haunt of prostitutes – when they saw a girl getting into a Rover V8 3500. They stopped the driver, a short, bearded man, who gave his name as Peter Williams. It was discovered that his number plates were false and had been stolen from that town.

The bushes in Melbourne Avenue were searched, and officers found a ball-pen hammer and a knife, which eventually were to be matched to the Ripper's crimes. Then Sutcliffe finally confessed to the Dewsbury police. 'I'm glad it's all over. I would have killed that girl if I hadn't been caught.'

What made him do it? Some experts argued that he was a paranoid schizophrenic who had little control over the delusions and impulses that haunted him, while one of the Home Office pathologists who worked on the case echoed the thoughts of the general public: 'He was quite simply a wilfully evil bastard.'

While awaiting trial in Armley gaol, Leeds, Sutcliffe was overheard by a warder planning with his wife Sonia that he would fake 'madness' and 'be out in ten years'. As it was, his plot failed. He was sent to Parkhurst maximum security prison on the Isle of Wight.

Peter Sutcliffe's mental condition did begin to deteriorate, and in March 1984 he was moved to Ward One of Somerset House, Broadmoor Institution for the Criminally Insane, where he remains.

HAROLD SHIPMAN
Doctor Death

Until recently Britain's worst serial killer was Victorian serial poisoner, Mary Ann Cotton, who murdered an estimated 21 people in the 1870s. Now that dubious distinction is claimed by Dr. Harold Shipman.

Dr Shipman ran a one-man practice in Hyde in the north of England. Most of Harold Shipman's patients were elderly women, living alone and vulnerable. They adored their doctor, Harold 'Fred' Shipman, and even when their contemporaries began dying in unusually high numbers, patients remained loyal to the murderous M.D. It seemed that as long as he spared them, his victims loved their doctor – to death.

A KILLER'S CHILDHOOD

Harold Frederick Shipman was born into a working class family on June 14, 1946 and was known as Fred or Freddy. His childhood, however, was far from normal. He always kept a distance between himself and his contemporaries – mainly due to the influence of his mother, Vera. The reason for this distance was to become clear in later years.

It was Vera who decided who Harold could play with, and when. For some reason she wanted to distinguish him from the other boys – he was the one who always wore a tie when the others were allowed to dress more casually. His sister Pauline was seven years older, his brother Clive, four years his junior, but in his mother's eyes, Harold

'VERA WAS FRIENDLY ENOUGH, BUT SHE REALLY DID SEE HER FAMILY AS SUPERIOR TO THE REST OF US. NOT ONLY THAT, YOU COULD TELL HAROLD (FREDDY) WAS HER FAVOURITE — THE ONE SHE SAW AS THE MOST PROMISING OF HER THREE CHILDREN.'

was the one she held the most hope for.

Shipman was comparatively bright in his early school years, but rather mediocre when he reached upper school level. Nonetheless, he was a plodder determined to succeed, even down to re-sitting his entrance examinations for medical school.

Funnily enough, he had every opportunity to be part of the group – he was an accomplished athlete on the football field and the running track. In spite of this, his belief in his superiority appears to have prevented him from forming any meaningful friendships.

There was something else that isolated him from the group – his beloved mother had terminal lung cancer. As her condition deteriorated, Harold willingly played a major supportive role.

WATCHING VERA DIE

Shipman's behaviour in his mother's final months closely paralleled that of Shipman the serial killer. Every day after classes, he would hurry home, make Vera a cup of tea and chat with

Above: *Dr Shipman's surgery in Hyde, Greater Manchester*

her. She found great solace in his company and always eagerly awaited his return. This is probably where Shipman learned the endearing bedside manner he would later adopt in his practice as a family physician. Towards the end, Vera experienced severe pain, but, because pumps to self-administer painkillers did not exist at that time, Vera's sole relief from the agony of cancer came with the family physician.

No doubt young Harold watched in fascination as his mother's distress miraculously subsided whenever the family doctor injected her with morphine. Ms. Shipman grew thinner and frailer day by day, until on June 21, 1963, the cancer claimed her life. Harold felt a tremendous sense of loss following his mother's death. After all, she was the one who made him feel special, different from the rest. Her passing also left him with an indelible image – the patient with a cup of tea nearby, finding sweet relief in morphine.

This must have made a great impact on the 17-year-old, as it was a scene he would recreate hundreds of times in the future once he became a doctor – with no regard for human life or feeling.

HAROLD THE STUDENT

Two years after his mother died, Harold Shipman was finally admitted to Leeds University medical school. Getting in had been a struggle – he'd had to re-write the exams he'd failed first time around. His grades, however, were sufficient enough for him to collect a degree and serve his mandatory hospital internship.

It is surprising to learn that so many of his teachers and fellow students can barely remember Shipman. Those who do remember claim that he looked down on them and seemed bemused by the way most young men behaved. 'It was as if he tolerated us. If someone told a joke he would smile patiently, but Fred never wanted to join in. It

> HE WAS OFTEN UNNECESSARILY RUDE AND MADE SOME OF HIS COLLEAGUES FEEL 'STUPID' – A WORD HE FREQUENTLY USED TO DESCRIBE ANYONE HE DIDN'T LIKE. HE WAS CONFRONTATIONAL AND COMBATIVE WITH MANY PEOPLE, TO THE POINT WHERE HE BELITTLED AND EMBARRASSED THEM. NOT YET THIRTY, SHIPMAN HAD BECOME A CONTROL FREAK.

seems funny, because I later heard he'd been a good athlete, so you'd have thought he'd be more of a team player.' He was simply remembered as a loner. The one place his personality changed, however, was the football field. Here, he unleashed his aggression and his dedication to win was intense.

Shipman finally found companionship in a girl, Primrose, who was three years his junior. He married her when he was only nineteen years old.

Above: *Primrose, Shipman's wife.*

Primrose's background was similar to Fred's, whereby her mother restricted her friendships and controlled her activities. Being rather a plain girl, Primrose was delighted to have finally found a boyfriend. Shipman married her when she was only seventeen and 5 months pregnant.

By 1974 he was a father of two and had joined a medical practice in the Yorkshire town of Todmorden. At this stage in his life Fred seemed to undergo a transformation. He became an outgoing, respected member of the community in the eyes of his fellow medics and patients.

But the staff in the medical offices where he worked saw a different side of the young practitioner. He had a way of getting things done his way – even with the more experienced doctors in the practice.

ADDICTION

His career in Todmorden came to a sudden halt when he started having blackouts. His partners were devastated when he gave them the reason – epilepsy. He used this faulty diagnosis as a cover-up. The truth soon came to the surface, when the practice receptionist Marjorie Walker came across some disturbing entries in a druggist's controlled narcotics ledger. These records showed how Shipman had been prescribing large and frequent amounts of pethidine in the names of several of his patients, when in fact the pethidine had found its way into the doctor's very own veins.

Not only that, he'd also written numerous prescriptions for the drug on behalf of the practice. Although this was not unusual because drugs were kept for emergencies, the prescribed amounts were excessive.

Following the discovery of Shipman's over-prescribing, an investigation by the practice uncovered the fact that many patients on the prescription list had neither required nor received the drug.

When confronted in a staff meeting, Shipman's way of dealing with the problem was to provide an insight into his true personality. Realizing his

SHIPMAN WAS CHALLENGED IN A STAFF MEETING. THEY PUT BEFORE HIM EVIDENCE THAT HE HAD BEEN PRESCRIBING PETHIDINE TO PATIENTS, THAT THEY'D NEVER RECEIVED THE PETHIDINE, AND IN FACT THE PETHIDINE HAD FOUND ITS WAY INTO HIS VERY OWN VEINS.

career was on the line, he first begged for a second chance.

When this request was denied, he became furious and stormed out, threw his medical bag to the ground and threatened to resign. The partners were dumbfounded by this violent – and seemingly uncharacteristic – behaviour.

Soon afterwards, his wife Primrose stormed into the room where his peers were discussing the best way to dismiss him. Rudely, she informed the people at the meeting that her husband would never resign, proclaiming, 'You'll have to force him out!'

And this was exactly what they had to do. They forced him out of the practice and into a drug rehabilitation centre in 1975.

Two years later, his many convictions for drug offences, prescription fraud and forgery cost him a surprisingly low fine – just over £600. Shipman's conviction for forgery is worth noting, because he was to use this skill later when faking signatures on a patently counterfeit will – that of his last victim, Katherine Grundy.

BACK TO WORK

Today, it is unlikely Harold Shipman would be allowed to handle drugs unsupervised, given his previous track record. However, within two years, he was back in business as a general practitioner in the Donneybrook Medical Centre in Hyde in the north of England. How readily he was accepted demonstrates his absolute self-confidence – and his ability to convince his peers of his sincerity. Again, he played the role of a dedicated, hardworking and community-minded doctor. He gained his patients' absolute trust and earned his colleagues' respect, but perhaps he was not watched carefully enough. In Hyde, Harold Shipman was home free – and free to kill!

A DIARY OF DEATH

Because of the nature of the Shipman case, it may never be possible to document every murder he committed, but it is estimated that he is responsible for the deaths of at least 236 patients over a 24-year period.

KATHLEEN GRUNDY, 81 (RIGHT)

A former mayoress of Hyde and the last victim, Mrs Grundy died on June 24 1998. She was found fully clothed on a settee at home. Dr Shipman killed her with a heroin overdose on a visit to take a blood sample. He has also been found guilty of forging her will and two letters to secure her £386,000 estate, as well as altering his medical records to suggest that the widow was addicted to morphine.

JEAN LILLEY, 58

Mrs Lilley was visited by Dr Shipman on the morning of her death on April 25, 1997. A neighbour became increasingly concerned about the length of time that the GP had been with Mrs Lilley, who was suffering from a cold. She found her friend's body within moments of the doctor leaving her home. An ambulance crew later said Mrs Lilley had been dead for some time, killed by a lethal dose of morphine. She was the only one of the 15 victims to have been married at the time of her death. Shipman contacted her husband by mobile phone to tell him his wife had died.

MARIE WEST, 81

On March 6, 1995, Harold Shipman injected Mrs West, his first victim, with a fatal dose of diamorphine (the medical term for heroine), unaware that her friend was in the next room. Shipman first told Mrs West's son that she had died of a massive stroke, then said it was a heart attack. Mrs West ran a clothes shop in Hyde, a suburb of Manchester, where all the victims came from.

IRENE TURNER, 67

Mrs Turner was found dead fully clothed on her bed by her neighbour, after Dr Shipman had called at Mrs Turner's house on July 11, 1996. Earlier, he had asked the neighbour if she could help pack Mrs Turner's belongings for hospital, but told her to wait for a few minutes before going over. Morphine was later found in Mrs Turner's body.

KATHLEEN WAGSTAFF, 81

Shipman confused Mrs Wagstaff with another patient, Anne Royal, whose daughter was married to Kathleen's son Peter, and called on the wrong person on December 9 1997 to announce she had died. Harold Shipman visited Angela Wagstaff at her workplace to tell her her mother had died, but the dead woman was in fact her mother-in-law Kathleen. After injecting Mrs Wagstaff with morphine, Shipman put her death down to heart disease.

BIANKA POMFRET, 49 (RIGHT)

Mrs Pomfret, a German divorcee, was found dead at her home by her son William on the same day she had been visited by Shipman, on December 10, 1997. Excessive morphine levels were found in her body, but the GP claimed Mrs Pomfret had complained to him of chest pains on the day of her death. He fabricated a false medical history to cover his tracks after killing her.

LIZZIE ADAMS, 77

Mrs Adams, a retired sewing machinist, died at home on February 28 1997. Dr Shipman stated that she had died of pneumonia and pretended to call for an ambulance, although no such call was made.

NORAH NUTTALL, 65

Mrs Nuttall, a widow, died on January 26 1998 after visiting Shipman's surgery for cough medicine. The GP later visited Mrs Nuttall at her home, where her son Anthony found his mother slumped in a chair.

MAUREEN WARD, 57

Mrs Ward, a former college lecturer, died on February 18 1998. Although she had been suffering from cancer, she was not ill at the time of her death. Dr Shipman claimed she died of a brain tumour.

WINIFRED MELLOR, 73

Mrs Mellor, a widow who had been Dr Shipman's patient for 18 years, was found dead on May 11 1998 in a chair at home with her left sleeve rolled up to suggest a heroin habit, following an earlier visit by Dr Shipman. He killed her with a fatal injection of morphine, and then returned to his surgery to create a false medical history to support a cause of death from coronary thrombosis.

JOAN MELIA, 73

Shipman murdered the divorcee on a visit to her home in Hyde on June 12 1998. She was found dead by a neighbour in her living room, having earlier visited Dr Shipman at his surgery about a chest infection. Shipman issued a death certificate stating she had died from pneumonia and emphysema. Her body, later exhumed, was found to contain morphine. The GP also claimed to have phoned for an ambulance, but didn't.

IVY LOMAS, 63

Dr Shipman killed Mrs Lomas at his surgery on May 29 1997 in Market Street, Hyde. He then saw three more patients before telling his receptionist that he had failed to resuscitate her. Morphine was later found in her body. She was such a regular there that Shipman told a police sergeant who was called after her death he thought her a nuisance. He joked that part of the seating area should be reserved for her and a plaque put up.

MURIEL GRIMSHAW, 76

Mrs Grimshaw was found dead at her home on July 14 1997. Shipman, who was called to examine her, said there was no need for a postmortem. Morphine was later found in her body.

MARIE QUINN, 67

Dr Shipman injected Mrs Quinn with morphine at her home on November 24 1997. Shipman claimed she had contacted him complaining of feeling unwell before her death. But her telephone bills showed no such call was made.

PAMELA HILLIER, 68

Shipman gave Mrs Hillier's family a confusing account of how she had died, on Feb 9 1998, saying she had high blood pressure, but that it wasn't high enough to give him major concern, although she had died from high blood pressure. He had in fact given her a lethal dose of morphine.

ANGELA WOODRUFF

In this macabre and still unfinished story, Shipman's former patients are grateful indeed he was finally stopped. The feeling that they could have been next will always haunt them, and there is little doubt that some owe their lives to a determined and intelligent woman named Angela Woodruff.

This lady's dogged determination to solve a mystery helped ensure that, on Monday, January 31, 2000, the jury at Preston Crown Court found Shipman guilty of murdering 15 of his patients and forging the will of Angela's beloved mother, Katherine Grundy.

Following her mother's burial Ms. Woodruff returned to her home, where she received a troubling phone call from solicitors. They claimed to have a copy of Ms. Grundy's will.

A solicitor herself, Angela's own firm had always handled her mother's affairs, in fact her firm held the original document lodged in 1986. The moment she saw the badly typed, poorly worded paper, Angela Woodruff knew it was a fake. It left £386,000 to Dr Shipman.

It was at this time that Angela went to her local police. Her investigation results ultimately reached Detective Superintendent Bernard Postles. His own investigation convinced him Angela Woodruff's conclusions were accurate.

THE TRIAL BEGINS

To get solid proof of Kathleen Grundy's murder, a post mortem was required which, in turn, required an exhumation order from the coroner. By the time the trial had begun, Det. Supt Postles' team would be uncomfortably familiar with the process. Of the fifteen killed, nine were buried and six cremated. Katherine Grundy's was the first grave opened. Her body was the first of the ongoing post mortems. Her tissue and hair samples were sent to different labs for analysis, and the wait for results began.

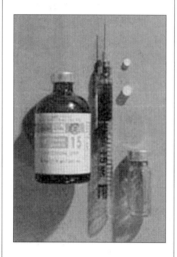

IT WAS DISCOVERED THAT THE MORPHINE LEVELS IN THE DEAD WOMAN'S BODY WOULD UNDOUBTEDLY HAVE BEEN THE CAUSE OF DEATH.

At the same time, police raided the doctor's home and offices. It was timed so that Shipman had no chance of learning a body had been exhumed for a post mortem. Police had to be certain no evidence could be destroyed or concealed before their search. When the police arrived, Shipman showed no surprise; his approach was one of arrogance and contempt as the search warrant was read out.

One item crucial to police investigations was the typewriter used to type the bogus will. Shipman produced an old Brother manual portable, telling an improbable tale of how Ms Grundy sometimes borrowed it. This unbelievable story was to go against Shipman – especially when forensic scientists confirmed it was the machine used to type the counterfeit will and other such fraudulent documents.

The search of his house also yielded medical records, some mysterious jewellery and a surprise. The Shipman home was littered with filthy clothes, old newspapers and, for a doctor's home, it was nothing short of unsanitary. But an even bigger surprise was due.

When toxicologist Julie Evans filed her report on the cause of Ms Grundy's death, Det. Supt Postles was astounded. It was discovered that the morphine level in the dead woman's body would undoubtedly have been the cause of death. Not only that, her death would have occurred within three hours of having received the fatal overdose.

Shipman would claim later that the stylish and conservative old lady was a junkie. Even today psychologists speculate on the possibility that he wanted to be caught. Otherwise, why would he hand them the typewriter and use a drug so easily traced back to him? Others believe he saw himself as invincible, believing that, as a doctor, his word would never be questioned.

The detective realized the case went far beyond one death, and the scope of the investigation was broadened immediately.

THE VERDICT AND SENTENCE

The outcome of all the tests carried out was consistent. In case after case, it was proved that the victims had not died from old age or natural disease. Typically, morphine toxicity was the cause of death.

It took the judge, Mr. Justice Forbes, two weeks to meticulously dissect the evidence heard by the jury. He urged caution, noting that no witness had actually seen Shipman kill, and he also urged the jurors to use common sense in arriving at their verdict.

At 4:43 pm on Monday January 31, 2000, the foreman declared all the jury's verdicts were unanimous – they found Shipman GUILTY on 15 counts of murder and one of forgery.

THE SHIPMAN LETTERS WERE WRITTEN BETWEEN SEPTEMBER 1998 WHEN HE WAS FIRST ON REMAND, AND JANUARY 2000 WHEN HE KNEW HIS TRIAL DEFENCE WAS DOOMED – THESE INTIMATE LETTERS ARE THE ONLY INSIGHT TO THE TRUE THOUGHTS OF DOCTOR DEATH.

Judge Justice Forbes presided in Shipman's trial .

The disgraced doctor stood motion-less showing no sign of emotion as he heard the jurors' verdicts read. Wearing black, Shipman's wife, Primrose, also remained impassive. Her boys – one beside her and the other seated behind – looked down and seemed to visibly shrink on hearing the results.

In the public gallery, some gasped as Shipman's previous forgeries were described. The defence counsel asked that sentence be passed immediately.

The judge passed fifteen life sentences for the murders and a four-year sentence for forgery.

Then the Judge broke with the tradition that usually involves writing to the Home Secretary about his recommendations on length of the sentence:

> 'In the ordinary way, I would not do this in open court, but in your case I am satisfied justice de-mands that I make my views known at the conclusion of this trial . . . My recommendation will be that you spend the remainder of your days in prison.'

Fifteen murders, a mere fraction of the suspected death toll, had been dealt with and the fifty-seven day trial was over. But there was one last life for Shipman to take.

At 6.20 a.m. on Tuesday January 13, 2004, Harold Shipman was found hanging from the window bars in his cell in Wakefield Prison by a ligature made of bed sheets. Staff at the prison tried to revive him but he was pronounced dead at 8.10 a.m.

As Shipman died before his 60th birthday, his widow, Primrose, will receive a pension of £10,000 per year, and a tax-free lump sum reported to be in excess of £100,000. Had he died after 60, the pension would have been halved, with no additional sum. This, it is believed, is the reason for his suicide.

Within hours of his suicide, the word "justice" had been graffitied 12 times across his former Hyde surgery.

IAN HUNTLEY
Child Killer

The mother of Holly Wells could not have known that when she took the picture of her 10 year-old daughter with best friend Jessica Chapman at just after 5 p.m. on Sunday, August 4 2002, in their beloved Manchester United football shirts, it would be a photo which would dominate front pages of both national and international newspapers for weeks to come – used first in the search for two missing girls and then in the hunt for their murderer.

The truth of exactly what horror befell Jessica Chapman and Holly Wells after leaving Holly's house on that fateful day may never be completely revealed.

'TEENAGERS SCREAMING'

There were just two confirmed sightings of the girls before they simply vanished. The first, at 6.17pm, was CCTV footage, which showed them walking happily together across the car park of the Ross Peers sports centre in Soham. The second, and last, sighting was at 6.30p.m. when they were seen walking along Sand Street by somebody who knew them. A jogger claims to have heard what he believed to be 'teenagers screaming' between 10 and 11p.m. in the Warren Hill area near to Newmarket, but did not report it to the police until two days later.

The alarm was raised at 7.30 p.m. by Holly's parents when they realised that the girls were not upstairs playing, as they had originally thought. Consequently, at the break of dawn the following morning, police and volunteers began the search for the girls in Soham, and by midday, following the broadcast of a national appeal, the search was on not only in

Above: The last ever photograph of Holly Wells and Jessica Chapman alive. After the photograph was taken, they changed into trousers and set off on a walk from which they were never to return

Above: Reward posters for Holly Wells and Jessica Chapman are shown outside St. Andrew's Church in Soham, Cambridgeshire

Below: Parents of murdered Soham schoolgirls Holly Wells and Jessica Chapman, Kevin and Nicola Wells and Leslie and Sharon Chapman hold a press conference

Soham but across the country. By the end of the day, the girls' parents had attended a press conference in which they appealed for information regarding their daughters' safety and whereabouts. The police search continued into the night.

NATIONWIDE SEARCH

The girls' disappearance triggered one of the biggest police searches in British history. Hundreds of local people, friends and neighbours had joined the police in the search for the girls, and amongst the volunteers was 29 year-old Ian Huntley, the caretaker at Soham Village College, which occupied the same site as the primary school that the girls attended. He not only helped in the search, but also informed the police that he too had seen the girls on the day they went missing. He told them how the girls had come to his door, 'happy' and 'giggly', and he had watched them walk away and continue down the road. He spoke to the media and even sought out Holly Wells's father, 'Kev' as he called him, to offer his condolences.

On Tuesday August 6, the football star David Beckham joined the parents and families of the girls in appealing for Holly and Jessica to come home, and a reconstruction of the girls' last confirmed movements was filmed on Saturday August 10.

The news that everyone had been dreading came a week later, on August 17. Two naked and decomposing bodies had been found in a ditch in Lakenheath, Suffolk, approximately 10 miles from the village of Soham where the girls lived. The nation's worst fears were confirmed when the police announced that these were indeed the bodies of Holly and Jessica. The following week, the burnt remains of the clothing that the girls had been wearing when they disappeared was discovered by police in a bin in the Soham Village College.

THE CARING CARETAKER

It had very quickly become clear to the police that Ian Huntley, the Soham caretaker who had been so helpful with their enquires and who had been happy to talk to the media, was one of the last people to see the girls alive. They arrested him on the day the bodies of the two girls were found, and three days later he was charged with both of their murders. His girlfriend, Maxine Carr, a temporary teaching assistant in Holly and Jessica's class, was also arrested, although charged not in connection

Above: A cordoned off search area in Warren Hill, Suffolk. The area was investigated when a jogger claimed to have heard 'teenagers screaming' there on the night of the girls' disappearance

Left: The burnt remains of one of the red Manchester United shirts belonging to the two murdered ten year old girls which were found along with traces of Huntley's hair in the school grounds where he worked

Holly sat on the edge of the bath while he dampened a tissue to hold to her face. However, as he approached her with the tissue, he stumbled and bumped into her, causing her to fall backwards into the bath, already filled with approx 45cm of water. She banged her head as she fell which caused Jessica to begin screaming at Huntley accusing him of pushing her friend. To stop Jessica screaming, Huntley placed his hand over her mouth, where it remained until he realised that instead of simply calming the second little girl, her body was now limp and no longer supporting itself. As he let go of Jessica, her body slumped to the floor. He turned to the bath, where Holly's lifeless body lay. He checked her pulse, no longer beating, and then put his face close to Jessica's, where there was no longer breath. He said he 'panicked and froze' when he realised what had happened, unable even to attempt to revive them. His next memory of the events was being sat on the carpet in his bathroom, next to a pile of his own vomit. He knew he should call the police, he said, but also knew that they would never believe that such a tragedy had occurred when he failed to believe it himself.

He pleaded guilty to manslaughter only, but went on to concede all the other given facts of the case – that he had bundled the bodies of Holly and Jessica into his car, bending their legs to make them fit, cut the clothing from them - their red Manchester United shirts, trousers, underwear, the bra which Holly's mother had bought for her only the day before - and left the corpses to burn in a remote ditch

with the murder of the girls, but for lying to the police and perverting the course of justice in providing a false alibi for Huntley's whereabouts on the day of the murder. Both denied the charges against them.

'PANICKED AND FROZE'

The court-case which lasted over a year, made headline news nationally and worldwide, and in it, Huntley did finally admit that the girls had died in his house. However, he denied murder. Rather, he claimed that the deaths of both girls were the result of a tragic sequence of events. He claims to have been outside his house washing his dog when the girls passed by, and he noticed that Holly was suffering with a nose bleed. He therefore invited the girls into his house and took them up to his bathroom, where he intended to curb the flow of blood from Holly's nose.

'ONE DIED AS A RESULT OF MY INABILITY TO ACT AND THE OTHER DIED AS A DIRECT RESULT OF MY ACTIONS'

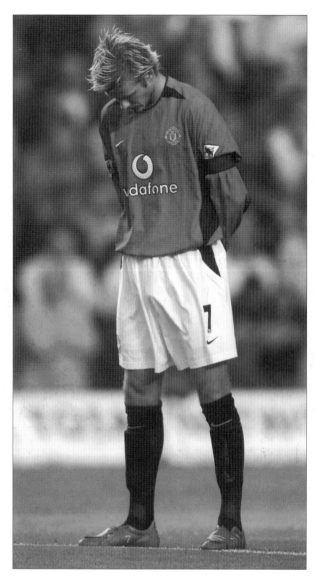

Above: Holly and Jessica's football hero, David Beckham, looks to the ground during the minute silence during the Barclaycard Premiership match between Chelsea and Manchester United in London on August 23, 2002, a tribute to the two murdered school children

Right: Flowers laid down in memory of Jessica and Holly

where the nettles grew thickly. He had then taken the girls' clothing and deposited it in a bin at Soham Village College.

Prosecutor Richard Latham supported this with forensic evidence that hairs, proven to be Huntley's, were found amongst the charred remains of the clothes in the bin, and that his fingerprints were present on the bin liner. He also presented evidence regarding Huntley's car. All four tyres on the car had been replaced the day following Jessica and Holly's disappearance. Latham claimed that this was to prevent his car being traced in any way to the girls' bodies.

Latham went on further to claim that Huntley's primary motive had been sexual. He asserts that the girls were lured into Huntley's house, possibly in the belief that Maxine Carr

was inside, and that when his advances towards one or the other had been rejected, both girls had had to die. 'They had to die in his own selfish self-interest. Each were potential witnesses - he was quite merciless.'

Huntley's version of events, that the death of the two girls had simply been the result of a tragic accident, was believed neither by the public, nor the jury who found him guilty on two counts of murder, the most serious of all the charges he could have faced, and when trial judge Justice Moses sentenced him to two life imprisonments a hushed 'yes' echoed around the courtroom. Moses told Huntley that he was '...the only person who knows how you murdered them.', and said that he displayed 'no regret' after the murders, even increasing the pain of the families by continuing to lie and deceive the police and investigators.

CATALOGUE OF OFFENCES

Information regarding Huntley's past had to be kept private during the trial in order not to influence the court, but on the conclusion of his case, a dark and disturbing catalogue of offences against children and teenagers was made public. It

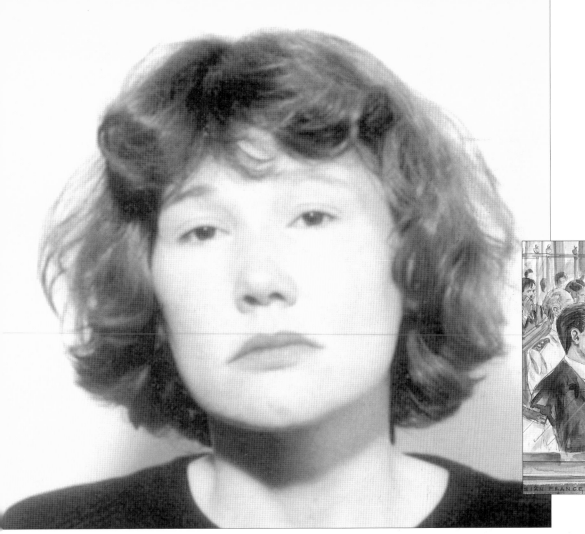

"I'M NOT GOING TO BE BLAMED FOR WHAT THAT THING IN THE BOX HAS DONE TO ME OR THOSE CHILDREN."

emerged that between the years of 1995 to 1999, Huntley was investigated by police no less than 10 times following accusations of rape, underage sex, assault on children and adults, and burglary.

Current regulations state that anybody applying to work with or around children has to undergo local police checks to ensure their suitability. Huntley's past went undetected by two police forces, Cambridgeshire and Humberside. Humberside, where the alleged offences had been reported, defended themselves by saying that the data protection act declares it unlawful to hold data concerning allegations which did not lead to a conviction. They have faced criticism from other police forces who believe this to be too strict an enforcement of the act. Perhaps aware of these regulations anyway, Huntley had changed his name when applying for the job in Soham to Ian Nixon - his mother's maiden name.

Much is still not known about what actually happened inside Huntley's house. It is reported that Huntley and Carr had cleaned the house of every DNA trace of the girls. There were no hairs, blood or saliva and not a single fingerprint. The clean-up operation had centred around the dining room, although what happened to the girls in that room has never emerged.

'LOVELY GIRLS'

Maxine Carr, although not present on the day of the girls' deaths, was living with Huntley in the house where the girls died. On that fateful Sunday, she was in fact visiting her parents in Grimsby, although told police that she had been at home with Huntley all day in order to protect him. On August 20, she was charged with lying to the police. She appeared in

Above: Court drawing by artist Sian Frances. Ian Huntley and Maxine Carr stand to hear the verdict being read out December 17, 2003 in London

Above left: Police photograph of Maxine Carr following her arrest in August 2002. She was found guilty of conspiring to pervert the course of justice, but cleared of helping an offender

court on charges of assisting an offender and perverting the course of justice. In response to the first charge, she claimed that she had no knowledge of what had actually transpired in the house, and had only lied to protect Huntley, believing him to be innocent. She was found not guilty. She was therefore, found guilty of the second, less serious, charge of perverting the course of justice and received a sentence of three and a half years imprisonment. By the time the trial had concluded though, she had already served 16 months in prison, almost half of her sentence, and was later released on probation on May 10, 2004. During the trial she spoke of Holly and Jessica as 'lovely girls', and referred to Huntley as 'that thing', saying that she would not take the blame for his actions, and had been feeling guilty for long enough believing that she could have prevented Holly and Jessica's deaths had she been in the house on the Sunday. The judge proclaimed her imminent release to be a sentence in itself, and that she would lead a terrible existence, forever looking over her shoulder.

For her involvement with Ian Huntley, Carr is now a hate figure and considered to be at such a risk from the public that she is to be issued with a new identity. Threats have already been made on her life, some claiming

Above: Queen's Council for the prosecution Richard Latham arrives at the Old Bailey on December 12, 2003 in London

HOW DID IT FEEL TO CARRY JESSICA'S DEAD BODY DOWN THE STAIRS?" HUNTLEY DID NOT REPLY. "WELL?" "NOT GOOD," SAID HUNTLEY IN A LOW VOICE

that she would be dead within a week of her release from prison. Consequently, on her release from Foxton Hall Prison in Derbyshire, Maxine Carr was moved to a secret location pending her official release.

As a result of speculation by British newspapers on whether Carr would be given plastic surgery, or sent to live abroad, an injunction was granted by London's High Court preventing any photographs of Carr, or details of her whereabouts, treatment or new life, being published. Her movements may be protected by the courts for the rest of her life. This was granted for reasons of her health and safety, and also to enable the Probation Service to supervise her and ensure that she settles back into society and doesn't re-offend.

However, documents containing full details of her release and new identity were stolen from the car of a Home Office official parked in Hampstead Heath just days before her release date. In spite of this, the Home Office confirmed that her release had

Right: Parents of Holly Wells and Jessica Chapman arrive for the first day of the murder trial. They sat together in the courtroom, remaining silent. They were commended for their strength and dignity throughout the proceedings.

not been compromised and would go ahead as planned. They stated that there was nothing in the stolen documents which could give away her new location and identity.

Ian Huntley is no safer in prison than Maxine Carr is out of it. Knocked unconscious by another inmate who is now considered a 'hero' by fellow prisoners, Huntley has reportedly become the target of a deadly 'race' between two prison gangs to murder him. Bets have been placed on which will succeed, and prison guards are on 'extra high alert' for his safety. Rumours have leaked to the prison authorities that plans are first to disfigure Huntley by throwing boiling water on him, and then to kill him. An unnamed source described Huntley as a 'scared rabbit' in prison. He had previously been rushed to hospital in a 'life-threatening condition' having taken an overdose in an attempt to take his own life.

HUNTLEY'S HOUSE OF HORROR

The house, 5 College Close, owned by the local education authority, is due to be pulled down, along with the hangar at the Soham Village College in which the burned clothing was discovered. Until recently, for legal reasons, the house could not be touched, but lawyers for Huntley have given their consent to demolition, stating that no further evidence from the house would need to be used in any appeal. Plans for the sites are to be discussed with the relatives of Jessica and Holly.

Above: Candles are lit in remembrance of Holly Wells and Jessica Chapman inside St Andrew's Church August 18, 2002 in Soham, Cambridgeshire

YOUR RIGHT TO GROW, TO MATURE AND PLAY
SO CRUELLY DENIED IN A SINISTER WAY
ATTENTIVE AND CARING, A PARENT'S DELIGHT.
BUT SO YOUNG AT HEART, NEEDING COMFORT AT NIGHT.

- First verse of a poem written and read by Kevin Wells, in a service to celebrate the girls' lives at Ely Cathedral

GRAHAM YOUNG
The Broadmoor Poisoner

Is it possible for a child to be born evil? Graham Young was a prodigy in poison, experimenting with deadly potions even before he was sixteen. And he killed his family and friends as if they were laboratory rats.

Even as a small child, Graham Young was entranced by poisons. Other people may regard such substances with alarm and caution but Graham played with them, learnt their various deadly properties and longed to use them.

Like Ian Brady, the infamous Moors Murderer, Graham Young had a lonely childhood, and in his sullen resentment of the world, turned to other outsiders in his search for role models. Dr Crippen, the wife murderer, was an idol, as was the Victorian poisoner, William Palmer. In contemplating their lives and dreadful acts, Graham Young found a kind of solace which he never got from his family.

He was born in September 1947, and his mother died when he was just three months old. He was cared for by his father's sister, Auntie Winifred, and her husband, Uncle Jack and their's was an affectionate household. But at the age of two his life changed when he was sent to live with his father, who had married a twenty-six-year-old woman called Molly. Psychologists would later say that 'the terrible coldness' that characterised Young was formed by the truama of separation from his first home. He never trusted any affection after that, believing only that it would end in pain and rejection.

Relations with his stepmother were cordial but she never lavished on him the brand of intense loving he craved. Perhaps she found it difficult, for Graham was rummaging through the chemist's rubbish bins in his search for poisons, and was reading books on Satanism by the time he was nine years old. He began wearing a swastika badge that he found at a jumble sale and refused to take it off, even for his teachers at school. Yet Graham was an exceptionally intelligent child, with a strong scientific ability. To celebrate his achievement in passing the eleven-plus examination, his father gave the boy his first chemistry set.

This gift was the key to the wonderful world of poisons that Graham longed to master. The phials and bunsen burners, the laboratory pipettes and crucibles became his toys at an age when most boys have their pockets stuffed with conkers and fudge. His private games were also more sinister than those of the normal child. Graham liked to witness the death throes of the mice that he fed with the poisons he brewed from his chemistry set. When his stepmother angrily removed a live mouse, and demanded that he stop bringing them into the house, he drew a picture of a craggy tombstone toppling over a mound, inscribed with the words: 'In Hateful Memory of Molly Young, R.I.P.' Graham made sure that the poor woman saw this nasty little drawing.

Opposite: *The child prodigy in poison, Graham Young, is led into custody.*

Below: *David Tilson, a victim who survived the poisons.*

HE NEVER TRUSTED ANY AFFECTION, BELIEVING ONLY THAT IT WOULD END IN PAIN AND REJECTION.

The youngster took to stealing chemicals from his school and he took to carrying a bottle of ether from which he would frequently take sniffs; he raided his stepmother's cosmetics cabinet to get at nail polish remover, which he used to kill a frog in one of his experiments in the effects of poison. By the time he was twelve, his teachers at the John Kelly Secondary School in Willesden knew that Graham had an unusual expertise, not only in poisons, but in his general pharmaceutical knowledge. The child knew the ingredients

of most household medicines, and was able to diagnose minor illnesses.

But medicine and its life-saving properties were not of real interest to the child boffin. He preferred poisons and their deadly effects. When he was thirteen, Graham found a book that would forever change his life. It was the story of the nineteenth-century poisoner Dr Edward Pritchard, who killed his wife and his mother with the poison antimony. Antimony, a slow working toxin, causes cramps, nausea and swellings in the victim. These symptoms have often led to an incorrect diagnoses from doctors, and this fact has, naturally, made the poison a favourite among murderers.

CHRIS HAD TO BE PUNISHED. GRAHAM BEGAN TO LACE HIS FRIEND'S SANDWICHES WITH ANTIMONY AND WATCHED THE RESULTS WITH SATISFACTION.

Left: *Graham Young was incarcerated in hospitals and prisons, but he still managed to experiment with his poisons.*

Opposite, above: *The poisoner, whose youth and ruthlessness horrified the nation, was obscured by a blanket as he was bundled into a police van.*

Opposite, below: *The sweet face of a boy but the Young family were not entirley fooled. They knew something was wrong with the child, Graham.*

MRS YOUNG SUFFERED SEVERE VOMITING ATTACKS. THEN GRAHAM'S FATHER EXPERIENCED SIMILAR SYMPTOMS, AS DID HIS AUNTIE WINIFRED.

Chemist Geoffrey Reis in High Street, Neasden, sold Graham Young the poison antimony. The boy lied about his age and claimed he was seventeen. Reis explained to the police that the boy's knowledge of poisons was so vast, and he outlined in such detail the chemical experiments in which he intended to use the restricted merchandise, that the chemist naturally assumed him to be older than a mere thirteen-year-old. And neither was Graham Young strictly truthful in describing his experiments to the chemist.

Chris Williams was one of Graham's few schoolboy friends who shared his love of chemistry. He had even invited Chris to his bedroom laboratory to share the pleasure of watching mice die in agony. But Chris Williams began hanging around with another boy, and Graham interpreted this as a persoanl rejection. Chris had to be punished. Graham began to lace his friend's sandwiches with antimony and watched the results with satisfaction. After Chris had suffered two violent vomiting attacks, his family sent him to a specialist who was unable to diagnose the problem. Throughout the early part of 1961, Graham continued to administer doses of poison to his school chum.

EPIDEMIC OF POISONING

Young took to carrying a phial of antimony around with him all the time, calling it 'my little friend'. But his stepmother found the bottle, marked with a skull and crossbones, and put a stop to her stepson's shopping trips when she herself informed the chemist, Mr Reis, of Graham's age. Thwarted but by no means defeated, Graham switched to a new supplier, and a new target. Molly Young would be punished for this.

In October and November, 1961, Mrs Young suffered severe vomiting attacks. Then Graham's father experienced similar symptoms, as did his Auntie Winifred. On one occasion, Graham spiked his own food in error, and he, too, was violently ill, but this did not deter the young poisoner. Using antimony tartrate which he bought from Edgar Davies – another chemist similarly fooled by his advanced knowledge of poisons – he moved on to his step-sister. The girl tasted something odd, and spat out her tea, accusing her mother of leaving some washing-up liquid in the cup.

Winifred was the first to be diagnosed as a poison victim when she had to be helped from a London Underground train on her way to work one morning, in the summer of 1962. Dizzy, her eyes blinded with pain and feeling very ill, she was rushed by ambulance to the Middlesex Hospital where a doctor said she was suffering from belladonna poisoning, the toxin released from the berries of the deadly nightshade

> HIS FATHER WAS INFORMED THAT HE WAS LUCKY TO BE ALIVE, BUT THAT HIS LIVER WAS PERMANENTLY DAMAGED.

father in hospital. 'Fancy not knowing how to tell the difference between antimony and arsenic poisoning!' He explained to the doctors that his father showed all the symptoms of antimony poisoning, but offered no explanation as to how the poison entered his father's system. His father was informed that he was lucky to be alive, but that his liver was permanently damaged. He was allowed home, but was back in hospital within a couple of days because Graham could not resist giving his father another dose in his morning tea.

The Young family were, by now, thoroughly alarmed by their suspicions that their own Graham might be causing their various illnesses. They did not like the way Graham seemed to brighten up and become keenly interested whenever he was discussing the finer points of poison with hospital staff. His father told Aunt Winifred to keep an eye on him, but it was to be his chemistry master at school who spotted the boy's toxic ways. The teacher went through Graham's desk at school, discovering notebooks with lurid pictures of men in their death throes, empty bottles of poison

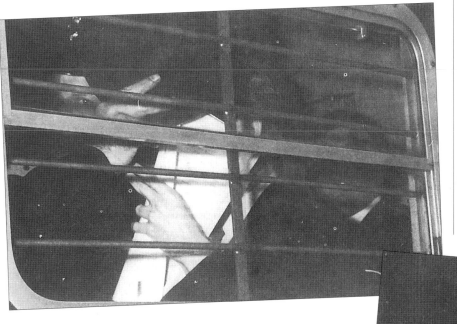

weed. Winifred believed that her nephew was to blame, but a search of his room failed to give evidence to her fears. Molly Young's health continued to decline as Graham fed her increasing doses of the antimony tartrate. Early in 1962 she died. At the age of fourteen, Graham Young had committed the perfect murder. He was arrested on suspicion of causing his stepmother's death, but he was released without charge. Molly was cremated and the evidence, the poison in her bloodstream, went with her.

Graham Young was now assured of his powers to punish those who annoyed or rejected him. Besides, he still had some unfinished business. Dad was to be fed further doses of antimony, as was his unfortunate schoolfriend who continued to suffer violent attacks of nausea, but was still alive. Fred Young collapsed and was rushed to Willesden Hospital where doctors diagnosed arsenic poisoning. 'How ridiculous!' sneered Graham when he visited his by their sides. He discovered phials of antimony tartrate alongside the drawings, plus detailed notes of what doseages of particular poisons are needed to kill an adult human being. After voicing his concerns to the school headmaster, the two teachers decided to inform the police. The police, in turn, decided to get a psychiatrist to help them trap Graham.

Posing as a careers guidance officer, the psychiatrist interviewed the boy, asking him what he would like to do when he left

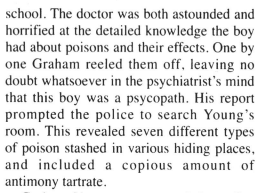

school. The doctor was both astounded and horrified at the detailed knowledge the boy had about poisons and their effects. One by one Graham reeled them off, leaving no doubt whatsoever in the psychiatrist's mind that this boy was a psycopath. His report prompted the police to search Young's room. This revealed seven different types of poison stashed in various hiding places, and included a copious amount of antimony tartrate.

Graham Young encountered the police when he came home from school. He reeked of the ether he habitually sniffed, and vehemently denied any involvement in the poisoning of his family. But Young's vanity overcame him. As he liked to brag to the doctors and the psychiatrist, showing off his knowledge of poison, so he could not resist telling the police that he was a successful poisoner. He confessed all, listing the doseages, the times and the methods he used to dispense the poison.

Left: *Jethro Batt whose evidence helped convict the mad poisoner.*

Below: *John Williams who told the court of Young's repeated attempts to kill him with poison.*

At Ashford Remand Centre he was subjected to a battery of psychiatric and psychological testing. The doctors who examined him recognised that his was a rare problem, for Young was incapable of comprehending his guilt. 'He has a distinct lack of moral sense, an idea that he is neither bound to nor governed by the rules which apply to other members in society,' was the official verdict. Indeed, Young relished telling the doctors, who were probing his warped emotional state, about his potions and how he loved his father, but that he came to view his parent as a guinea pig for experiments in poison. He told them: 'I chose my family because they were close at hand, where I could observe and note the results of my experiments.' There was no remorse, however. 'I love my antimony,' he explained. 'I love the power it gives me.'

The case of the schoolboy poisoner captured the public imagination when he came before the stern judge Mr Justice

Melford Stevenson on 6 July, 1962, at the Old Bailey. This is Britain's highest court, where half-a-century before, Graham's hero Dr Crippen, had been condemned to death.

Graham Young was charged with poisoning his father, his aunt and his school chum. He spoke only once at his trial, to plead guilty to the charges, but a statement that he made while in custody was read out. Graham told the police: 'I knew that the doses I was giving were not fatal, but I knew I was doing wrong. It grew on me like a drug habit, except it was not me who was taking the drugs. I realised how stupid I have been with these poisons. I knew this all along but I could not stop it.'

A psychiatrist, after testifying that Young was suffering from a psychopathic disorder, recommended the accused be incarcerated in Broadmoor, Britain's top security mental hospital. The judge asked whether a grim, forbidding place such as Broadmoor was the right institution for such a young boy, but after further testimony from Dr Donald Blair, a psychiatrist who had also examined Young, he – the judge – was left with little choice. Blair told the court: 'There is no doubt in my mind that this youth is, at present, a very serious danger to other people. His intense obsession and almost exclusive interest in drugs and their poisoning effect is not likely to change, and he could well repeat his cool, calm, calculating administration of these poisons at any time.'

Young was sent to Broadmoor with an instruction that he should not be released without the permission of the Home Secretary. It was not, however, the last that the world would hear of Graham Young and his potions.

POISONER BEHIND BARS

Far from being an unsuitable place for Graham, Broadmoor was actually a home-from-home for him. The institute is a hospital, after all, and the young poisoner was surrounded by all the medicines and drugs and poisons that he could wish for. He enjoyed lecturing the staff on toxins, and often gave advice to nurses on drugs when no doctors were on hand. Suspicion, however, fell upon him when a fellow inmate, twenty-three-year-old double-murderer John Berridge, died of cyanide

poisoning. But Graham was never charged with his murder, although he spent many hours explaining to other inmates how the poison could be extracted from the leaves of the laurel bushes which grew in the hospital grounds.

Young's room in Broadmoor became a shrine to Nazism, heavily decorated with swastikas. He even grew a toothbrush moustache and combed his hair in a fashion that imitated that of Adolf Hitler. He managed to secure a 'green card' – the special pass allowing him to freely roam the hospital wards and gardens. The pass was issued by the psychiatric staff in contradiction to the wishes and advice of the day-to-day nursing staff. The card gave Young the opportunity to collect leaves and plants that contained poisonous materials, and to steal chemicals. The nursing staff often found jars of poison, not on the shelves where they were supposed to be, but in odd places. Young owned up to hiding some of these, but not all. Inexplicable outbreaks of stomach aches and cramps were endured by both staff and

Above: *Winifred Young, Graham's sister, and his aunt who listened intently to the court evidence against him.*

'THERE IS NO DOUBT IN MY MIND THAT THIS YOUTH IS, AT PRESENT, A VERY SERIOUS DANGER TO OTHER PEOPLE.'

patients; hindsight dictates that Young had been busy dispensing his potions freely-round the large prison hospital.

With the support of two senior doctors who did not want to see him institution-alised for the rest of his life, Graham was able to convince the parole board to free him for Christmas in 1970. He spent it with his Auntie Win, but his return to Broadmoor after the holidays made him more resentful than ever. He wrote a note that nursing staff found, saying: 'When I get out of here I intend to kill one person for every year I have spent inside.'

Nursing staff say they heard him boasting, when he thought no staff were listening, how he wanted to be the most infamous poisoner since Crippen. And the note he wrote remained on their files. Yet Graham Young was released after nine years. At the age of twenty-three he returned to his forgiving Auntie Winifred at her home in Hemel Hempstead, Hertfordshire, before moving on to a hostel in Chippenham where he began his new life.

ANOTHER FRIEND POISONED

Within weeks he was up to his old tricks again. A keen amateur footballer called Trevor Sparkes, who was with Young at a training centre, suffered cramps and pain over a six-month period, and was so debili-tated by the mysterious 'illness' that he would never play football again. Sparkes would testify that he and Young enjoyed a friendship, and it never occurred to the

Above: *Broadmoor, the mental hospital where Young was confined.*
Below: *Frederick Young, the father who nearly died.*

footballer that he was being systematically poisoned by his friend.

In April, 1971, Graham saw an advertisement, offering employment for a storeman with the John Hadland Company of Bovingdon, in Hertfordshire. Hadland's was a well-established family firm that manufactured high grade optical and photographic equipment. Graham impressed Managing Director, Godfrey Foster, at the interview, and explained that his long break from regular employment was due to a nervous breakdown. Foster checked up with the training centre and also Broadmoor, and he received such glowing references as to the young man's abilities and recovery that he offered him the job without hesitation..

On Monday 10 May, 1971, Graham Young arrived at Hadlands. The company thought they were getting a storeman. In reality, they had hired an angel of death. Young rented a bedsitter, and the cupboards and shelves were soon filled with a collec-

tion of poisons. At work he was regarded as a quiet, remote young man unless the conversation turned to politics or chemistry when he became belligerent and articulate. His best friend at work was forty-one-year-old Ron Hewitt whose job he was taking.

inquest on his body because doctors diagnosed his illness as bronchial-pneumonia linked to polyneuritis.

In September, after a relatively pain-free summer for the staff at Hadlands, because

Below: *Frederick Young, Graham's father and the long-suffering Aunt Winnie. Graham tried to poison both of them.*

old Ron Hewitt whose job he was taking. Ron stayed on to show the new man the ropes and introduced him to the other hands in the plant. Many showed great kindness to Young, lending him money and giving him cigarettes when he had none. Young repaid their warmth by rushing to serve them from the morning tea trolley.

On Thursday 3 June, less than a month after Graham started work, Bob Egle, fifty-nine, who worked as storeroom boss, was taken ill with diarrhoea, cramps and nausea. Next, Ron Hewitt fell violently ill, suffering the same symptoms but with burning sensations at the back of his throat. Workers at Hadlands called the mystery pains 'the bug'. In fact, the symptoms were caused by doses of Thallium, an extremely toxic poison. Young bought the poison from chemists in London, and then laced his workmates' tea with the deadly, but tasteless and odourless chemical. On Wednesday, 7 July, Bob Egle died. His was a horrible, painful death, yet there was no

Young was often absent from work, Fred Biggs, a part-time worker, died after suffering agonising cramps and pains over a twenty-day period. Young feigned sympathy for him, as he had for his other victims. 'Poor old Fred,' he said to colleague, Diana Smart. 'It's terrible. I wonder what went wrong with him. I was very fond of Fred.' Four other workers fell victim to awful illnesses, two of them losing all their hair, followed by severe cases of depression.

The company became so concerned by the poor health of their workforce, that they called in a local doctor, Iain Anderson, to check the employees, but he was unable to determine the source of the 'bug'. But then Anderson talked to Graham Young, who unable to suppress his vanity, reeled off mind-numbing statistics about poisons and their effects and Anderson's amazement turned to suspicion. He consulted the company management, who called Scotland Yard. The police ran a background check on

IT WAS A RELATIVELY PAIN-FREE SUMMER FOR THE STAFF AT HADLANDS BECAUSE YOUNG WAS OFTEN ABSENT FROM WORK.

FOUR OTHER WORKERS FELL VICTIM TO AWFUL ILLNESSES, TWO OF THEM LOSING ALL THEIR HAIR, FOLLOWED BY SEVERE CASES OF DEPRESSION.

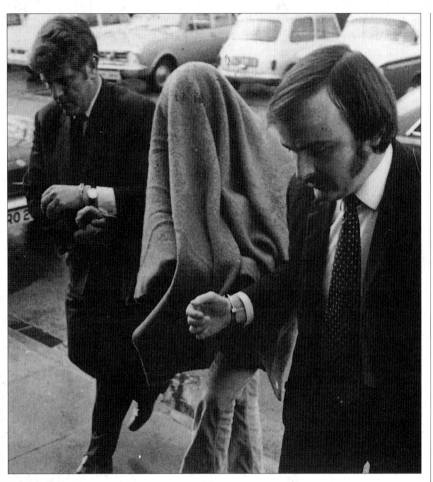

Above: *Graham Young taken into court by law officers. He was given a long sentence, but died in prison – not of self-administered poison, but a heart attack.*

this confession could put him in jail for life. But the prisoner said: 'You have to prove that I did it.' He intended to withdraw his statement in court, which in due course he did.

On 3 December, Graham Young was charged with murdering Egle after the analysis of the ashes of his cremated corpse showed traces of Thallium in them. He pleaded Not Guilty. He was also charged with the murder of Fred Biggs and the attempted murders of two others and of further administering poison to two others.

In prison , Young enquired of his guards whether Madame Tussaud's waxworks in London were planning to put his effigy next to those of his heroes, Hitler and the poisoner, Palmer. He threatened to kill himself in the dock of the court if he were found Guilty. But there were no theatricals from the prisoner when he was convicted on all charges by a jury that took less than an hour to deliberate on the evidence.After a brief chat with his family, he was taken away to begin a life sentence in July 1972.

A DEADLY FUNGUS

Young was not sent back to Broadmoor but, initially, was sent to Wormwood Scrubs, then, to the top security Park Lane Mental Hospital near Liverpool. He was in this institution for two years before officials realised he had lost none of his madness. In 1990, they discovered that Graham had grown, in the prison grounds, a deadly fungus that he mixed with his own excrement to concoct a deadly toxin.

He was transferred to the top security prison of Parkhurst on the Isle of Wight where he was found dead in his cell on 2 August 1990. At first, officials thought that he had killed himself with one of his own poisons, but a post mortem revealed that a heart attack had been cause of death.

There were few people to weep for him, his sister, also called Winifred, felt sad for him. She said that he craved publicity and infamy, and he certainly achieved these ambitions. But she said that he was depressive and lonely. When she suggested he ease his loneliness by going to social clubs or dances, he replied; 'Nothing like that can help me, I'm afraid. You see, there is this terrible coldness inside of me...'

all company employees, while forensic scientists from the government research station at Aldermaston were asked to analyse samples taken from the poorly members of staff. The scientists proved that Thallium had caused the deaths and the illnesses among the staff at Hadlands. Graham Young was arrested at his father's house, and as he was led away, asked the police: 'Which ones are they doing me for, then?'

However, in custody Young claimed that he was innocent, despite the fact that a phial of Thallium was found in his jacket pocket, and a list of six names of Hadland's employees was found in his bedsitter. The list was significant: it included the two men who had died, and the four stricken with horrible illnesses. But Young could not resist for long his need to boast.

He detailed his first murder, that of his stepmother, and explained why he decided to poison his workmates. Graham Young said: 'I suppose I had ceased to see them as people – or, more correctly, a part of me had. They became guinea pigs.' Detective Chief Superintendent Harvey Young, in charge of the case, warned Graham that

WAR CRIMES

POL POT
The Murder Machine

A gentle nation, ancient in its culture, pious in its faith, was cruelly dismembered by a Marxist fanatic. Pol Pot turned Cambodia into a killing field while the world turned its back on this lost nation.

Above: *The grinning face of evil – Pol Pot is a study in tyranny and murder. He turned his gentle land into a vast 'killing field'.*

AS MANY AS THREE MILLION PEOPLE MAY HAVE PERISHED DURING POL POT'S REGIME IN CAMBODIA.

Imagine a government that comes to power, then declares that money is banned. Not only money, but the forces which provide money – commerce, industry, banking – are also proscribed. The new government decrees that society will become agrarian again, just like it had been in the Middle Ages. Great cities and towns will be de-populated and the people will be moved to the countryside, where they will live and work raising crops and cattle. But families will not be allowed to stay together. The government, in its infinite wisdom, realises that children must not be influenced by outdated and archaic bourgois thoughts passed down by their parents. So they are taken away and brought up as the vanguard of the regime, imbued with and steeped in the philosophy of the new order. No messing about with books until they are in the late teens – there is no need for books anymore, so they are burned – and children from the age of seven will begin working for the state.

For the new agrarian class, there are eighteen-hour days, back-breaking work, followed by 're-education' in Marxist-Leninist thought from their new masters. Anyone who dissents, or who shows signs of 'regression' to the old ways is not allowed to live – nor are intellectuals, teachers and college professors; nor those people who are literate because they might read thoughts which are not Marxist-Leninist, and spread a poisonous philosophy among the re-educated workers in the fields. Priests, with their outmoded theology, politicians of any hue other than that of the ruling party and those who made fortunes under previous governments are no longer needed: they too are eliminated. There is no trade, there are no telephones, there are no churches or temples, here are no bicycles, birthday parties, marriages, anniversaries, love or kindness. At best, there is work for the state – torture, degradation and at worst, death.

This nightmare scenario was not a figment of some science fiction writer's imagination. It became a terrible reality in Cambodia, where leader Pol Pot turned the clock back and pushed civilisation out, hoping to find his own warped vision of a classless society. His 'killing fields' were littered with the corpses of those who did not fit into the new world that his brutal

subordinates were shaping. As many as three million people may have perished during Pol Pot's regime in Cambodia – the same number of unfortunates killed in the gas chambers of the Auschwitz death factory run by the Nazis in the Second World War. Life under Pol Pot was intolerable and Cambodians were forced to tragically re-christen their South-East Asian country. They gave it the macabre name of the Land of the Walking Dead.

The Cambodian tragedy was a legacy of the Vietnam War that first marked the end of French colonialism before escalating into the conflict against the Americans. Fifty-three thousand Cambodians were slain on the fields of battle. Between 1969 and 1973 American B-52 aircraft carpet-bombed huge tracts of Cambodia, dropping as many tons of high-explosive on the tiny land as had fallen on Germany in the last two years of the Second World War. The Viet Cong fighters in Vietnam used its neighbour's lush jungles as encampments

Above: *Leading a column of his faithful followers, Pol Pot treks through the Cambodian jungle.*

HE ORDERED THE ABOLI-
TION OF ALL MARKETS,
THE DESTRUCTION OF
CHURCHES AND THE
PERSECUTION OF ALL
RELIGIOUS ORDERS.

and staging posts for operations against the Americans, and these hideouts were the targets of the war planes.

Prince Norodom Sihanouk, ruler of Cambodia and heir to its great religious and cultural traditions, renounced his royal title ten years before the onset of the Vietnam War, but remained the head of his country. He tried to guide his country along a path of neutrality, a delicate balancing act for a country surrounded by warring states and conflicting ideologies. He had been crowned King of Cambodia, a French protectorate, in 1941, but abdicated in 1955. However, he returned, after free and fair elections, as head of state.

Between 1966 and 1969, as the Vietnam War escalated in intensity, he upset policy-makers in Washington by ignoring the arms smuggling and the Vietnamese guerilla camps in the jungles of Cambodia. At the same time, he was only mildly critical of the punishing air raids being launched by America. On 18 March, 1970, while he was in Moscow, his prime minister, General Lon Nol, with the backing of the White House, staged a coup, after which he changed the name of Cambodia back to its ancient title, Khmer. The Khmer Republic was recognised by the United States, which, however, one month later, chose to launch an invasion against the newly-named land. Sihanouk went into exile in Peking... and here the ex-king chose to form an alliance with the devil himself.

Not much is known about Pol Pot, the man with the fat face and sparkling eyes, the man with the face of an avuncular old grandfather and the heart of a murderous tyrant. He was the monster with whom

Sihanouk threw in his lot, swearing with this Communist guerilla chief that they would mould their forces into a single entity with the aim of destroying American forces. Pot, brought up by a peasant family in the Kampong Thom province of the country, had been educated at a Buddhist monastery where, for two years, he lived as a monk. In the 1950s he won a scholarship to study electronics in Paris where, like so many other students of the time, he became involved in left-wing causes. Here he heard about – although it is unclear whether they actually met – another Cambodian student, Khieu Samphan, a political science student whose controversial but exhilarating plans for an 'agrarian revolution' were to inspire the ambitions of the peasant, Pol Pot.

Above: *Government troops surround refugees during the Khmer Rouge fighting.*

Top: *Refugees flee from the city of Phnom Penh.*

POL POT, THE MAN WITH THE FACE OF AN AVUNCULAR OLD GRANDFATHER AND THE HEART OF A MURDEROUS TYRANT.

A TERRIBLE REALITY

Samphan's theory was that, in order to progress, Cambodia must regress; it must turn its back on capitalist exploitation, fat-cat bosses created by the former French colonial overlords, reject corrupted bourgeois values and ideals. Samphan's twisted theory decreed that people must live in the fields and that all the trappings of modern life must be annihilated. If Pol Pot himself had remained an obscure figure, this theory may have remained a coffee bar philosopy rattling around the boulevards and parks of Paris. Instead, it became a terrible reality.

Between 1970 and 1975 the Khmer Rouge – the Red Army led by Pol Pot – became a formidable force in Cambodia, controlling huge tracts of the countryside. On 17 April, 1975, Pol Pot's dream of power became a reality when his armies, marching under the red flag, entered the capital, Phnom Penh. Within hours of the coup, Pol Pot called a special meeting of his new cabinet members and told them the country was now called Kampuchea. He outlined the plans for his brave new world which would begin taking shape within days.

He ordered the evacuation of all cities and towns, a process to be overseen by newly-created regional and zonal chiefs. He ordered the abolition of all markets, the destruction of churches and the persecution of all religious orders. Although privileged himself, in having been educated abroad, he harboured a loathing for the educated classes, and so all teachers, professors and even kindergarten teachers were ordered to be executed. The educated peasant, Pol Pot, feared the educated classes.

The first to die were the senior cabinet members and functionaries of Lon Nol's regime, followed by the officer corps of the old army. All were buried in mass graves. Then came the evacuation of the city, towns and villages. Pol Pot's twisted dream was to put the clock back and make his people the dwellers of an agrarian, Marxist society. Pol Pot was aided by his evil deputy, Ieng Sary. Doctors were murdered because they, too, were 'educated'. All religious groups were exterminated because they were 'reactionary'. The term Pol Pot used for his extermination policy was '*Khchat-khchay os roling*' – it translates as 'scatter them out of sight'. The sinister reality meant the death of thousands.

Buddhist temples were desecrated or turned into whorehouses for the troops or even became abbatoirs. Before the terror, there were some sixty thousand monks in Cambodia; after it was over, just three thousand returned to their shattered shrines and their holy places of worship.

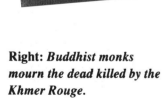

Below: *Cambodian defence minister, Keieu Sampen receives a warm hug from Prince Sihanouk (right).*

Pol Pot also decreed that ethnic minorities did not, in fact, exist. Vietnamese, Thai and Chinese festivals, languages and cultures were ruled illegal, to be practised under punishment of death. His was to be a pure Khmer society. The deliberate and forceful eradication of ethnic groups fell most heavily on the 'Cham' people. Their ancestors had formed the Kingdom of Champa, once a country in what is now Vietnam. The Cham migrated to Cambodia during the eighteenth century to live as fishermen along Cambodia's rivers and the Tonle Sap lake. They were an Islamic people and were, perhaps, the most distinctive ethnic group in modern Cambodia, for they never adandoned or diluted their language, cuisine, costume, hairstyles, burial customs or religion.

The Cham were obvious targets for the young fanatics of the Khmer Rouge who fell upon them like a plague of locusts. The villages were torched, the people marched into the swampy, mosquito-plagued hinterland, fed pork – strictly against their religion – and the religious leaders executed. When villagers resisted whole communities were murdered, their bodies flung into huge pits and covered over with lime. Of two hundred thousand Cham people alive before the new order, barely one hundred thousand survive today. Those who survived the initial terror found that life

Right: *Buddhist monks mourn the dead killed by the Khmer Rouge.*

BUDDHIST TEMPLES WERE DESECRATED OR TURNED INTO WHOREHOUSES FOR THE TROOPS.

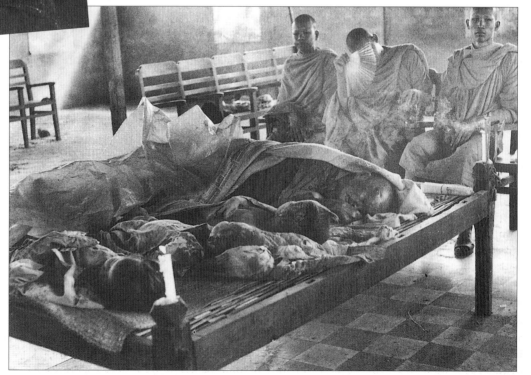

under the new regime was infinitely harder than a quick death – hence the phrase 'Land of the Living Dead', coined by those forced to live under these conditions.

BOURGEOIS CRIMINALS

Pol Pot believed that all adults were tainted by feudal, bourgeois attitudes, with 'sympathies' for foreign regimes which Pol Pot had decreed were alien to the national way of life. Urbanites, in particular, were rooted out and placed in work camps where hundreds of thousands were literally worked to death or murdered if they spoke French – a major crime in Khmer Rouge eyes because it showed a bourgeois attitude, with a link to, and sympathy with, the colonial reign of the past.

In vast encampments, devoid of any comforts save a straw mat to sleep on and a bowl of rice at the end of every day, the tradesmen, dockers, clerks, bankers – many alive only because they managed to hide their professions – and numerous other citizens, toiled in conditions that would have shamed Japanese prison-of-war camps in the Second World War. The camps were organized, much like the concentration camps of the Nazis, to ensure that 'natural' selection' took its toll of the aged and the ill, the very young, and pregnant women. Given a poor diet, deprived of strength, hundreds and thousands succumbed to disease, starvation and the clubbings of their brutal overseers. With no medical men to treat them, save for the attention of a few 'traditional' herbalists whom the new government tolerated, the life span of a prisoner in the camps was pathetically low. They were frog-marched out at dawn into malaria-ridden swamps where they worked twelve hours a day, planting rice and clearing jungles in futile attempts to reclaim more farmland. Then they were frog-marched back at night, under gunpoint and often under the blows and bayonet-thrusts of their guards, to a bowl of rice, gruel and a morsel of dried fish. Then, exhausted though they were, they had to endure Marxist indoctrination sessions, when irredeemable bourgeois elements were rooted out to be taken away for punishment while the others chanted, parrot-fashion, the benefits and joys of the new state. There was one day off in every ten, when people could look forward to twelve hours of indoctrination. Wives were separated from

THEY WERE FROG-MARCHED OUT AT DAWN INTO MALARIA-RIDDEN SWAMPS WHERE THEY WORKED TWELVE HOURS A DAY

To re-inforce his battle against enemies real and imagined, Pol Pot set up a system of interrogations, tortures and executions in his prison camps. Much like the Spanish Inquisition of old, Pol Pot and his henchmen knew that all who came through the portals of these grim places were guilty – all they had to do was to confess that guilt. To convince its followers that cruelty was necessary and good for the nation, the regime taught its young bureacrats that torture had a special, political significance.

Taught by the Chinese, the Khmer security officers were enmeshed in a hard and cruel ideology, revealed in documents captured after the overthrow of Pol Pot. These dossiers show that torture attained a high level in his nation. One document, the 'S-21 Interrogator's Manual', later handed over to United Nations' investigators, reads: 'The purpose of doing torture is to get their responses. It's not something we do for the fun of it. Thus, we must make them hurt so they will respond quickly. Another purpose is to break them psychologically and make them lose their will. It's not something that is done out of individual anger or for self-satisfaction. Thus we beat them to make them afraid but absolutely not to kill them. When torturing them it is necessary to examine their state of health first and necessary to examine the whip. Don't greedily want to kill them. Politics is very important whereas torture is secondary. Thus the question of doing politics takes the lead at all times. Even when

their husbands, their children were either put to work at the age of seven or given away to the barren wives of party functionaries, so as to be brought up in the mould of fanatical warriors of the revolution. Pol Pot was a thorough man.

Bonfires were made of the books from universities and schools, as wretched, maltreated citizens were forced to chant as the works of civilisation perished in the flames. There were 'hate-ins', when people were whipped before pictures of members of the old regime. It was a nightmare world, sinister and hopeless, for the Cambodian people were literally isolated from the world. There was no postal service, no diplomatic ties with any country, no telephones and no travel; it was truly a nation lost to the world.

questioning it is always necessary to do constant propaganda.

TORTURE WITHOUT REASON

'At the same time it is necessary to avoid any question of hesitancy or half-heartedness, of not daring to do torture, which makes it impossible to get answers to our questions from our enemies, which slows down and delays our work. In sum, whether doing propaganda or torturing or bringing up questions to ask them or accusing them of something, it is necessary to hold steadfastly to a stance of not being half-hearted or hesitant. We must be absolute. Only thus can we work to good effect. We torture them but forget to give the reason first. Only then do they become totally helpless.' The notorious Chinese water torture, crucifictions and suffocations with a plastic bag were three among numerous torture methods practiced by the evil men of the Khmer Rouge.

The S21 facility, from which the document took its name, was the most infamous institution in the whole of Cambodia. Based in the north-east of the country, at least thirty thousand victims of the regime died there. Only seven prisoners are known to have survived – prisoners kept alive because they had administrative skills necessary to their overlords in the running of the dreadful place.

Torture was only one instrument of fear brandished over the heads of the cowed populace. The frequency with which people were executed was another. Many times, inmates in the new country camps were caught eating the flesh of their dead comrades in their desperation for food. The penalty for this was a horrible death of being buried up to the neck in mud and left to starve and thirst while ants and other creatures gnawed at the victim. Then the heads were cut off and stuck on pikes around the settlement with the words painted on a sign hanging from the neck: 'I am a traitor of the revolution!'

Dith Pran, a Cambodian interpreter for American journalist, Sydney Schanberg, emerged from the years of slaughter as a witness to the horrors of Pol Pot's reign. His own experiences, including his threatened execution, were chronicled in the film 'The Killing Fields', in which the torment of the Cambodian people was, for the first time, starkly revealed to the world. Pran's journey from his civilised childhood to a prison camp, where he pretended to be illiterate in order to survive, was a harrowing tale that reduced audiences to tears of pity. 'Many times,' said Pran, 'I prayed that I was dead rather than having to endure the life that I was forced to live. But some of my family had gotten away to America and it was for them that I carried on living. It was a nightmare time.'

Below: *A Khmer Rouge soldier menaces civilians with his gun. The population of Phnom Penh were quickly subdued by the thugs of Pol Pot's army.*

STACKS OF SKULLS

Pran was one of the lucky ones who survived the Asian holocaust to be reunited with his family in 1979 in San Francisco. Even now, the mass graves of the unknown, unnamed dead continue to be unearthed in remote corners of the sad country, the skulls stacked against the graves like so many footballs.

It was military muscle and not moral right that, in the end, halted the bloodbath and allowed for some semblance of sanity to return to the blighted land. Britain had, it must be acknowledged, spoken out in 1978 against alleged human rights abuses, after receiving reports, through intermediaries in Thailand, about the reign of terror in Cambodia, but the protest was ignored.

Opposite, top: *Peasants feared that they would be forced to join the 'intellectuals' in the labour camps.*

Opposite, bellow: *Coils of barbed wire marked the Cambodian border with Thailand.*

Above: *The fall of Phnom Penh is celebrated by young guerillas of the Khmer Rouge.*

Britain reported to the United Nations Commission on Human Rights, but the hysterical Khmer Rouge representative responded: 'The British Imperialists have no right to speak of the rights of man. The world knows well their barbarous and abject nature. Britain's leaders are living in opulence atop a pile of rotting corpses while the proletariat have only the right to be unemployed, to steal and prostitute.' Regrets were sent from Pol Pot flunkies who said that they were too busy to attend UN enquiries on the allegations to the commission hearings in New York.

In December, 1978, Vietnamese forces, who had been skirmishing for years with the Khmer Rouge over a disputed border region, launched a major offensive with mechanised infantry divisions and full armoured support. The infrastructure of Cambodia had disintegrated so badly by this time, that battlefield reports had to be biked great distances to Khmer Rouge command posts because there were no telephones left in operation.

The Vietnamese, early in 1979, found themselves masters of a blighted land. Pol Pot had fled in his white armoured Mercedes from Phnom Penh, just hours before the Vietnamese troops arrived to liberate the ghostly city. He went scurrying back to his masters in China, glad of the sanctuary, but bitter that they had not come to his aid in resisting the well-armed and determined North Vietnamese onslaught.

'US SURVIVORS REMEMBER OUR FAMILIES BEING TAKEN AWAY, MANY OF THEM, AND OUR FRIENDS BRUTALLY MURDERED.'

Massive amounts of aid flooded into Cambodia as the world realized the full horror of the Khmer Rouge regime and the devastation of the country. The Khmer Rouge were, like the Nazis, particularly methodical when it came to detailing their crimes; investigators found daily logs of shootings, torture, hundreds of photo albums of those to be executed – including those of wives and children of 'intellectuals' liquidated in the earliest days of the terror – and the detailed loggings of the infamous killing fields. These fields, intended to be the basis of the worker's Utopia, a land without money or want, became, instead, the burial pits of a people crushed under the yoke of a cruel tyranny.

Pol Pot seemed to fade into the background but has emerged in recent years to become a major political force vying for power in this embitttered region. Like all tyrants, he said that mistakes were made by those under him, that he had faced rebellions on all fronts and that those who died were 'enemies of the state'. In 1981, back in Cambodia, he told a meeting of old friends at a secret location near the Thai border that he was 'too trusting. My policies were sound. Over-zealous regional commanders and sub-district personnel may have mis-interpreted orders. To talk about systematic murder is odious. If we had really killed at that rate, we would have had no one left to fight the Vietnamese. I have been seriously mis-interpreted.'

ANGEL OF DEATH

Misinterpretation on the scale of three million dead – almost twenty-five per cent of the population of the nation – seems too small a word to describe what was done in his name and under his orders. But following Hitler's code, that the bigger the lie, the more people will believe it, Pol Pot has, once again, become a power-player in the region and is able to rally forces in the countryside that continue to believe in him, and are still loyal to him. Now he is a major force once again, only waiting to ride into the country, like some avenging angel of death, to finish off what he started before: his great agrarian revolution.

For Dith Pran and other survivors, the prospect of Pol Pot's return to power, the possibility that he will plunge his tortured land into new depths of depravity, fills them with horror. When the United Nations first announced that the Khmer Rouge would be part of the power-sharing peace process in Cambodia, Pran said: 'I am still shocked when I see the Khmer Rouge flag flying on UN territory. How would you feel if you were Jewish and you saw Hitler's flag flying at the United Nations? Some people went on a fast for three days to protest this, but I did not. I have starved for four years and that is enough for any man.'

There is international lobbying for world governments to have the Cambodian massacres recognized as war crimes in the same way as the Hitlerian genocide of the Jews has been recognised. Yang Sam, of the Cambodian Documentation Commission in New York, is the Cambodian equivalent of Simon Wiesenthal, the Nazi death camp survivor who, from his office in Vienna, devotes his life to tracing and collating evidence against Nazi war criminals. Sam, a survivor of the terror, collects information against the butchers of his own land. He said: 'Those most responsible for the Cambodian genocide – the cabinet members of Pol Pot's regime, the central committee of his Communist party, the Khmer Rouge military commanders whose troops committed so much of the killing, those officials who oversaw, directed and ran the nationwide network of torture chambers, prison-execution centres and extermination facilities – continue to remain active in Cambodia and international political life. Based in enclaves along the Thai-Cambodian border, they conduct guerilla war seeking to return to power in Phnom Penh. They have not been held accountable for their crime under international law and that is a tragedy of monumental proportions.

'Us survivors remember our families being taken away, many of them, and our friends brutally murdered. We witnessed members of our families and others die of exhaustion from forced marches and slave labour, and from the brutal conditions of life to which the Cambodian people were subjected by the Khmer Rouge.

'We also saw Pol Pot's soldiers destroy our Buddhist temples, end schooling for our children, suppress our culture and eradicate our ethnic minorities. It is difficult for us to understand why the free and democratic nations of the world do not take action against the guilty. Surely this cries out for justice?' But there is no justice here.

WE WITNESSED MEMBERS OF OUR FAMILIES AND OTHERS DIE OF EXHAUSTION FROM FORCED MARCHES AND SLAVE LABOUR.

Below: *The legacy of the Pol Pot years. The skulls of the anonymous dead serve to remind the world of the man's dreadful regime.*

STALIN
Crime at Katyn Wood

In the secret heart of the forest, the proud officers of the Polish army were brutally executed. Even their murderers were so shamed by the killings that they denied the facts. But the dreadful truth of Katyn Wood has not remained hidden.

Adolf Hitler, leader of the German Nazi party, sent his emissary Joachim von Ribbentrop to Moscow in August 1939. He wanted a pact with Josef Stalin, bloodthirsty leader of the Soviet peoples. Yet Stalin represented the Slavic races that Hitler had threatened time and time again, in his manic outpourings, to destroy for ever. And Hitler, in Stalin's eyes, was a fascist running dog who persecuted without mercy the Communists. The former champagne salesman, von Ribbentrop, emerged after several days of diplomatic niceties with his Soviet counterpart, foreign minister Vyacheslav Molotov, to proclaim to a stunned world that a new non-aggression pact had been signed between the two former adversaries. This was *Realpolitik* at its most cynical – the conclusion of distasteful business for the mutual benefit of mutual enemies.

The West viewed the Molotov-Ribbentrop Pact as the precursor to an aggressive war of conquest in Western Europe. With the Soviets promising no action if Germany made 'territorial claims' upon her neighbours, strategists saw that Hitler had effectively silenced his biggest, and a potentially lethal, foe without a shot being fired in anger.

But what the West did not know – and would not find out until a month later, when the armies of Hitler launched their attack on Poland that was to start the Second World War – was that 'the pact' contained a secret clause that divided Poland between Hitler

and Stalin. Between them, the two great dictators, who despised each other and the systems each represented, had forged a compact to ensure that this independent nation should cease to exist.

Betwixt the two, Poland became a vassal state. Polish Jews were soon earmarked for destruction by the Nazis, while under the Soviets, the intelligentsia and anti-Communist elements were rooted out for 'special treatment' by the NKVD, the forerunner of the KGB, but that concentrated less on espionage and more on mass murder and political suppression.

Opposite: *Josef Stalin, the man of steel. He has more blood on his hands than any other man this century.*

Below: *Polish women weep over their loved ones after the bodies were disinterred.*

Bottom: *German investigators and Russian peasants exhume the vast mass grave.*

One other segment of Polish national life was hated by both sides – the officer corps of the army who were proud, disciplined, fiercely independent men.

It was precisely because they were troublesome to both dictators, that one of the most heinous crimes in wartime history went unsolved for over forty years. In 1940, four thousand Polish officers, from generals to lieutenants, were bound, shot in the back of the head and buried in massive lime pits, surrounded by thick fir trees that made up the forest of Katyn, near Smolensk in western Russia. All the victims had their hands tied to nooses around their necks which tightened when they struggled; all bore the same single-entry head wound testifying to methodical execution by shooting.

For close on five decades the crime at Katyn Wood was not acknowledged or admitted by the perpetrators. The Germans claimed the Russians did it; the Russians that the Germans were the perpetrators. It was not until the demise of the Soviet Union and the release of KGB files that the

truth was out – that the Poles were executed because they were the 'class enemy' of the Soviet people. On 13 April, 1990 Mikhail Gorbachev acknowledged his nation's culpability... forty–seven years after the day that Germany claimed her soldiers in the east had stumbled across the mass graves in the forest.

The events in the clearings of the Katyn Forest during those days of April 1940 make for grim reading. Even now the scars left by the liquidation of these proud warriors remain deep. This is the story of Stalin's massacre of the army allied to Britain – the nation for whom Britain went to war in the first place.

The tale, from being part of the first national army to stand up to Hitler to that degrading execution in the vast mass grave of the Katyn Forest, was a short one for these Polish officers.

Opposite, top: *Molotov, seated, signs a non-aggression pact with Germany.*

Opposite, below: *The Russian admission of responsibility for the massacre at Katyn Wood made headlines all over the world.*

Below: *The villages of Poland were burnt and abandoned as columns of German troops marched through the conquered land.*

IN THESE CAMPS WAS THE BEST OF THE BEST OF POLISH NATIONAL LIFE; EDUCATED, CULTURED, PASSIONATE MEN.

MOLOTOV INFORMED THE POLISH AMBASSADOR: 'THE POLISH STATE CEASES TO EXIST.'

First, Hitler's Stuka dive-bombers and armoured columns brought terror to the civilian population as Operation Case White – the conquest of Poland – began on 1 September. Hitler used a transparently lame excuse for sending his troops across the border; namely, that German soldiers in a frontier post had been killed by marauding Poles. Sixteen days later, with their cities in flames and their armies all but routed, the desperate Poles then had to endure an attack from their eastern neighbour, Russia. Again, it was a flimsy excuse that brought the Red Army pouring over the frontier. In reality, it was the fulfillment of the secret clause in the contemptible Molotov-Ribbentrop Pact.

Stalin camouflaged his military intervention by claiming his soldiers were being sent merely to protect the rights of Byelorussians and Ukrainians, living in Polish territory near the border with the Soviet Union. At 3am on 17 December, hours after Soviet troops, backed up by the death squads of the NKVD, were pouring across the border, Waclaw Grzybowski, the Polish ambassador to Moscow, was summoned to the foreign ministry where he was confronted by Molotov who, shedding all diplomatic niceties, informed him: 'The Polish state ceases to exist. We are aiding you to extricate your people from an unfortunate war in which they have been dragged by unwise leaders and to enable them to live a peaceful life.'

By 5 October, the day the last Polish units ceased fighting, Germany had two-thirds and the Soviet Union one third of Polish territory. Germany took close to six hundred thousand prisoners-of-war; the Red Army captured another two hundred and thirty thousand men. In the wake of the fighting troops came the SS battalions, on the German side, and the NKVD secret police units of Stalin. Both groups were remarkably similar in their initial actions. Round-ups began of intellectuals, university professors, nobles, known radicals, truculent churchmen; anyone who was deemed to pose the smallest threat.

Hitler had used the state as his instrument of repression and murder since he achieved power in 1933, but he was a mere apprentice in the art of massacre compared to Stalin. On his hands was the blood of *tens of millions* of people, murdered across

May, five weeks later. In the previous week the prisoners were rounded up in their camps at Kozelsk, Starobelsk and Ostashkov and taken in batches to railheads to board cattlewagons for unknown destinations. However, the four thousand four hundred Poles from Kozelsk camp were bound for the forest at Katyn.

HOPE OF REPATRIATION

Since their capture, these men had existed on meagre rations and were given few facilities to communicate with their families. During the days that they were herded into trains, they were given a better diet, kindling hope among them that they were

the vast steppes, shot in the cellars of the NKVD prisons, worked to death in the great Gulag archipelago that stretched over the frozen Siberian wastes. Stalin, in his Kremlin office, decreed that the vanquished Poles in the territory he now ruled would, indeed, receive no treatment that had not already been meted out in large measure to his own suffering masses. None could accuse the Man of Steel of inconsistency in his harshness.

Early in November, after a secret edict from Stalin, NKVD units began separating and moving out from a vast string of POW camps the fifteen thousand Polish officers whom they had captured. They were taken to camps set up in old monasteries that had perished under Bolshevism, all of them within Russian territory. In these camps was the best of the best of Polish national life; educated, cultured, passionate men, many of them reservists who had simply abandoned their comfortable lives to put on a uniform and fight for the land they loved.

Only a handful would ever see it again.

The NKVD were preparing for *mokrara rabota* – the agency's slang for bloodletting. For months the NKVD superiors at the prison camps, that held the Poles, had been sending reports back to their Lubyanka masters, suggesting that some of the Polish officers might be transported to Moscow, where they could be assimilated and indoctrinated into the Soviet system. But Josef Stalin had already made up his mind about their fate.

The liquidations at the Katyn Forest began on 3 April and did not end until 13

indeed being repatriated to a new life. Each man received three dried herrings, half-a-pound of bread and some sugar. For some lucky few there was even an issue of Russian cigarettes to treasure.

The NKVD wanted the officers lulled into a state of well-being. Had there been any inkling of what lay in store for them,

Above right: *Red Cross and other officials are shown the grave site by a German officer.*

Above: *German Red Cross workers search for anything to help identify the corpses.*

Right: *Jewellery and military insignia found on one Polish corpse.*

'I AM NOW COMING TO THE CONCLUSION THAT THIS JOURNEY DOES NOT BODE WELL.'

there would have been bloody mutinies from the brave prisoners in the camps.

But once at the railheads, away from the camps and their comrades, the treatment changed immediately. New NKVD men were waiting to board them on the trains, men armed with clubs and dogs and with the vicious, four-sided bayonets issued to the NKVD. Many prisoners were severely,

gratuitously beaten as they clambered aboard the trains. Waclaw Kruk, a lieutenant, was one of the officers never to return from Katyn.

A diary was later found near his body in which he wrote down his feelings – feelings that must have been those of all the Poles as they moved out of the camps into the unknown. 'Yesterday a convoy of senior officers left: three generals, twenty to twenty-five colonels and the same number of majors. We were in the best of spirits because of the manner of their departure. Today, my turn came. But at the station we were loaded into prison cars under strict guard. Now we are waiting to depart. Optimistic as I was before, I am now coming to the conclusion that this journey does not bode well.' His diary was found in 1943, near a body tagged 'number 424'.

Another corpse, that of Major Adam Solski, also had a journal near it. Experts who examined it concur that the condemned man wrote the final words less than twenty minutes before he was murdered. It makes sad reading. 'Few minutes before five in the morning: reveille in the prison train. Preparing to get off. We are to go somewhere by car. What next? Five o'clock: ever since dawn the day has run an exceptional course. Departure in prison van with tiny cell-like compartments; horrible. Driven somewhere in the woods, somewhere like a holiday place. Here a detailed search. I was relieved of my watch, which showed 6.30am, asked for my wedding ring. Roubles, belt and pocket knife taken away.'

Journey's end for the soldiers was the Katyn Forest, sloping towards the Dnieper River and not far from the town of Smolensk. Here, gigantic pits had been dug in the sandy soil, within the leafy groves of fir trees and silver birch. Not far from the pits was a building known innocently as The Little Castle of the Dnieper; in reality it was a summer house, a dacha, of the local NKVD and now served as the headquarters of the killing squads who were about to despatch the cream of the Polish army to their deaths.

A SINISTER JOURNEY

The prisoners were taken from the rail cars in what were known as the *chorny voron* – the police buses, which had been a grim feature of Soviet life for years. A glimpse of one of them, in a Soviet street, was enough to send shivers up the back of any innocent observer. These buses were divided into separate steel compartments, each little bigger than a kennel, in which the Polish officers were kept until their turn for execution arrived.

Only one man, a Polish professor, Stanislaw Swianiewicz, saw the killing of his comrades and lived to tell the tale. He was on board one of the trains, but was locked into a compartment by himself, only to be transported to Moscow to face charges of espionage. But he witnessed the scene as his fellow officers were led to their deaths. In the authoritative book 'Katyn' by Allen Paul, the professor was quoted: 'wondered what kind of operation it was. Clearly, my companions were being taken to a place in the vicinity, probably only a few miles away. It was a fine spring day and I wondered why they were not told to march there, as was the usual procedure at camps. The presence of a high-ranking NKVD officer, at what was apparently the simple transferal of several hundred prisoners from one camp to another, could be explained if we were actually going to be handed over to the Germans. But, in such a

case, why these extraordinary precautions? Why the fixed bayonets of the escort? I could think of no reasonable explanation. But then, on that brilliant spring day, it never even occurred to me that the operation might entail the execution of my companions.' Such an act was unthinkable.

Execution at the pits was to be cold, methodical, production-line work. Machine guns or grenades could not be used; people would run, there would be survivors, there

WHY THESE EXTRAORDINARY PRECAUTIONS? WHY THE FIXED BAYONETS OF THE ESCORT? I COULD THINK OF NO REASONABLE EXPLANATION.

Above: *A German officer holds up the decomposing jacket of a murdered Polish officer.*

would be an immediate panic among those prisoners awaiting transport from the train to the execution place. Instead the NKVD agents used 7.65mm Walther German-police issue pistols, considered by handgun experts to be the best pistols of their type in the world. NKVD squads would be waiting with fresh guns to replace those that over-heated in the ceaseless slaughter, others with mounds of ammunition.

Once taken, one by one from the buses, the individual prisoners were bound in a particularly gruesome manner – a manner perfected over the years by the murderers from the NKVD. The victim's hands were first tied behind his back, then a second cord was tied over his head at neck level

> AS THE LAST OF THE SAND WAS BULLDOZED OVER THE GRAVES, THE BUTCHERS PLANTED TINY BIRCH SAPLINGS ON TOP.

Below: Joachim von Ribbentrop announces details of the cynical pact with the Soviet Union to carve up Poland.

with the victim's greatcoat pulled up over it, like a shroud. From the neck the cord was passed down the prisoner's back, looped around the bound hands and tied again at the neck, forcing the arms painfully upwards towards his shoulder blades. Any attempt to lower his arms put pressure on the neck; repeated pressure would result in strangulation.

One by one these brave, noble men were led to the edge of the pits. Many bodies bore the brutal stab-marks of the four-squared NKVD bayonets – proof that, agonizing though their bonds were, they had attempted to struggle for their lives. Each one was despatched with what the Germans called the *Nackenschuss* – a shot through the nape of the neck which caused instant death and limited blood loss. This method had been perfected in countless

> I SENSED A PROPAGANDA EXERCISE. I HATED THE GERMANS. I DID NOT WANT TO BELIEVE THEM.

cellars and execution dens of the NKVD over many years of Stalinist terror.

They fell into the pits and were stacked like cordwood, one on one, in layers of twelve before lime was sprinkled over them and tons of sand bulldozed back over them. But the tons of sand helped to press the corpses down and literally 'mummify' them as the body fluids and blood was squeezed out. The lime failed to work, so when the advancing Germans discovered the graves of Katyn, the thousands of corpses were well preserved.

On and on went the killing. The NKVD butchers fuelled their spirits with massive quantities of vodka consumed in the nearby dacha. Twelve hours a day for six weeks, nothing but the sound of gunshots echoed from those lonely groves until, finally, four thousand one hundred and forty-three victims were dead. As the last of the sand was bulldozed over the graves, the butchers planted tiny birch saplings on top.

The remaining eleven thousand Polish officers, held in other camps were liquidated at killing sites deeper in Russia. Their graves have never been exhumed but there has since been an admission from the now-defunct Soviet Union that all these Polish officers had been annihilated on Stalin's personal orders.

But Katyn was, and remains, the most significant massacre site. It was a known site, yet for decades it was surrounded by lies and duplicity. It justified a deep-rooted hatred of the Soviet state felt by all the people of Poland.

FRIENDS TURN ON EACH OTHER

It was only a matter of time before those arch-enemies, Hitler and Stalin, were to turn on each other. Hitler had written in *Mein Kampf* that *Lebensraum* – living space – in the east was his single greatest goal. On 22 June, 1941 he set out to achieve that with Operation Barbarossa, the attack on the Soviet Union.

Fifteen hundred miles away from Stalingrad, in the dacha where the NKVD executioners planned the killing of the Polish officers, the soldiers in Lt Col Friedrich Ahrens' signal regiment were having a relatively quiet war.

Ahrens and his men had a strange fore-boding about Katyn Wood, the site of the dacha. They heard rumours from the local people about NKVD executions taking place there, and hidden graves. Then, in February 1943, when the German 6th Army was routed at Stalingrad, a wolf unearthed bones in one of the mass grave sites. Ivan Krivozertsev, a local peasant, approached Ahrens and formally informed him of the dark secrets of the forest. NKVD secrecy and planning had not been hidden from the sharp eyes of the peasants.

Below: *British prisoners-of-war were taken to the site. The Germans wanted to convince the Allies that the massacre was a Russian act.*

The Germans prepared to tell the world of the slaughter of the Polish officers, and Dr Gerhard Buhtz, a professor of forensic medicine from a leading German university, was put in charge of the exhumation and examination of the grave pits, which were opened in early March. For ten weeks the stink of rotten flesh and Egyptian tobacco − the Germans smoked it to mask the smell of the dead − mingled with the scents of moss and pine sap as the murdered men were disinterred and laid out. Some prisoners-of-war, American Lt Col John Van Vliet among them, were taken by the Germans to witness the massacre site. He recalled: 'I sensed a propaganda exercise. I hated the Germans. I did not want to believe them. But after seeing the bodies there, piled up like cordwood, I changed my mind. I told the Allies, after the War, that I thought the Soviets were responsible.'

On 13 April, 1943, at 3.10pm Berlin time, the German radio network officially announced the finding of the graves where

the Polish officers had been 'bestially murdered by the Bolsheviks'. The world was stunned into silence, choosing to believe that the report was fabricated by the Nazis. But the Polish government-in-exile, in London, had long harboured suspicions that the Russians had copious amounts of Polish blood on their hands.

On 15 April the Soviets counter-attacked, claiming: 'In launching this monsterous invention the German-Fascist scoundrels did not hesitate at the most unscrupulous and base lies, in their attempts to cover up crimes which, as has now become evident, were perpetrated by themselves. The Hitlerite murders will not escape a just and bloody retribution for their bloody crimes.' Three separate commissions were invited to visit Katyn by the Germans. The first was entirely German, the second composed of scientists and forensic experts from Switzerland, Belgium, Hungary and Bulgaria, and the third was entirely Polish. The evidence was mightily in favour of the German view-point. Although the ammunition was

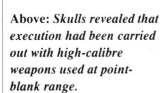

Above: *Skulls revealed that execution had been carried out with high-calibre weapons used at point-blank range.*

German, records from the manufacturing plants showed it to be batches sold, before the war, to Lithuania only to be siezed later by NKVD police units.

The Soviets claimed that the men were killed by the advancing Germans in 1941 − although not one document with a date later than 6 May, 1940 was ever found on a single corpse. The bayonet thrusts on the bodies were of the four-cornered NKVD type. The fact that there were no insects found in the graves indicated cold weather-burial, not summer as the Soviets claimed – and besides, all the murdered soldiers wore heavy winter clothing.

But their military fight against Hitler had, for the Allied commanders, at that time, a higher priority than a search for justice and truth. Churchill remarked in a cabinet meeting: 'We must not take sides in the Russo-Polish quarrel.' He assured Stalin in a secret communique that he would do his personal best to silence Free Polish newspapers in London over the affair, while he told Wadyslaw Sikorski, the prime minister in exile: 'If they are dead, nothing you can do will bring them back.' President Roosevelt in the White House preferred to believe the Soviet leader's explanation that the murders were committed by the Nazis.

Right: *A priest prays at the graveside for the Polish officers, who were denied the blessing of the last rites at their death.*

Below: *Row upon row of corpses, all tied in the same fashion, were pulled from the mass burial pit.*

When the Soviets finally overran the Katyn territory in their great push westwards, they took the opportunity to cover up the massacre of the Polish officers. The ponderously-named 'Special Commission for Ascertaining and Investigating the Circumstances of the Shooting of Polish Officer Prisoners by the German Invaders in the Katyn Forest' went into overdrive to persuade the world that the murders were the work of the Gestapo and *Einsatzgruppen*. The Soviets stuck to their story that the officers had been murdered a year later than was actually the case – and

as stories of German atrocities throughout the War began to emerge from all over Europe, there were plenty of people willing to believe the Soviets.

By the time the triumphant Red Army rolled into Berlin in May 1945, the myth that the Germans were responsible for Katyn was firmly planted around the world and in the satellite Eastern European nations over which, in Churchill's words, the Kremlin had drawn an 'Iron Curtain'. In Warsaw, the monument to the dead at Katyn blamed the Nazi invaders; at Katyn itself the inscription read: 'To the victims of Fascism. Polish officers shot by the Nazis in 1941.' The Soviets were operating under the maxim that Hitler once used – tell a lie big enough for long enough and it will metamorphose into truth. They denied any reference to the atrocity if it cast suspicion on their forces. Ewa Solska, the daughter of Major Solski whose diary was found on him, wrote 'killed at Katyn' in the box on her university application form which asked for information about her father. She was expelled for giving this information.

Even at Nuremberg, the great post-war trial for the crimes of Nazism, the Soviets were able to bluff the tribunals that Katyn was a Nazi crime. They could not bluff the Polish people, nor the many people around the world who were slowly caming to realise the enormity of Stalin's crimes.

It wasn't until 1990, at a ceremony inside the Kremlin, that Gorbachev, in keeping with the spirit of his Glasnost reforms, handed President Jaruzelski of Poland a box containing NKVD documents and other files, showing that the officers had indeed been murdered by the NKVD. These revealed that the executioners themselves had been 'liquidated' under Stalin's orders, then buried at an unknown grave site somewhere in Russia. Only four hundred prisoners-of-war from the entire Polish officer corps survived, to be taken to Moscow and other Russian cities, where they proved to be willing Communists. Gorbachev labelled the massacre 'one of the gravest crimes of Stalinism'.

Was it all a big mistake on Stalin's part? Some historians believe that his orders may have been 'misinterpreted' by underlings. Stanislaw Mikolajczyk, the successor to Sikorski in London for the Polish government-in-exile, has his view and claims a Soviet bureaucrat secretly gave him the following interpretation of what happened:

A MISSINTERPERATED ORDER

'Early in 1940 the Red Army sent a staff officer to find what Stalin planned to do with the Polish officers. A planned swap in which the officers would be turned over to the Germans in return for thirty thousand Ukrainians had just fallen through. The Ukrainians were Polish Army conscripts captured by Germany the previous September, and were interned in two camps in eastern Poland. The Germans, at first agreed to the exchange but backed out at the last possible moment, telling the Soviets to take the Ukrainians and keep the Poles. Then came rumours in Moscow that the Ukrainian conscripts and the Polish officers would be organised into special units of the Red Army. Senior commanders were aware of such talk but had nothing specific to go on. The staff officer was sent to get Stalin's clarification. The staff officer saw Stalin and briefly explained the problem. Stalin listened patiently. When the staff officer finished, Stalin supplied him with a written order. Such orders were common, often requested by subordinates as a matter of self-protection. In this case. said the informant, Josef Stalin took a sheet of his personal

Above: *The soil in Katyn Wood served to preserve the bodies. This was of considerable help when investigators came to identify bodies and buried papers.*

STALIN TOOK A SHEET OF HIS PERSONAL STATIONERY AND WROTE ONLY ONE WORD ON IT: 'LIQUIDATE'.

stationery and wrote only one dreadful word on it: 'Liquidate'.

The staff officer returned the one-word order to his superiors, but they were uncertain what it meant. Did Stalin mean to liquidate the camps or to liquidate the men? He might have meant that the men should be released, sent to other prisons, or to work in the Gulag system. He might also have meant that the men should be shot, or otherwise eliminated. No one knew for sure what the order meant, but no one wanted to risk Stalin's ire by asking him to clarify it. To delay a decision was also risky and could invite retribution. The army took the safe way out and turned the whole matter over to the NKVD. For the NKVD, there was no ambiguity in Stalin's order. It could only mean one thing: that the Poles were to be executed immediately. That is, of course, exactly what happened.'

Many thought Stalin, the Man of Steel would never have had it any other way.

ADOLF HITLER
The Holocaust

Germany was humiliated by defeat after the Great War. Despair gripped the nation. But one man promised to return their pride. All they had to do was build gas chambers and kill, kill, kill. So began the most shocking mass murder in the history of the world.

They met at a place called Wannsee, a charming suburb of Berlin with ornate houses and tree-lined streets that looked out over the lake which gave the area its name. It was 20 January, 1942 and the Reich had reached the zenith of its military victories. The swastika flew over the Russian steppes, over the Balkans and Greece, France, the Low Countries, North Africa, Poland, Norway and Denmark. The wars of conquest had ended in total triumph for Hitler's armies so it was now time to put into effect phase two of his doctrine of Nazism. It was time to implement 'The final solution of the Jewish question in Europe'.

No one who followed the rise of Adolf Hitler and his Nazi party was surprised that he had a diabolical plan to eradicate the Jews. Hitler began his campaign of state terror against the Jews soon after he came to power. He passed the infamous Nuremberg Laws which stripped them of property, valuables, human rights and political power. Then he organized the terror, which culminated in the *Kristallnacht* – 'Night of Broken Glass' – in 1938. This involved the destruction of synagogues and Jewish property throughout Germany during a frenzied night of state-sponsored terror. But Hitler wanted 'a final solution to the Jewish problem' and this was to become a euphemism for mass murder.

That is why at Wannsee, in 1942, SS and Gestapo chiefs, led by Reinhard 'Hangman' Heydrich, gathered at a villa, once owned by a Jewish merchant, to plot the logistics for the collection, transportation and extermination of millions of men, women and children who had no place in the new world order. The men in black and grey uniforms drew up blueprints for the greatest state-sponsored murder in history.

Since the Nazi seizure of power Hitler had experimented with mass-killing techniques at euthanasia laboratories where the mentally ill were killed in gas-vans or by lethal injection. When his armies overran Poland and parts of Russia he walled his Jewish enemies up in medieval-style ghettoes where he allowed starvation and disease to kill the people locked within. In Russia his *Einsatzgruppen* – action squad – SS commandos shot hundreds upon thousands of Jews and other 'undesirables'. But

Opposite: *Adolf Hitler salutes to his followers. Rudolf Hess stands before him.*

Below: *An SA stormtrooper ensures that shoppers follow the order on the sign: 'Do not buy from Jews'.*

HOESS TOOK A SCIENTIFIC
DELIGHT IN SOLVING THE
PROBLEMS OF MASS
MURDER.

NAMES LIKE TREBLINKA,
SOBIBOR, BUCHENWALD,
DACHAU AND AUSCHWITZ
HAVE NOW BECOME
HOUSEHOLD WORDS
FOR EVIL.

Right: *Survivors stand in bitter mourning for their lost families at the memorial erected to the victims of the Holocaust.*

HITLERDEUTSCHLAND – EIN ZUCHTHAUS

200 000 POLITISCHE GEFANGENE IN KONZENTRATIONS-
LAGERN, GEFÄNGNISSEN UND ZUCHTHÄUSERN

it was not enough. These methods were cumbersome, slow and inefficient. Hitler was determined to bring some Henry Ford principles into the process of mass murder – a production line of death camps that would dispatch the unfortunates at the greatest speed possible.

Herman Goering, Luftwaffe chief whose first task for the Nazis was setting up the dreaded Gestapo, had Heydrich's orders in a letter, written six months before the Wannsee conference. It read: 'I hereby charge you with making all necessary preparation with regard to organizational and financial matters for bringing about a complete solution of the Jewish problem in the German sphere of influence in Europe.'

Heinrich Himmler, head of the SS; Heydrich, head of the SD, the security arm of the same organisation; Adolf Eichmann, and Ernst Kaltenbrunner, Heydrich's successor after his master was assassinated in Prague in May 1942, can be said to be the architects of the final solution. They built the concentration camp network which spanned all conquered Europe.

Names like Treblinka, Sobibor, Buchenwald, Dachau and Auschwitz – Auschwitz, particularly, the most infamous human abbatoir of them all – have now become household words for evil. In these death factories Jews from all over Europe made a one-way trip to hell. And not only Jews – Gypsies, Poles, Slavs, Russian prisoners-of-war, intellectuals, revolutionaries, homosexuals and artists who did not fit into the racial or political mould were despatched. A new breed of men and

Below: *Former inmates of the death camps show the identity numbers tattooed on their arms by the Nazis.*

Below, right: *A synagogue in ruins after the attacks against Jews during Crystal Night, 9 November, 1938.*

Hoess took a scientific delight in solving the problems of mass murder. Auschwitz, like the other camps, had used mass shootings and hangings to eradicate the inmates, but this was precisely the inefficiency that Hitler and the SS wanted to do away with. Later in 1942 a gas made from prussic acid, that was used to kill rats and mice in German factories, was deployed for the first time against Russian POWs. The Russians were led into a long, sealed room, the walls of which were lined with showers. But the shower faucets were false and the plugholes sealed. And then they heard the rattle of hard crystals dropped on to a wire grating above their heads, before the room filled with a gas, called Zyklon-B, that was released from the crystals. They were all dead within twenty minutes.

At the far south end of the Birkenau camp two massive gas chambers and adjacent crematoriums were built by the inmates themselves. Trains arriving at a railhead were greeted by one Dr Josef Mengele – about whom more will be said later – the SS doctor who became supreme arbiter of life and death within the electrified fences of Auschwitz. With a flick of his riding crop he dictated the fate of the inmates. Those who were to work for the Reich on starvation rations, under the blows of whips and cudgels, marched one way while their elderly parents, sisters brothers, and toddlers walked the other.

women, inconceivable in their cruelty, depraved beyond belief, were recruited to administer these extermination centres.

Such a man was Rudolf Hoess, commandant of Auschwitz where the final solution was to reach remarkable heights of cruel efficiency. Hoess, at his peak, oversaw a complex where men and women lived in filth, were worked like dogs and finally executed when they were no longer of any use to the Reich. Auschwitz, and its annexe camp of Birkenau, where the gas chambers and crematorium were situated, were two miles from the main town of the same name in southern Poland. Every day, in the camps, twelve thousand people died in the gas chambers before being burned in the massive crematorium.

Loudspeakers told the latter group that they were heading off for showers and de-lousing before they were to be re-united with their families in barracks. In fact, they were taken to a long wooden hut where they were told to strip and place all valuables in a locker. Then their heads were shaved and the hair collected in giant sacks by other prisoners. Then they were marched in to the giant shower-rooms. But these showers did not flow with water and the naked humiliated prisoners were actually in giant death chambers

BODILY REMAINS

Afterwards, men working for the *Sonderkommando* or special commando squads set up by their SS overlords, entered to disentangle the corpses and remove the gold fillings from their teeth. The bodies were then pushed into the ovens, the ashes raked out and spread over nearby woodland or dumped in the River Vistula.

Cruel and inhuman as the killing machine was, death was often the one thing the living prayed for. The camp culture spawned a sadistic, warped race of guards who took morbid pleasure in the mistreatment of their charges. Irma Greese, the 'Blonde Angel of Hell' from Belsen, delighted in flaying women's breasts with a knotted whip. Karl Babor, the camp doctor

Below, left: *Inmates were used to clear away the bodies of their fellow prisoners and feed them into the crematoriums of the death camps.*

Below: *Hitler with his mistress, Eva Braun, relaxes in his mountain retreat at Berchtesgaden.*

of the Gross-Rosen camp, amused himself by burning new-born babies on an open fire. And at Auschwitz there was the infamous Dr Mengele, whose smiling face was always there to greet the new arrivals as they arived in stinking cattle wagons.

Mengele was a doctor of medicine who betrayed his Hippocratic oath each and every day, while convincing himself that his scientific research in the camp was carried out on mere 'subhumans'.

His greetings at the train ramp for the Auschwitz arrivals had a dual purpose; he

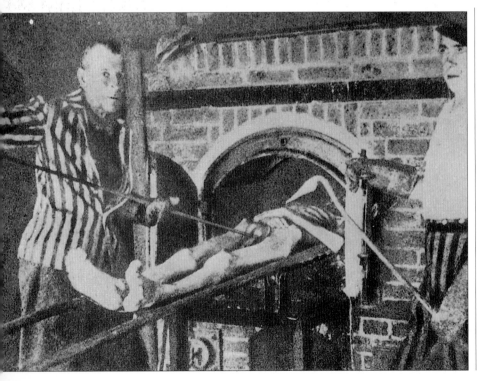

sorted out those who could work for the Reich before their deaths, and he sought blue-eyed twins so he could perform experiments aimed at cloning the Nordic super-men which Hitler had decreed were to be the new chosen race. And all the while he salved the shreds of his wicked conscience by claiming that *he* was saving life for the future! Yet all experts concur that on his personal orders alone some four hundred thousand Jews were executed. Prisoners, infected with lice, TB, typhus, typhoid and grotesque medieval-style infections – infections bred by the poor diet and insanitary conditions which prevailed in the camps – existed in a twilight zone of brutality that could only be eased by death. When they were no longer able to function in the armaments plants and quarries adjacent to the camps they were eliminated. The gold teeth from the corpses were sent to the Reichsbank in Berlin, their hair was

Left: *Those destined for the concentration camps were packed into cattle trucks for the journey.*

Below: *Grim photographs are both proof of, and constant reminders of, the barbaric slaughter of millions of innocent Europeans in the Nazi camps.*

used to stuff mattresses for troops on the Russian front and the fat from their bodies was processed into soap. Such was the efficiency that Adolf Hitler demanded and got from his loyal servants of evil.

Adolf Eichmann, like Mengele, was a classic product of the twisted logic of Nazism. He saw no evil in what he was doing, believed that he was a 'good soldier' who was only obeying orders. Day after day, as Germany was losing the war on all fronts, this son of an accountant re-routed armaments trains headed for the troops with supplies and rations, and cancelled returning hospital trains, so he could use the rolling stock to clear out the ghettoes of Eastern Europe and thus feed the furnaces at the extermination camps. But he was not flamboyant, more a grey bureaucrat and his cruelty only became public after the collapse of the Reich in May 1945.

During the height of the Holocaust one thousand trains a week were criss-crossing Europe with people destined for the camps. In the middle of 1943 fully a third of all camp inmates assigned to work details died each week. Survival became a matter of co-operating with the SS – by getting a job in a camp clinic, becoming a block captain, seizing any chance to please the SS – anything that might bring a chance of survival. The overwhelming horror of these places was belied by the cynical slogan

Himmler placed above the entrance gates of the camps – *Arbeit Macht Frei* – Work Brings Freedom. It was a bitter lie.

Not the camps were not the only disgrace. As brave German soldiers fought valiantly at places like Stalingrad and Kharkhov, the *Einsatzgruppen* squads were forever besmirching Germany's name with their mass executions. Herman Graebe, a German civilian engineer working on road-building in the Ukraine, witnessed just such

HIMMLER PLACED ABOVE THE ENTRANCE GATES OF THE CAMPS – *ARBEIT MACHT FREI* – WORK BRINGS FREEDOM.

Above: *Allied soldiers guard captured Nazi leaders during the massive war crimes trial held in Nurnberg after the defeat of Nazi Germany*

Right: *Adolf Eichmann was finally captured in the Sixties. He pleaded his cause before a weary Judge Moishe Landau (far right).*

Opposite, far right: *Herman Goering in prison, awaiting sentence, during the war crimes trial.*

'WITHOUT SCREAMING OR WEEPING THESE PEOPLE UNDRESSED, STOOD AROUND IN FAMILY GROUPS, KISSED EACH OTHER, SAID FAREWELLS, AND WAITED FOR THE SIGN FROM THE SS MAN WHO STOOD BESIDE THE PIT.

a scene. He wrote: 'Without screaming or weeping these people undressed, stood around in family groups, kissed each other, said farewells, and waited for the sign from the SS man who stood beside the pit with a whip in his hand. During the fifteen minutes I stood near, I heard no complaint

or plea for mercy. I watched a family... An old woman with snow-white hair was holding a child of about one in her arms, singing to it and tickling it. The child was cooing with delight. The parents were looking on with tears in their eyes. The father was holding the hand of a boy about

ten years old and speaking to him softly; the boy was fighting back tears. The father pointed to the sky, stroked his head and seemed to explain something to him.

'At that moment the SS man at the pit started shouting something to his comrade. The comrade counted off about twenty people and instructed them to go behind the earth mound. Among them was the family I have just mentioned. I well remember a slim girl with black hair who, as she passed me, pointed to herself and said: 'Twenty-three'. I walked around the mound and stood in front of a tremendous grave. People were closely wedged together and lying on top of each other so that only their heads were visible. Nearly all had blood running over their shoulders from their heads. Some were lifting their heads and moving their arms to show that they were still alive. The pit was nearly two-thirds full and I estimated that it contained about one thousand people. I looked at the man who did the shooting. He was an SS man who sat at the edge of the narrow end of the pit, his feet dangling into it. He had a tommy-gun on his knees and was smoking a cigarette. The people, completely naked, went down some steps which were cut in the clay wall of the pit and clambered over the heads of the people lying there, to the place to which the SS man directed them. Some caressed those who were still alive and spoke to them in low voices.'

Above: A rogues' gallery of Nazis. From the left, Propaganda minister, Goebbels; SS Chief, Himmler; Deputy Hess and Hitler, all together at a pre-War rally.

A DIGNITY IN DEATH

Towards the end of the war the Nazis increased their frantic efforts to wipe out the estimated nine million Jews within the conquered lands. One of Eichmann's greatest coups in the desperate days of 1944, as the Russians were advancing rapidly throughout Eastern Europe, was to get the Hungarians to hand over half of their population of eight hundred thousand Jews. They were all gassed at Auschwitz – an achievement which Eichmann said gave him 'intense satisfaction'.

Most Jews and other Nazi victims went nobly and quietly to their deaths. They had a dignity which mocked the brutality of their tormentors, yet the Nazis liked to crow that the Jews had continually shown their weakness in life's struggle because they did not fight, but meekly submitted to the sword. But in reality, there was nowhere for these tortured people to go if they had escaped, no prospect of victory over well-trained and well-fed guards.

The Nazis did not have it entirely their own way. At Sachsenhausen many guards were killed in an armed breakout and, in 1944, the Jewish Underground in Auschwitz placed explosives in one of the ovens and blew it to smithereens. The most impressive display of defiance came when Hitler ordered the destruction of the Warsaw Ghetto in 1944. Here, the Jews of Poland were housed, but they refused to be taken to the trains and, with smuggled weaponry, killed SS men.

It took half-a-division of SS men with full anti-tank and armour facilities to rout the defenders in four months of bitter fighting. It cost the Jews fifty-six thousand lives and kept valuable German soldiers away from the fight on the front. Such were the twisted values of Nazism – the defenceless Jew always considered more of an enemy than guns, tanks and armed soldiers.

While they may have salved their own consciences about what took place in the death camps, with the excuse that they were 'only obeying orders', the guilty men knew what awaited them. Auschwitz personnel fled the camp just twenty-four hours before Russian troops arrived to liberate the wretches left inside. The air was still heavy with the sickly-sweet stench of burned human flesh and the crematorium, the one that was still working, had corpses awaiting burning. In a warehouse barracks that the Nazis dubbed 'Canada' because of its vast size, the Russians found a mountain of human hair, gold teeth, underwear, clothing and jewellery – the last destined for the Reichsbank. Hoess had planned to demolish Auschwitz but he left it too late. But Franz Stangl, commandant of Treblinka, managed to destroy his camp. The only testimonies to its existence are the tracks of the railway line, and the deep green hue of the grass over the rich, fertile ground that, in places, is twelve feet thick with human bonemeal.

In the west, it was the Americans and the British who liberated the Nazi charnel houses of Belsen and Buchenwald.

Josef Kramer, the commandant of Belsen, was puzzled by the fury of the ordinary British squaddies who liberated his fiefdom; could not understand why they were so belligerent towards him. At his

'I DIDN'T FEEL ANYTHING TOWARDS THE PRISONERS. I RECEIVED ORDERS TO KILL THEM AND THAT'S WHAT I DID. SURELY YOU CANNOT EXPECT A SOLDIER IN WARTIME TO DISOBEY AN ORDER?'

Left: *His charm and determination gave Adolf Hitler a terrible power over a nation broken by their defeat in the Great War.*

Below: *A unique picture of Jews arriving from a train at the Czech concentration camp of Terezin.*

from Swiss banks the names of wealthy Jewish clients, now used the same good offices of secrecy for their own flight.

REFUGE FOR THE WICKED

South America, where military regimes had long expressed solidarity and sympathy with the Nazi cause, was a favourite destination. Eichmann headed for Argentina; Mengele for Brazil; Joseph Schwammberger, commandant of the concentration camp at Przemysl, to Argentina; Alois Brunner, designer of the mobile gaswagons and the brains behind the deportation of forty-six thousand Greek Jews to Auschwitz, made it to Damascus where he still lives under Arab protection.

Justice for those left behind was swift; many camp guards were executed within days of liberation. The Nuremberg trials despatched many more, including Kramer and Greese. But it was left to people like Simon Wiesenthal, who lost eighty members of his family in the Holocaust, to become the conscience of the world – to ensure that mankind never forgot what revolting crimes had taken place.

Wiesenthal is an old man now, his shoulders slightly hunched and his hair grey, but his eyes have lost none of their fire. He survived the death camps and has pledged his life to tracking down Nazi war criminals and bringing them to justice. His determination and diligence led to the capture of Eichmann in Argentina and the deportation from South America of Lyons Gestapo chief Klaus Barbie.

Weisenthal's small office in central Vienna is called the Documentation Centre and it is a museum to the memory of the slain. Wiesenthal calculates that as many as fourteen million were claimed by the Nazis in their war of racial purification. From 22 March, 1933, when Dachau, twelve miles from Munich, opened as the Reich's first concentration camp, until the Allies liberated the entire network, Hitler had managed to dispose of over a third of Europe's Jews. Wiesenthal inflates his figures because of the special 'actions' undertaken in Russia, the enormity of which has still to be fully understood.

Even now Weisenthal is still hunting, still ceaselessly bringing to justice those who perpetrated mankind's biggest mass

trial after the war for his crimes at the Natzweiler, Auschwitz and Belsen camps, he told those judging him: 'I didn't feel anything towards the prisoners. I received orders to kill them and that's what I did. Surely you cannot expect a soldier in wartime to disobey an order?'

But Kramer and all the others – Babor of Gross-Rosen, Mengele of Auschwitz, Heinrich 'Gestapo' Mueller, Adolf Eichmann, Franz Stangl of Treblinka – all tried to escape. They knew that their blind obedience to orders would never stand up in a courtroom whose loyalty was not to Adolf Hitler. Using the services of the ODESSA – the Organization of Former Members of the SS – they drew on secret Swiss bank accounts to pay for new identities and lives in distant lands. Much of the money came from the victims whose butchery they had overseen in the camps. It was a final bitter twist of irony that the SS who had tried, without success, to wheedle

Above: *The power-mad, ruthless Herman Goering started the Gestapo to enforce the more ruthless aspects of Nazi rule.*

Opposite, top: *The Nazis sought to whip up anti-semitic feelings with crude caricatures meant to persaude citizens that the Jews were untrustworthy.*

Opposite, below: *Gold was extracted from the teeth of concentration camp victims. The gold was boxed and delivered to the Reichsbank.*

murder. He cannot stop, not while revision-ist historians and neo-Nazi sympathisers, now on the rise in Europe and Russia, are busy denying that the Holocaust with its death camps ever happened.

Wiesenthal would die a happy man if he could get Alois Brunner, the committed Nazi, who, in 1965, said to reporters from a German newspaper: 'I'm glad! I'm proud of what I did. If I could have fed more Yids into the flame I would. I don't regret a thing – we were only destroying vermin.'

Simon Wiesenthal finds some solace in the report he will give to the Lord when it is his time to depart. this life

'We will all be called before the Lord for judgement,' he said, 'and we will be asked to give an account of ourselves. One man will say: "I became a tailor". Another will say: "I became a doctor". Yet another will say: "I became a jeweller".

'And I will be able to say: "I did not forget you…".'

ALFREDO ASTIZ
The Dirty war

The new military government promised to return Argentina to its former glory. Instead, they unleashed a gang of sadists upon the nation – men like Astiz who led a dirty war of murder and torture against his own people.

Between 1976 and 1982 Argentina waged a full-scale war within its own borders. The enemy were classified as those who acted or sympathised with anyone who had a viewpoint other than that espoused by the government. The military junta in power called their reign of terror The Process of National Reorganization. But it was a fancy euphemism for mass murder, whereby people vanished into human slaughterhouses, were tortured there and murdered. Coffee-bar socialists, mothers of radicals, babies of dissidents, long-lost cousins of intellectuals who had once read a Communist pamphlet – these were the victims of this 'Process' known to the rest of the world as the 'Dirty War'. And working within this state terror machine were individuals like Lt Alfredo Astiz.

THE CLEANSING OF SOCIETY

Astiz was a member of the officer corps which took upon itself the burden of 'cleansing' Argentinian society. The military throughout South America has had a long and shameful history of interference in civilian governments but none more so than the Argentinian army. Military rule has dominated Argentina and between 1930 and 1982, the only civilian government to last its full term was that of Juan Peron. For years, after no less than six coups, the men in uniform guided – or rather, misguided – the fortunes of this land rich in minerals, farming and cattle.

When the sophisticated and cosmopolitan citizens of Buenos Aries woke up to the clatter of tank tracks on the cobbled streets of their gracious city on 23 March, 1976 they did not panic; they had, after all, heard and seen it all before.

This time, it was a General Jorge Videla telling the people that massive unemployment, inflation running at eight hundred per cent and a resurgence of left-wing violence had driven the military to grab power. Videla, having seized the radio and

television stations, put it to his people like this: 'Since all constitutional mechanisms have been exhausted, and since the impossibility of recovery through normal processes has been irrefutably demonstrated, the armed forces must put an end to this situation which has burdened the nation. This government will be imbued with a profound national spirit, and will respond only to the most sacred interests of the nation and its inhabitants.'

There was a tone of determination in his voice which made the people of Argentina embrace rather than shrink from military government. Leftist guerillas had, since 1966, been rampant in the countryside, murdering, kidnapping, committing atrocities among the civil population. The country was on an inexorable slide into anarchy as it battled against these guerilla groups, most notably the *Ejercito*

THIS GOVERNMENT WILL BE IMBUED WITH A PROFOUND NATIONAL SPIRIT.

Above: *The Mothers of the Plaza de Mayo defied arrest, torture and even death as they paraded before the junta headquarters in frequent mass demands for the return of their children.*

Opposite: *The raffish, handsome exterior of naval officer, Alfredo Astiz, hid the ugly torturer of the death squads.*

Revolucionarioa del Pueblo – People's Revolutionary Army – and the *Montoneros*. There is a school of thought which says that, had these terrorists not created a climate of fear which brought the army out of its barracks and put the torturers in government, fifteen thousand innocent people might still be alive today. But Videla and his henchmen were welcomed by a tired population who were glad to listen to his ideas on The Process of National Reorganization.

While Videla uttered platitudes and told his own people, and the world at large, that his government would respect human rights, his machinery of terror was being secretly assembled, soon to be unleashed on an unsuspecting population.

The officer corps of the Argentinian armed forces saw themselves as an elite group, imbued with the national spirit as no other body within Argentina. Many proved very happy to oversee the terror required to reorganize their countrymen, but none

Above: Dagmar Hagelin, a young Swedish woman, disappeared after the junta kidnapped her.

Opposite, top: Alfredo Astiz enters the court where he faced charges regarding the disappearance of Dagmar Hagelin.

Opposite, below: Ragnar Hagelin stands outside the military court after he was notified of the acquittal of Astiz who was charged with the disappearance of Hagelin's daughter.

more so than Alfredo Astiz, who was to develop into an infamous torturer, his name forever linked with this shameful period of Argentina's sad history.

THE DEATH SQUADS

Astiz, a handsome naval lieutenant of wealthy parents, drank deeply from the poisoned chalice offered by Videla. He believed the General when he said that the enemies of Argentina were within its own frontiers. With the zeal of a Spanish Inquisition cardinal, Astiz helped enthusiastically in the founding and operation of ESMA, the Navy Mechanics School in Buenos Aries, which was nothing more than a human abbatoir hiding behind the name of an institute of marine engineering.

Thousands of victims of 'The Process' were brought as prisoners to the Navy Mechanics School where they were subjected to the most horrific beatings and torture, then taken out for execution; very few made it back to families and loved ones. It was not only the navy that organized this kind of torture centre; the army, air force and police were also involved, each one vying for glory as they hunted the 'enemy within'. They operated in squads called *patotas* and they each found places to turn into centres of hell, where they dragged the dissidents who, they believed, were destroying the Argentinian way of life and its cultural traditions.

One of the few victims to survive after Astiz and his men had captured her has a horrifying story to tell. Twenty-seven-year-old nursery school teacher Isabel Gamba de Negrotti was pregnant when she was seized at gunpoint by the *patotas* and taken away in a green Ford Falcon car – a make of car that came to be indelibly linked with death – and dumped in the Navy Mechanics School. The young woman described her ordeal: 'They took me to a room after arrival where they kicked me and punched me in the head. Then they undressed me and beat me on the legs, buttocks and shoulders with something made of rubber. This lasted a long time. I fell down several times and they made me stand by supporting myself on a table... While all this was going on they talked to me, insulted me, and asked me about people I didn't know and things I didn't understand.

The junta was going after the children, the students and the trade unionists, the journalists and the teachers – all were swept up in the vortex of terror. Victims were picked up at random and, as these citizens were bundled into the death cars, they would yell out their names and addresses to passers-by who, in turn, would inform families that their relations had joined *los desparecidos* – 'the disappeared'.

Often the military disposed of their victims by pushing bodies, dead or alive, out of helicopters as they flew over rivers. Almost five thousand people are believed to have met their deaths on these 'NN' – 'No-Name' – flights. Others were buried in mass graves on the pampas or in remote corners of country churchyards, buried without name, sacrament or ceremony.

Inside the Navy Mechanics School, Astiz and other torturers preferred even crueller forms of death and practised bizarre forms of torture and sadism against men, women and children.

Many people who came across Astiz compared him to Dr Josef Mengele, the Nazi death camp doctor at Auschwitz. Astiz who was fair-haired and blue-eyed,

'I pleaded with them to leave me alone, otherwise I would lose my baby. I hadn't the strength to speak, the pain was so bad. They started to give me electric shocks on my breasts, the side of my body and under my arms. They kept questioning me. They gave me electric shocks in the vagina and put a pillow over my mouth to stop me screaming. Someone called 'The Colonel' came and said they were going to increase the voltage until I talked, but I didn't know what they wanted me to talk about. They kept throwing water over my body and applying electric shocks all over. Two days later I miscarried.' She survived the ordeal.

Enemies real and imagined were seen everywhere by officers of the junta. Their paranoia is revealed in a telling comment from Fifth Army Corps Commander General Adel Vilas, that he made some months after 'The Process' had started: 'Up to now only the tip of the iceberg has been affected by our war against subversion... it is necessary to destroy the sources which feed, form and indoctrinate the subversive delinquent, and the source is the universities and secondary schools themselves.'

OFTEN THE MILITARY DISPOSED OF THEIR VICTIMS BY PUSHING BODIES, DEAD OR ALIVE, OUT OF HELICOPTERS AS THEY FLEW OVER RIVERS.

THEY ROAMED AT WILL, AT ANY HOUR OF THE DAY OR NIGHT, SATISFYING WHATEVER GROTESQUE LUSTS CAME UPON THEM WITH ANY VICTIM THEY HAPPENED UPON.

SOMEONE CALLED 'THE COLONEL' CAME AND SAID THEY WERE GOING TO INCREASE THE VOLTAGE UNTIL I TALKED, BUT I DIDN'T KNOW WHAT THEY WANTED ME TO TALK ABOUT.

Right: *These men of the Junta faced murder charges. Clockwise: Jorge Videla, Emilio Massera, Orlando Agosti, Omar Graffigna, Basilio Lami Dozo, Jorge Anaya, Leopoldo Galtieri, Roberta Viola and, centre, Armando Lambruschini.*

Opposite: *Alfredo Astiz in his role as naval officer signs his surrender to the British during the Falklands War, and in the lower picture, he goes to court as a suspected criminal to face charges of kidnap and murder.*

was nicknamed 'the blonde angel' and he revelled in his sadistic work. He was keen from the very beginning of 'The Process' to take on the dirty, murderous tasks that many of his naval comrades refused.

Raul Vilarano, the killer who later confessed to the horrible deeds perpetrated by himself and Astiz, said that he and his cohorts did not work to any pattern at the Navy Mechanics School; rather, they roamed at will, at any hour of the day or night, satisfying whatever grotesque lusts came upon them with any victim they happened upon. Dagmar Hagelin happened to be one of those victims.

Dagmar was arrested on 27 January, 1977. She had Swedish nationality even though she was raised in Argentina, and

was a gifted eighteen-year-old classical music student with coffee-table ideas about socialism, but no affiliation with any guerilla groups or other Communist subversives. As she rang the bell at a friend's house two men – a *patota* squad from the Navy Mechanics School – appeared and Dagmar ran, only to be shot down in the street. She was dumped in the boot of a Ford Falcon and driven away. The man who had fired the shot was Astiz.

Unlike other 'no-names' who had disappeared, Dagmar did not come from the poor and powerless. Her father ran a profitable business and was on good terms with the Swedish ambassador but, though he used every influence to trace his daughter, his efforts were to no avail. Dagmar, another innocent among thousands, died in the Navy Mechanics School and her remains have never been found. The Swedish ambassador refused to accept honours from his host country when it came time for him to take up another diplomatic posting – he did not want to give credence to a regime that, he was convinced, murdered young girls.

Jacobo Timerman, a Jewish newspaper editor who was deemed sympathetic to the enemies of the state, was tortured by Astiz but he survived to shame the military men with an account of his suffering in the book 'Prisoner Without a Name, Cell Without a Number'. He wrote: 'When electric shocks are applied, all that a man feels is that they're ripping his flesh apart. And he howls. Afterwards, he doesn't feel the blows. Nor does he feel them the next day, when there's no electricity, but only blows. The man spends days confined in a cell without windows, without light, either seated or lying down. The man spends a month without being allowed to wash himself, transported on the floor of an automobile to various places of interrogation, fed badly, smelling bad. The man is left enclosed in a small cell for forty-eight hours, his eyes blindfolded, his hands tied behind him, hearing no voice, seeing no sign of life, having to perform his bodily

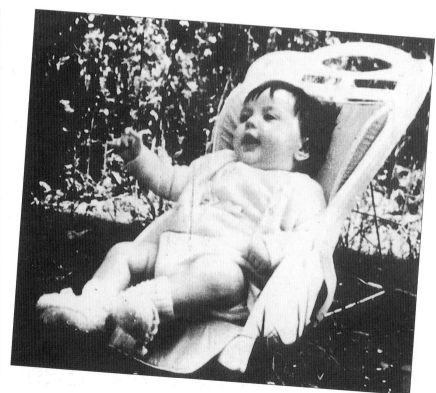

functions upon himself. And there is not much more. Objectively, nothing more.'

Astiz reached new heights of cynicism and cruelty when he posed as Gustavo Nino, a peasant boy who had lost relatives to the *patotas*. He infiltrated the ranks of the women who came to be called 'The Mothers of the Plaza de Mayo,' the head-scarved women who paraded silently in front of the junta's pink palace with the names of missing loved ones on boards hanging from their necks. These women were the true heroines of the Dirty War, defying truncheons and tear-gas to stage their weekly vigil, a vigil that played a powerful role in bringing the world's atten-

'WHEN ELECTRIC SHOCKS ARE APPLIED, ALL THAT A MAN FEELS IS THAT THEY'RE RIPPING HIS FLESH APART. AND HE HOWLS.'

THESE WOMEN WERE THE TRUE HEROINES OF THE DIRTY WAR, DEFYING TRUNCHEONE AND TEAR GAS TO STAGE THEIR WEEKLY VIGIL IN DEFIANCE OF THE JUNTA

THE MAN SPENDS DAYS CONFINED IN A CELL WITHOUT WINDOWS, WITHOUT LIGHT.

Opposite, top: *A woman weeps at a 'No-Name' cemetery where thousands of Argentinians were dumped in unmarked graves after their murder by the junta.*

Opposite, below: *The baby Clara Anahi Mariani disappeared after her parents were murdered. This baby was either abducted or killed by the junta.*

Left: *The Mothers grew bolder and bolder. They knew they had to attract world attention to their plight if they were to defeat the regime.*

Above: *After the junta fell, Argentinians began to dig up the unmarked graves.*

Opposite, top: *The military roll their weapons through Buenos Aires.*

Opposite, below: *Soldiers were seen as heroes before the ignoble Dirty War.*

who were waiting with the whips and the electric cattle prods and the flames.

For a time Astiz also worked out of his government's naval bureau in Paris, where he spied on exiled Argentinian human rights groups. After he was rumbled in Paris he headed for South Africa on a naval posting, but was hounded out of the country in 1981 when journalists learned of his unsavoury work at the Mechanics School. His superiors decided to pack him off to the war against Britain in the Falkland Islands in 1982.

THE TORTURER IS FREED

Astiz was captured by Royal Marines and when his name appeared in British newspapers, alarm bells began to ring in the capitals of the world. There were calls for his blood from Stockholm to Paris to the capital of his homeland, where thousands had a righteous claim on his murdering hide. But, under the terms of the Geneva Convention, Astiz was a prisoner-of-war and could not be handed over to foreign powers who suspected him of domestic crimes. He returned home after the war.

In Argentina, the following year, Raul Alfonsin was sworn in as the democratic president, the forty-first in the nation's history. His mandate was not only to steer the country towards democratic reforms, but also to exorcise the evil perpetrated upon his people by the junta. Some of the guilty men were brought to trial – including the suave torturer, Astiz. But he was never punished, never served time in a prison. At his pre-trial hearing his lawyers refused to admit that he had abducted and killed Dagmar – but in a supreme Orwellian twist said that if he had, it did not matter, because he was operating in a 'war time' situation. The military really did believe they were at war with their own people. He is now free in Argentina, a forty-two-year-old man with a wicked past but not a troubled conscience.

A commission was established after the war by the Alfonsin government to probe the terror. It found that the 'final purpose' of the terror was to exterminate the detainees and disfigure the bodies, so they could never be identified. The commission found no common factor to link the victims – they came from every level of

tion to the mass killings taking place in what the West had long regarded as the most 'civilised' of the South American nations. However, when the women's ranks were depleted by arrests, when their homes were raided or set on fire, when more members of their family disappeared, Gustavo Nino was always there to comfort them, never letting on that he had been the one who fed the damning information about their families back to his colleagues,

Argentinian society. Almost nine thousand of 'the disappeared' have never been found, despite the fact that more than sixty per cent of those seized were abducted in front of witnesses in public places. Three hundred and forty torture centres were unearthed – centres which, according to the junta, never existed. The commission produced a report fifty thousand pages long but the government failed to bring any of these state murderers to account.

Democracy now rules in Argentina, the dark days of 'The Process' are over. But the men in the olive green uniforms with the dark glasses are still there, lurking, waiting their next chance. Hebe Bonafini hopes they stay hidden. She was one of the founding members of the Mothers of the Plaza de Mayo and lost two sons and a daughter-in-law in the terror. She said: 'The military went to war against people who spoke their own tongue. They never got the right ones anyway, just children, really, no one who was ever a threat. What happened to us must serve as a warning to all people all the time. It can happen anywhere you know, making people disappear. That is the tragedy of it. It can happen to anyone...'.

SEPTEMBER 11
World Trade Center

On September 11, 2001, terrorists unleashed a shocking air assault on America's military and financial powers by hijacking four commercial jets and then crashing them into the World Trade Center in New York, the Pentagon and the Pennsylvania countryside.

Above: *The second plane hits the south tower of the World Trade Center.*

It was the most dramatic attack on American soil since Pearl Harbor and caused the most incredible scenes of chaos and carnage. With the estimated death toll at over 5,300, this was definitely one of the most devastating terrorist operations in American history.

HIJACKED PLANES

The terrorists hijacked four California-bound planes from three airports on the Eastern Seaboard. The planes were loaded with the maximum amount of fuel, which suggested a well-financed and well-co-ordinated plan. The planes were identified as American Airlines flight #11 and United Airlines flight #175 both flying from Boston, Massachusetts to Los Angeles, California. There were a total of 157 people on board the two planes.

At 8.45 a.m. the first hijacked passenger jet, Flight #11, crashes into the north tower of the 110-storey World Trade Center, tearing a gaping hole in the building and setting it on fire.

As if this wasn't horrifying enough, at precisely 9.03 a.m. the second hijacked airliner, Flight #175, crashes

THE WORLD TRADE CENTER'S NORTH TOWER COLLAPSES FROM THE TOP DOWN AS IF IT WERE BEING PEELED APART, RELEASING A TREMENDOUS CLOUD OF DEBRIS AND SMOKE.

into the south tower of the World Trade Center and explodes – both buildings are now burning. They had ripped a blazing path through the Defence Department, bringing the domestic air traffic system to a halt and plunging the whole nation into an unparalleled state of panic.

Immediately the Federal Aviation Administration shut down all New York City area airports, halting all flight operations for the first time in US history. The Port Authority of New York and New Jersey ordered that all bridges and tunnels in the New York area were to be closed.

President Bush put US military forces, both at home and abroad, on their highest state of alert, and navy

Above: *Firefighters attempting to put out the blaze at The Pentagon.*

In a grim address to the nation, President Bush condemned the attacks as a failed attempt to frighten the United States and promised a relentless hunt to find those responsible. 'We will make no distinction,' he said, 'between the terrorists who committed these acts and those who harbour them.' Bush also promised that America would continue to function 'without interruption'.

Below: *The collapse of the south tower at the World Trade Center.*

warships were deployed along both coasts for air defence.

The horrors of the attack, however, were not yet over. At 9:43 a.m. American Airlines Flight #77 out of Dulles International Airport, ripped through the newly renovated walls of the Pentagon – perhaps the world's most secure office building.

Evacuation of The Pentagon and the White House began immediately.

At 10:05 a.m. the south tower of the World Trade Center collapses, plummeting into the streets below. A massive cloud of dust and debris forms and slowly drifts away from the building. At the same time as the collapse of the tower, a fourth jet, Flight #93, is reported to have crashed 80 miles southeast of Pittsburgh, shortly after it was hijacked and turned in the direction of Washington.

None of the 266 people aboard the four planes survived. There were even more horrific casualties in the World Trade Center and the Pentagon, which together provided office space for more than 70,000 people.

The spectacular collapse of the historic twin towers and another not so famous skyscraper during the rescue operations caused even more bloodshed. At least 300 New York firefighters and 85 police officers lost their lives.

GROUND ZERO

The site of destruction became known as 'Ground Zero'. The extent of the devastation, even the limited view of it that could be seen from outside the perimeter, was a horrifying sign of just how evil mankind can be. However, you could also see many signs of the good side of humanity, in the numerous outpourings of love and support for the victims and their families that surrounded the site. You could see the tributes everywhere – in the yard of a describe the place as clean, the cleanup of the World Trade Center site is now complete. What was just a pile of jagged, knotted steel and concrete, is now a hole, a neatly squared-off, rectangular cavity of 16 acres.

One prominent reminder of the scale of the disaster that engulfed New York on that fatal day was the remains of 'The Sphere' which stood in the fountain. This was once the centrepiece of World Trade Center plaza.

The search for bodies has now officially been called off.

Above: *Recovering the body of the firefighter's chaplain from the Ground Zero site.*

church near the site, and along the fence surrounding the area. There were signs, posters, greeting cards, dolls, stuffed animals, flowers and numerous other messages and items indicating that people all over the world cared about the people who died in this tragedy. It seemed to show the sheer determination of the people to stand up against the terrorists.

Though it may never feel right to

THE GRIM AND EXHAUSTING TASK OF CARTING AWAY THE RUINS OF THE WORLD TRADE CENTER TOOK MONTHS AND A BILLION DOLLARS — AND FINISHED UNDER BUDGET AND AHEAD OF SCHEDULE.

WHO IS RESPONSIBLE?

Although no one claimed responsibility for the attacks on September 11, federal officials said they suspect the involvement of Islamic extremists with links to fugitive terrorist Osama bin Laden. Bin Laden has been implicated in the 1998 bombings of two US embassies in Africa and several other attacks. There is also a lot of evidence implicating bin Laden's militant network in the attack. Politicians from both parties predicted a major and immediate escalation in America's worldwide war against terrorism.

Following the cataclysmic events of September 11, the US authorities were quick to name Osama bin Laden as their prime suspect. The reasons for their suspicions were many, and the evidence collected during the ensuing investigation seemed to support their theory.

Although the evidence seemed compelling, at least two people weren't convinced. Milt Beardon, a former CIA agent who spent time in Afghanistan advising the mujahedeen during their fight against the Soviets,

> 'MY PRIME SUSPECT IS OSAMA BIN LADEN BECAUSE HE WAS INDICATING HE WAS GOING TO DO THIS, HE WAS CALLING FOR THE KILLING OF AMERICANS JUST RECENTLY AND HE HAD THE CAPABILITY, SO WHY WOULDN'T WE SUSPECT HIM — WE'D HAVE TO BE CRAZY.'
>
> Professor Bard O'Neil from the National War College in Washington

told ABC's Sunday programme that the attacks may have been the work of Shi'ite Muslims because the hijackers on the aircraft that crashed outside Philadelphia were described as wearing 'red head bands,' an adornment known to date back to the formation of the Shi'ite sect. While Pakistani journalist, Hamid Mir, also doubts that bin Laden was behind the September 11 attacks, saying the terrorist leader did not have the resources to pull it off.

Despite these doubts, another piece of information provided a chilling insight into what was to come. While recording a segment for the CBS *60 Minutes* programme, the show's producer George Creel, was travelling in a car with Khaled Kodja, a known bin Laden associate, when Kodja told him:

> 'America is a very vulnerable country, you are a very open country. I tell you, your White House is your most vulnerable target. It would be very simple to just get it. It is not difficult. It takes only one or two lives to have it, it's not difficult. We have people like this.'

Although the world intelligence community has been aware of bin Laden and his al-Qaeda network for some time, no one was able to predict where and when he would strike next. The organization is not only more sophisticated than past terrorist groups, but it is controlled and financed by a man who has dedicated most of his adult life to fighting a jihad against anyone he sees as an 'enemy of Islam', particularly America.

FROM A LARGE FAMILY

Osama bin Laden (Usamah bin Muhammad bin Awad bin Ladin) was born in 1957 or 1958 in Riyadh, Saudi Arabia. He was the seventh son in a family of 52 children.

His father, Sheik Mohammed Awad bin Laden, was a poor, uneducated

Above: *Osama bin Laden*

labourer from Hadramout in South Yemen who worked as a porter in Jeddah. In 1930, the elder bin Laden started his own construction business, which became so successful that his family grew to be known as 'the wealthiest non-royal family in the kingdom.'

Bin Laden tops the FBI's most wanted terrorist list and, until recently, has been living in exile under the protection of Afghanistan's Taliban regime. Since the collapse of the Taliban regime, he has been in hiding. Though his current whereabouts are unknown, most reports indicate that, if alive, bin Laden is probably in Afghanistan.

Although the September 11 attacks shocked the world with their audacity and far-reaching repercussions, one positive factor remains. A large percentage of the world's population was united in a collective resolve to never let it happen again. Perhaps, at least in this case, some good will come out of it and the thousands of victims will not have died in vain.

THE BIGGEST AL-QAEDA CATCH

The arrest and interrogation of Khalid Sheikh Mohammed is the biggest catch yet in the global hunt for al-Qaeda suspects. Western security sources say they have no doubts that Khalid played a major role as al-Qaeda's operational commander in the September 11 attacks.

Kuwaiti-born Mohammed was one of three al-Qaeda suspects detained in the city of Rawalpindi near the Pakistani capital Islamabad as part of Pakistan's support for US President George W. Bush's war on terror.

Nobody but a few Pakistani intelligence agents had heard of Khalid until a 1,200lb bomb of fertilizer, petrol and hydrogen exploded in the underground car part of the World Trade Center in New York on February 26, 1993. This attack, which killed six people and injured more than 1,000, was Khalid's spectacular debut in international terrorism.

Chilling details have begun to emerge regarding Khalid's alleged activities since September 11. He is reported to have commanded Richard Reid, the shoe-bomber now serving life in an American prison for attempting to blow up a US aircraft over the Atlantic. Jose Padilla, who was arrested in Chicago last June on suspicion of planning a 'dirty bomb' attack, is said to have been another one of his protégés. Attacks on an Israeli aircraft, bombings on the USS Cole in Yemen and a hotel in Kenya last October were planned by him, according to reports. He has also played an important role inspiring and fostering ties with Asian terrorist groups, particularly those responsible for the Bali bombings.

Witnesses in Pakistan are also reported to have confessed that Khalid personally killed Daniel Pearl, the Wall Street Journal reporter who was kidnapped in Karachi last year.

Some of America's most senior politicians are already saying that the normal rules governing the torture of terror suspects, should be set aside because Sheikh Mohammed is the repository of so much important information.

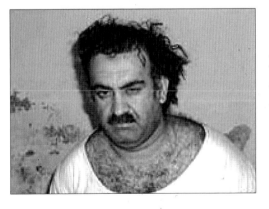

Left: *Khalid Sheikh Mohammed following his arrest.*

Sheikh Mohammed has already disclosed the names and descriptions of about a dozen key al-Qaeda operatives believed to be plotting terrorist attacks on American and other Western interests. He has also filled in important gaps in what U.S. intelligence knows about al-Qaeda's practices.

SADDAM HUSSEIN
Genocide of the Kurds

The proud warrior tribes refused to bend before a dictator. So he took his vicious revenge. He sprayed them with terrible chemicals, which brought painful and dreadful death to thousands of Kurdish men, women and children.

Long before the high-tech war visited on his country by the Allied forces during Operation Desert Storm, Iraqi despot Saddam Hussein had waged another, dirtier kind of war within his own borders. His enemy was the fiercely proud Kurdish tribe, the hot-blooded warrior race that, for centuries, had longed for an independent Kurdistan that would span the border between Iraq and Turkey.

Hussein assembled one of the greatest war machines ever seen, before it was dismantled during the Gulf War. In manpower alone, he had the fifth largest army in the world, plus a formidable array of conventional and chemical weaponry. He needed to ensure that he was the master of the Middle East, but part of his arsenal was developed for a plan every bit as sinister as that hatched by the Nazis. He wanted to wipe out the Kurdish people once and for all. In 1988, before his power was stunted, if not altogether broken by the West, Saddam unleashed his appalling chemical weapons against innocent Kurds, as part of his blueprint for their destruction, killing over four thousand people. Against his arch-enemy Iran, whom he fought for eight futile years, he used mustard gas.

His chemical weapons programme was one of the most advanced in the world. America and the former USSR had long ago curbed production of chemical weapons, which are forbidden under United Nations rulings and the Geneva Convention. The world did not want to repeat the horrors of the First World War where chemical weapons had been used. But Saddam realised that massive stockpiles of lethal gas would give him a huge military advantage over his enemies.

The technology had not changed a great deal in the years since the Great War - the poison is still delivered by shelf and bomb - but the chemical content has. Saddam developed hydrogen cyanide, a particularly lethal gas which causes death within two seconds when inhaled. He also developed new versions of the nerve gases Tabun and Sarin, pioneered by the Nazis during the Second World War, though never used by them. A very small quantity of either of these gases, will, when it falls on skin, cause a human being to go into convulsions, followed very quickly by death.

THE MEANS OF DESTRUCTION

The technology needed for his gas programme was provided by the Western

HUSSEIN ASSEMBLED ONE OF THE GREATEST WAR MACHINES EVER SEEN, BEFORE IT WAS DISMANTLED DURING THE GULF WAR.

Opposite: *Saddam Hussein, the butcher of Baghdad. He is feared because of his ruthless quest for power in the Middle East.*

nations that would one day be arrayed against him. As long as Saddam Hussein was keeping the forces of Islamic fundamentalism on the opposite bank of the Euphrates River, the West was happy to give him the means for mass destruction. Western companies salved their consciences by saying that much of the hardware necessary for the production of

Above: *Refugees wend their way to Piranshar in Iran to escape the persecution of Saddam Hussein in Iraq.*

chemical warfare was for fertilizer factories within Iraq, although any scientist knows that it is but a small step from producing fertilizers to poison gas. Some were merely duped. The Phillips Petroleum Company of Bartlesville, Ohio, was one of the American companies whose security system failed it. Phillips, through a Belgian unit, had sold the Iraqis five hundred tons of a complex chemical called thiodiglycol, believing it was for use as a fertilizer. Combined with hydrochloric acid, it makes mustard gas. An understanding of what had been made from their shipment to Saddam hit company executives, when in 1988, they read news reports of Iranian soldiers on a remote battlefield coughing up their lungs, and of corpses covered with horrifying chemical burns.

Germany, Holland and Britain also sold chemical weapon technology and raw materials to Iraq, enabling Saddam to build up stockpiles which sent shivers through his bitterest enemy - Israel. Israel, long before Saddam unleashed his Scud missiles on her cities during the Gulf War, feared a pre-emptive strike with chemical missiles.

When Saddam used his mustard gas on the battlefield, it was in limited quantities and aimed strategically at Iranian command posts and communications centres; rarely was it used against civilians. But in his war against the Kurds he had no such qualms.

The Kurds were Saddam Hussein's biggest political problem. They were not impressed by his bellicose speeches, the huge pictures of him that adorned public buildings and stretched over highways; nor did they pay anything other than lip-service to his regime. The Kurds, armed and virtually autonomous in the northern, mountainous region of Iraq were to be taught a tragic, final lesson that they would never be able to forget.

In March 1988, while the war against Iran was still raging, Saddam received reports from his battlefront commanders that Iranian troops, aided by Kurdish guerillas, had seized control of the Kurdish town of Halabja. The town was based near a vital hydro-electric dam. The information that Iranian troops were involved gave Saddam reason to unleash his deadliest poisons on the innocent civilian population.

Above: *A tent city, housing thousands of refugees, has arisen on the Turkish border as people flee the repression of Iraq.*

Yet he must have known that there were, in fact, no Iranian troops in the town because they left within hours of taking it.

THE DEADLY CLOUD

The sun was just rising over the mountain peaks when the first shells began to rain down on Halabja. But unlike the high explosives that the citizens had heard falling along the battlefront with Iran, there was only a soft 'plop-plopping' as the shells dropped without detonating. But soon palls of sickly yellow, white and grey gas began to swell and swirl, drifting like fog through the streets, creeping into every nook and

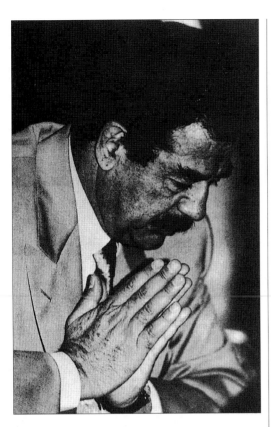

blurring the vision as the eyes smart and itch. There followed uncontrollable bouts of sneezing and vomiting. Their breath shortens in the hours following inhalation of the mustard as the inflammation spreads, swelling the internal lining. Many of them had horrible blisters on their necks, and thighs, causing huge patches of skin to fall off. Large lesions broke out over their genital areas. They were young and old but they were not soldiers. The youngest I treated was a baby of four months. I could not help but ask what they had done to deserve this.'

Iraq, usually so adept at controlling press coverage within its borders, made the mistake of allowing Western newsmen and foreign relief workers into the area. The pictures of thousands of bodies without any visible wounds whatsoever belied Bagdhad's statement that they had been

BUT SOON PALLS OF SICKLY YELLOW, WHITE AND GREY GAS BEGAN TO SWELL AND SWIRL, DRIFTING LIKE FOG THROUGH THE STREETS.

Left: *Hussein may not be a good man, but he is a devout one.*

Below: *Iranian soldiers cower in their trenches during the war against Iraq.*

cranny. Saddam had uncorked his evil weapons of Tabun, cyanide gas and mustard gas on the townspeople. Chaos and hysteria reigned as panic gripped the townsfolk. They ran through the streets, their skin peeling from their faces when the mustard-sulphur clouds hit them. If they ran into Tabun fumes, they were dead within seconds. A shocking photograph recorded a poignant death during this morning of carnage. It shows a mother clutching her dead baby in the main street, both killed as they ran in a frantic attempt to seek cover from the deadly clouds.

By the afternoon the donkeys and goats in the fields were all dead, the vegetation wilted. The sickly smell of rotten onion mixed with burned garlic hung over the air. It was as if someone had gone in with a giant fly spray and snuffed out the life of all the citizens. Only those who had been working in remote fields survived. In all, four thousand men, women and children died on that tragic day in Halabja.

Caglayan Cugen, a Turkish doctor who treated survivors who had burns and respiratory problems, said: 'They talked of seeing these blue canisters from which the gas came. There was an odd odour first and then they remember burning in their eyes,

Above: *Mustard gas killed this woman and her baby during a chemical warfare assault against Kurds in the town of Halabja.*

'DESPITE THE FACT THAT SADDAM HUSSEIN COMMITTED MAJOR ACTS OF GENOCIDE, THE FACT IS, IRAQ GOT AWAY WITH IT.'

killed in the cross-fire of shelling between the forces of Iraq and Iran. It was several months before the Iranian leadership admitted to the use of the gas as 'a necessary measure to drive out the Iranian infidels'.

A UN official who saw the carnage said: 'The bodies were lying in doorways, in streets, around tables set up for lunch and in cellars where people mistakenly sought shelter from the heavier-than-air gas. Many other corpses were found on the roads leading from the town, where residents had failed to outrun the spreading cloud. The victims seemed to have died quickly, as there were few signs of a struggle. The streets were also littered with the bloated carcasses of cows, dogs, cats, sheep and goats.

A TERRIBLE OUTRAGE

'Some thirty of the victims were flown for treatment at hospitals in the West, which confirmed that several poison gas agents were indeed deployed on the innocent civilians. Iranian doctors I spoke with, who treated those refugees who managed to cross over into their country, said their tests had shown that the gases were mustard, cyanide and nerve gas. The injured suffered from the most appalling burns and their lungs were all but destroyed.'

Western diplomats in Iraq were appalled at the outrage. 'Halabja was inexcuseable in every sense of the word,' said one indignant emissary at the time. 'The use of poison gas against enemy troops is bad enough, but to use it against civilians, and especially your own citizens, is quite unbelieveable.'

Steven Rose, a neurobiologist at Britain's Open University, said: 'Despite the fact that Saddam Hussein committed major acts of genocide, the fact is, Iraq got away with it.' There was no pressure to bring this criminal, a man who clearly and openly violated the rules of war, to justice. No less than six separate United Nations missions went to Iraq before and after the Halabja massacre, each time collecting more

Above: *Western newsmen recorded the murder of Kurds in the streets of Halabja.*

Left: *A frantic and terrified people trekked great distances to reach the safety of Turkey.*

information on Iraqi chemical assaults. One team was despatched to the town of Halabja and reported: 'This warns us that the use of chemical weapons against the Kurdish people may become more frequent, even commonplace.'

Saddam was well satisfied with this awesome display of his maniacal power. He had cocked a snook at world opinon, defied the conventions of the West - which he viewed as weak - and had dealt a stunning blow to his Kurdish enemies. He felt so good about it that he decided to do it again.

TWO BLEEDING NATIONS

In August 1988 the guns finally fell silent in his war with Iran. It had bled the

'IT IS ONE THING TO BE
BLOWN TO PIECES, BUT
IT IS ANOTHER TO BE
KILLED BY A WEAPON
YOU CANNOT HEAR AND
CANNOT SEE UNTIL IT IS
TOO LATE.'

SEFIKA ALI IS NOW
TWENTY-FOUR, BUT HER
PRETTY FACE IS WRINKLED
LIKE THAT OF A MUCH
OLDER WOMAN. THIS IS
THE RESULT OF CYANIDE
GAS BURNS.

Right: *The presence of their despot cannot be forgotten by the Iraqi people. His image looms on billboards across the country.*

two nations white, ravaged their economies, decimated their populations and cemented the politics of hate for generations to come. But the onset of peace for Saddam meant he could turn more manpower - and more chemical weaponry - against his Kurdish foes.

By the end of August Saddam had moved some sixty thousand troops into the Kurdish region, together with battalions of helicopter gunships, tanks and artillery, all effective methods of launching the gas blitz he intended. The first village to die under his onslaught was Butia.

Sefika Ali is now twenty-four, but her pretty face is wrinkled like that of a much older woman. This is the result of cynanide gas burns which happened when her village was wiped out in a gas attack launched from the air. She fled to Turkey with her husband and three children. They were the lucky ones. Left behind were an estimated two thousand neighbours, who suffered the same death as the victims of Halabja. She said: 'I was cooking breakfast for my family when I heard the sound of aircraft. I heard bombs whistling and the next thing I knew was that there was something wrong with my eyes. I started to vomit almost immediately. I knew what was happening. We had heard what had happened at Halabja. My family suffered the same effects. We all drank a lot of milk and then we ran. We ran to get as far away as we could. We know that not many made it out.'

REFUGEES FACING DEATH

In the refugee camps along the Turkish border the hordes of burned, coughing survivors of the latest outrage swelled the hospital tents as medical teams from the West struggled to cope with the aftermath of Saddam's attacks. The refugees were called *Pesh mergas* by the Iraqis - 'Those who face death' - and there were no apologies from Bagdhad for the fate of these victims. It was estimated that along with Butia, two other villages in the Danhuk region of the country were hit, but these suffered few fatalities because the populace were working in far-away fields and strong winds blowing that morning helped disperse the gas away from them.

Kurdish refugees, almost one hundred thousand of them, moved into Turkey, where they were accommodated in insanitary, overcrowded tented camps along the border. Massad Barzani, one of the Kurdish leaders, appealed to the UN to press Iraq not to use any more chemical weapons. He said: 'It is one thing to be blown to pieces, but it is another to be killed by a weapon you cannot hear and cannot see until it is too late. In the name of humanity, the governments of the west must come together to end this nightmare we are suffering. Many women and children who were gassed, but who survived the onslaught were later murdered by Iraqi

troops to prevent them from spreading information about what dark deeds were done to them. It is a crime against humanity we are talking about here.'

America finally woke up to the atrocities, realising that Saddam Hussein was becoming more of a liability than an ally in the region. The State Department said it had obtained proof of the latest outrages and called them abhorrent and unjustifiable. Secretary of State George Shultz met with Iraqi's Minister of State for Foreign Affairs, Saddoun Hammadi to tell him that the continued use of poison gas would severely affect the future of US - Iraq relations.

Hammadi insisted, despite all the evidence to the contrary, that no civilians had this time been killed by gas. Gwynne Roberts, a British television journalist, had himself collected soil samples from some of the villages he visited in Kurdistan and had them analysed by a laboratory. The laboratory report showed significant traces of mustard gas in the samples.

The anger felt by Shultz and other officials was supported by the American people and there was a popular feeling that

Below: *The strange dual role played by Saddam Hussein is revealed in this photograph: the militant warrior is also a pious man of God.*

maybe America had, after all, been backing the wrong horse in the long struggle between Iran and Iraq. Senator Claiborne Pell, a Democrat from Rhode Island, introduced a bill calling for sanctions against Iraq for what he called its 'anti-Kurdish genocide'. There was a period of an arms embargo after more UN evidence of the chemical atrocities was revealed, but sadly trade soon resumed again.

THE GULF WAR

In August 1990, Iraq invaded Kuwait. At the conclusion of a decade of war against Iran, Iraq was bankrupt and needed money to rebuild. Saddam claimed that oil was being stolen from Iraq through slant-drilling in Kuwait and took his complaint to the US. No action was taken. He further claimed that the border between Iraq and Kuwait had been incorrectly laid down, which meant that the oil companies in Kuwait were stealing even more Iraqi oil. Again, no action was taken. Having been told that the US would not get involved in border disputes, Saddam decided to resolve the problem his own way. Although poor economically, Iraq now had a massive army and arsenal - which the United States had

"THE FUNDAMENTAL PROBLEM WITH IRAQ REMAINS THE NATURE OF THE REGIME ITSELF. SADDAM HUSSEIN IS A HOMICIDAL DICTATOR WHO IS ADDICTED TO WEAPONS OF MASS DESTRUCTION"
President George Bush

Below: *George Bush Snr watches on as his son, George W. Bush, addresses the nation. He forced Iraq out of Kuwait during the Gulf War, and his son brought down Saddam Hussein's tyrannical regime in 2003.*

helped stockpile - and on August 2, Saddam drew it up to the border and stormed into Kuwait, taking the nation and the world by surprise.

It is likely that Saddam did not anticipate the reaction which this move provoked from the US. Or perhaps he had thought that their refusal to get involved in border disputes meant that they would not intervene in this invasion. He was wrong. President George Bush stepped up and declared that 'This will not stand'. The UN Security Council declared war on Iraq and gave the US permission to end Iraq's occupation of Kuwait using any means necessary.

The air campaign began in January 1991, and bombing continued for over a month. During this time, Saddam positioned human shields as defence. The ground attack began in February, and was instantly successful, with Iraqi forces either surrendering immediately, or pulling out of Kuwait completely. Before leaving though, those who retreated dropped millions of barrels of oil into the Persian Gulf, and set fire to a large amount. The effect on the environment, on people's health and on the landscape was devastating, and the damage can still be seen today.

With the primary goal of liberating Kuwait achieved, the US pulled their forces out, and received much criticism for doing so. Many felt that Saddam was still a threat and should be deposed. George Bush nevertheless decided to pass the problem over to the UN, and to celebrate the success they had already had. So Saddam remained as leader of Iraq.

In the aftermath of the Gulf War, during which Iraq lost an estimated 100,000 troops, Iraqis rose up against Saddam. But he brutally crushed every rebellion. Conditions worsened when a UN trade embargo was imposed on Iraq by the US, following Saddam's purge of the Marsh Arabs in the south. In retaliation, an assassination attempt was made on President Bush when he visited Kuwait to meet the restored Emir, but it was unsuccessful.

During the administration of President Clinton, Saddam was accused of violating the terms of the Gulf War cease-fire and producing weapons of mass destruction (WMD).

GEORGE W. BUSH

This accusation was pursued by President George W. Bush, when he came to office in 2000. Apparently picking up where his father had left off, Bush launched a diatribe against Saddam, declaring that he was ever-dangerous and that only the complete overthrow of the Saddam regime would remove the threat of the employment of the WMD which he alleged that Iraq possessed. When war on terror was declared following the September 11 attacks, Bush's belligerence intensified. Despite the lack of any evidence that Iraq actually possessed WMD, even after numerous inspections had been carried out to prove to the contrary, Bush declared Iraq to be a threat to national security.

After many months of threats and a long military build-up, the United States finally attacked Iraq on Thursday, March 20, 2003. The war faced strong opposition from France, Germany, Russia, China and the great majority of UN member states as well as world public opinion. The

combined military ground force of the US and the UK was around 300,000, and they encountered stiff Iraqi resistance.

THE ATTACK

Named 'Operation Iraqi Freedom', the attack was an attempt to target Saddam Hussein and other Iraqi leaders, using air strikes and ground troops which entered the country by crossing southern Iraq from Kuwait. The following day the major phase of the war began with heavy aerial attacks on Baghdad and other cities. There was also fighting in the north of the country, with some reports that it involved US Special Forces. During the day, a number of oil wells – seven, according to the British government – were reported to be on fire. According to the British government, two of the fires were extinguished by special firefighting troops. The Iraqi government denied that oil wells had been

Above: The statue of Saddam Hussein in Paradise Square is brought crashing down as Iraqi civilians, and the rest of the world, watch on.

set on fire, saying that it had set fire to oil-filled trenches as a defensive measure against airstrikes.

By March 23 US and British forces succeeded in taking the airport outside of Basra, and were in battle with Iraqi forces for control of the city itself. On April 9 Baghdad fell to US forces. Some Iraqis cheered in the streets after American infantrymen seized deserted Ba'ath Party ministries and pulled down a huge iron statue of Saddam Hussein, ending his brutal 24-year rule of Iraq.

The looting and unrest, especially in major cities Baghdad and Basra became a very serious issue. In Baghdad, with the notable exception of the Oil Ministry, which was guarded by American troops, the majority of government and public buildings were totally plundered. On April 13, Tikrit, the home town of Saddam Hussein, and the last town not under control of the coalition, was taken by American marines.

With the fall of the Tikrit region, the coalition partners declared the war effectively over on April 15.

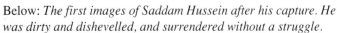

"LADIES AND GENTLEMEN, WE GOT HIM"

Paul Bremer
US Chief Administrator in Iraq

CAPTURE OF SADDAM HUSSEIN

On Saturday, December 13, 2003, US troops converged on a two-room mud hut, squatting between two houses on a Tigris farm near the village of Ad-Dawr. One room, which appeared to serve as a bedroom, was in disarray with clothes strewn about the place. Inside the hut, dirt and a rug covered the entryway to a subterranean hideaway. The US troops had finally caught up with the man who had eluded them for many months. Saddam Hussein's last hiding place was a miserable 8-foot hole dug in the mud. Although Saddam was armed with a pistol, he showed no resistance during his capture. The former dictator of Iraq appeared tired and disoriented when he was pulled from his hiding place, which was found to contain arms and around $750,000 in cash. The US proudly declared 'We got him', and paraded the once proud man, now unkempt and with a scraggy beard, around in front of a world audience.

The assumption that the capture of Saddam Hussein would solve all the problems surrounding Iraq soon seemed to lose its credence. Violence on the streets, and attacks against coalition forces continued with the same ferocity and fatalities that they had prior to Saddam's capture. Saddam, the pathetic, bedraggled man, living in a hole in the ground with only three guns and some cash, certainly was not the powerful figure behind the resistance forces in Iraq. The fact that he probably had very little control or influence is a disturbing and significant fact as it raises the question as to whether these were insurgents vying for power, or Iraqis demonstrating their continued hatred and aggression towards the US?

Below: *The first images of Saddam Hussein after his capture. He was dirty and dishevelled, and surrendered without a struggle.*